Survival Theory:
A Preparedness Guide

HOW TO SURVIVE THE END OF
THE WORLD ON A BUDGET

By:

Jonathan Hollerman

Apoc Publishing mass market 1st Edition: March 2016
1st Edition Edited by: Christina Hollerman

Published in the United States by:  APOC PUBLISHING
PO Box 279
McConnellsburg, PA 17233
www.apocpublishing.com

Back Cover author photo by Daniel Kuykendall – TheSurvivalSummit.com

Back Cover quote – from CenterForSecurityPolicy.org article titled, "Warning of Post-Sony Cyber Attacks on U.S. Grid Underscored by Penetration of South Korean Nuclear Plants' Computers" on Dec 22, 2014

ISBN: 069267280X
ISBN 13: 978-0692672808

Note to Reader:
Although every precaution has been taken to verify the accuracy of the information contained herein, the author and publisher assume no responsibility for any errors or omissions. No liability or responsibility is assumed for damages, losses, or injuries that may result from the use or misuse of information or ideas contained within. This book is published for entertainment purposes only and is not a substitute for specialized instruction with qualified professional consultants.

To contact author or for personalized consulting go to:
www.GridDownConsulting.com

Books by Jonathan Hollerman:

EMP: EQUIPPING MODERN PATRIOTS
"A STORY OF SURVIVAL"
Book 1

EMP: EQUIPPING MODERN PATRIOTS
"THE AFTERMATH"
Book 2

EMP: EQUIPPING MODERN PATRIOTS
"NEW BEGINNINGS"
Book 3

SURVIVAL THEORY
A PREPAREDNESS GUIDE:
How to Survive the End of the World on a Budget

ALONE: BETH ANN'S STORY OF SURVIVAL
Co-Authored with C.M. Hollerman

Forthcoming Works

SURVIVAL THEORY II
A follow-up to Survival Theory, A Preparedness Guide

DARK SKIES
The first novel in a new series inside the Equipping Modern Patriots world. It will follow a new character while describing life inside the Green Zones.

𝔇edication

This book is dedicated to my new daughter, Hannah Jane, as well as my wife and son who are always in my thoughts.

I also dedicate this book to all my close friends and family members who have endured endless hours of my rambling about preparedness. My hope and prayer is that they, as well as the rest of America, will one day wake up and see the potential threats against our comfy way of life, and take the needed steps to safeguard their families' futures.

I could only have brought this book to you by the grace of God and His unfailing love shown to an undeserving servant.

Psalm 91

Index

PART I: Preparedness Theory

PART II: The Preparation

Preface

Most people have no idea that the federal government (FEMA) instructs all Americans to prepare for hard times. Ready.gov recommends that every household in America have at least three days' worth of food, water, medical, and other supplies stored away in case of an emergency. Essentially they are saying, "We, the US government, are totally unable to come and rescue your family in a timely fashion should there be a localized natural disaster. Please take care of yourselves for at least three days until we can come to your rescue!" Comforting, isn't it? Have you done that already? Do have three days' worth of supplies for a potential disaster in your area?

You should prepare for hard times NOT because it may take the government three days to mobilize, but because there are multiple, verified scenarios that would cripple the US government leaving you on your own for months...or possibly years. That is not fear-mongering; it is the truth. Why is it that those of us that choose to prepare for potential hard times are so maligned and stigmatized in the media? All we are doing is planning ahead and taking precautions to ensure our family is fed should a collapse scenario come to pass. Shouldn't planning ahead and safeguarding your future be considered virtues? Per social norms, aren't we supposed to own home insurance, car insurance, fire insurance, flood insurance, medical insurance, and life insurance to protect us from potential calamity in the future? Aren't most people encouraged to have a savings account or "rainy day fund" in case they lose their job or come under a financial hardship? Why is it that putting some extra food in your basement to feed your family during hard times be considered so irrational?

The fact is, the reason people look down at "preppers" is that they don't see the threat of hard times ahead and in a lot of cases, when presented with concrete evidence, they still don't want to believe it. There is plenty of evidence and reliable information available to you, but most have never seen it and a lot of people don't want to. The information about a grid-down scenario, pandemic or financial collapse never enters the "information bubble" most people surround themselves with. What I mean by information bubble is the people, places, and media sources that most people surround themselves with is what dictates how they think and feel about the various issues facing our country. If they don't have a friend or co-worker who's into preparedness, their thoughts and opinions on "preppers" can then only be formed by their media and entertainment sources. Shows like *Doomsday Preppers* don't help our cause either. I believe they intentionally pick the craziest people they can find for that show.

Every single client I have ever worked with has been an absolute, down to earth, normal and sane individual. I have never met a single prepper like some of the nut jobs I see on *Doomsday Preppers* (though I obviously know they exist). So let's be honest. The main reason preppers and survivalists are thought of as crazy people is because that's how they are portrayed in the news and entertainment establishment. Believe me or not, but it's true. In fact, most of the things people believe and care about today are carefully crafted by those who set the "media narrative" and that includes every source of news, liberal and conservative.

People's opinions and worries are completely controlled by a media who TELLS YOU exactly what you should and shouldn't care about. Don't believe me? I can prove it with a single question. Has gun crime been on the rise over the last 20 years or has it decreased? What is absolutely astonishing is that 56% of respondents to the Pew Research study think gun crime is on the rise, while 26% think it has stayed the same, and only 12% think it decreased. The truth: the gun homicide rate has dropped 50% in the last twenty years! Over 82% of people were absolutely and totally dead wrong in their understanding of gun crime in America! How did they get that way? The media and academia has an anti-gun agenda which they have been pushing hard for a long time. It's not like gun violence had dropped a few percentage points over the last twenty years; gun murders were literally cut in half in only 20 years and yet nearly 60% of people think it's going up! Think about how unbelievably wrong these people's thoughts are about a simple provable fact (even the 26% who think it has merely stayed the same are way off). The point I'm making doesn't have anything to do with guns, gun control, or gun crime. The point is that the media and academia are capable of completely brainwashing a large percentage of the American population into believing things that are completely untrue and easily debunked by spending two minutes on Google! Look it up yourself. The gun crime data I just cited comes from a Pew Research study from 2013 titled, "Gun Homicide Rate Down 49% Since 1993 Peak; Public Unaware."

Let's take the example of Cecil the Lion, which was killed by a hunter in Africa in July of 2015. Now before I begin to talk about Cecil, it's important to realize that hundreds of lions have been legally killed every year in Africa by trophy hunters and almost NO ONE HAS EVER CARED! The media whipped up the entire US population into a frenzy with 24 hours-a-day coverage for a week straight of Cecil the Lion. The national outcry as a result of the sensationalized and emotional news coverage was amazing to behold. People organized marches, organizations raised hundreds of thousands of dollars in record time to protect lions, Twitter and Facebook were filled with emotional meme's and memorial photos for the poor feline, and the hunter who shot Cecil had to take his family and flee, losing his livelihood and going into hiding for weeks after receiving numerous credible death threats. The outcry even affected the laws in Africa when, under pressure, they banned hunting lions. What happened next? Nothing. The next media story came out a week later and all of a sudden no one gave a flying monkey about the lions in Africa anymore. Everyone was then concerned about terrorism, or the plight of transgenderism, mass shootings, or something some politician said. The craziest part of the story is that just before I sent this book to print in February 2016, while researching information about Cecil, I stumbled across a current story about how Africa is literally getting ready to kill over 200 lions in a single wildlife preserve because the population of lions has grown completely out of control since they have eliminated trophy hunting after the outcry over Cecil. You can't make this stuff up! They are calling it "the Cecil Effect." Where is the media and national outcry? Not a single major news outlet covered the story. All the hand wringing over lion hunting, and now Africa is getting ready to literally mow down a couple hundred lions at one time as a direct result of the Cecil reporting. It's insane!

The news stories come and go and people are off to taking up the next cause or caring about something else. It is next to impossible to know what to believe anymore and nearly EVERY SINGLE news story from EVERY SINGLE news outlet cover their stories with a pre-planned bias; they all push their own agenda. America, wake up! You are being used, manipulated, and intentionally brainwashed in a lot of cases. There is a really good chance that a fair percentage of the things you hold as truths are actually completely wrong and you've just been manipulated with misinformation for years into believing it as fact.

Preparedness and the risks of societal collapse are nowhere on the list of narratives the news media outlets regularly plug. On

November 20, 2014, Admiral Rogers, who is the Commander of US Cyber Command, testified before the Congressional Intelligence Committee that America's critical infrastructure (including the electric grid) is completely vulnerable to attack by multiple enemy nations and groups who currently have the knowledge and the ability to literally "flip the switch" on our electric grid **at any time**. It is his biggest fear as the Commander of US Cyber Command and he fears a traumatic attack in the very near future which will result in massive loss of life and property. You can watch his testimony on *CSPAN.org*. It will blow your mind that you've never heard of this or the fact that the media didn't feel it was important enough information to tell the American people. Do you know what the major media story was on Nov 20, 2014? The Supreme Court affirming same-sex marriages in South Carolina. You have the man in charge of US Cyber Command warning congress about an imminent cyber attack against the US that would result in millions of Americans dying in the aftermath, and the media is more concerned about who is marrying whom in South Carolina. Again I say it's time to wake up, America! It is *up to you* to do your own research on these various threats to our way of life because no one else is going to tell you about them.

In this guide, I will present the evidence and make the case that our country will experience hard times in your lifetime. I will help you prepare for a societal collapse and show you how to survive after things have fallen apart. What you do with that evidence and information is completely up to you.

If you don't heed my advice and prepare now, you will most likely die. Frank Gaffney, the President of the Center for Security Policy, had this to say about America losing the electric grid for an extended period of time after an EMP attack: "Within a year of that attack, 9 out of 10 Americans would be dead, because we can't support a population of the present size in urban centers and the like without electricity." Seriously think about that. Think of ten people you are close to and try to imagine nine of them dying of starvation or being murdered over the course of a single year.

If you are reading this and you haven't started preparing, it is most likely for one or more of the following three distinct reasons:

1. You aren't convinced that the threat is real.
2. You're overwhelmed and you don't even know where to start.
3. You don't want to be stigmatized by your friends and family as a "Survivalist."

If point 1 is your reason, I can assure you that if you continue reading this book, go to my website and click on the hundreds of links to supporting documentation, as well as DO YOUR OWN RESEARCH, you will come to the same conclusion that many others have come to. The threat of losing the electric grid is VERY real and VERY likely to happen in our lifetime. In the first few chapters of this book, I will lay out the evidence behind the threat of losing our national electric grid. Any words or text that you see underlined in the following chapters have supporting documents and videos available on my website (*GridDownConsulting.com*) where you can find the supporting evidence for yourself.

If point 2 is your reason, you have two options. You can buy dozens of books on the subject and try to decipher what your next step should be from the various survival experts (with varying levels of expertise and conflicting opinions), or you can hire an Emergency Preparedness and Survival Retreat Consultant like myself to guide you on your way. If point 3 is your reason, then you are doing it wrong. I cannot stress this enough. The number one rule of preparedness is "DON'T TELL ANYONE THAT YOU ARE PREPPING!" There are many more important reasons for this that we will get into later, but if no one knows about your plans, then you can easily avoid the label of being a "survivalist" or "prepper." How many of your friends know the value of your life insurance policy? Survival Insurance (prepping) is in all actuality a life insurance policy. Treat them the same way.

Please do not be one of the 95% of people unprepared when that day comes: starving, sick, and huddled in the corner of your house wondering when the government is coming to save you. You will discover that no help is on the way with deadly consequences for you and your family. However, before you make a hasty leap and buy into some monthly long-term food scam thinking you are covered, please educate yourself on what it will really take to make it through a long-term SHTF (S**t Hits The Fan) scenario. It's a lot more than storing up some food and water in your basement.

So, if you absolutely knew that there was a very real possibility that hard times would come in your lifetime, wouldn't you prepare for them? If you knew that a flood was coming, would you head to higher ground or would you put your faith and trust in our government to come and rescue you like so many did during Hurricane Katrina? If you heard a tornado off in the distance, would you take cover or continue whatever you were doing? Think of prepping as "Survival Insurance." The reason most people don't prep is because they don't see the need or understand the risk factors.

What are the chances that your house will burn down or flood? What are the chances that you will die an early death? These are all very unlikely events, yet you probably have car insurance, medical insurance, life insurance, home insurance, flood insurance, and probably even insurance on some of your more expensive electronics… all to protect yourself against unforeseen tragedies and accidents. Why do you have all these insurance plans? At some point, someone convinced you that it was the responsible and wise thing to do. My main desire would be that my book helps you see the threat of a SHTF scenario in our near future and convinces you that putting together a "survival insurance plan" for you and your family is the responsible thing to do. I am not saying that you need to drain your savings account and your child's college fund, but you should at least make it part of your monthly budget. Start getting a couple items each month. If you look at the amount of money you spend on those other insurances throughout the year, "Survival Insurance" will be considerably cheaper.

Chapter 1
What are you preparing for? Why?

In order to be prepared for hard times, you first need to know what you are preparing for. There are dozens of SHTF ("S**t Hits the Fan") scenarios that people are concerned about. Some of them are quite silly and very unlikely, but most of them have at least some legitimacy. When getting started, I ALWAYS recommend that you apply the age-old philosophy, "Prepare for the worst and hope for the best!" At the same time, you need to be able to balance the worst-case scenario with what is also most likely to come to fruition in the future.

So, what is the worst-case SHTF scenario? If you were to ask most threat assessment experts, without a doubt it would be a full-scale nuclear war with Russia or China. On the flipside of this threat is the fact that it is very unlikely to happen in the near future. While I know that many people who lived through the Cuban Missile Crisis may vehemently disagree with me, most experts say the possibility of all out nuclear war happening in today's political climate is very slim. The three largest nuclear nations, including the US, have amassed a nuclear arsenal that could destroy the entire earth a hundred times over.

What keeps nuclear war in check? Mutually assured destruction. In other words, if China were to fire on us, we would fire back and both countries would be completely destroyed. If an all-out nuclear war were to happen, large portions of the earth would likely be destroyed and the rest would be mostly uninhabitable afterward due to the radioactive fallout that would encircle the rest of the world. Everybody knows this and nobody wins or gains anything by doing this. In fact, everyone loses. Even if they could catch us off-guard, destroying solely our country would in essence destroy their own. China's entire economy relies on Americans buying their exports. If our economy crashes, theirs crashes right behind us.

Besides, there isn't much you can do to prepare for a surprise nuclear bomb being dropped on your head and there wouldn't be many places you could go to avoid the massive fallout. The nuclear threats we need to be concerned about are North Korea, Pakistan, and potentially Iran in the near future using a nuclear warhead as an EMP, but I'll get into that shortly. There is also a realistic risk of a smaller "dirty bomb" being set off in some major city; however, if you're not near ground zero, you shouldn't be affected. Even if you are in the outlying vicinity, you should be relatively capable of avoiding the fallout if you know what you are doing. A dirty bomb would be considered a localized disaster and the rest of the country would rally around the affected area(s) and come to their aid within days.

So what are some of the other threats we should be aware of? Before I discuss the loss of the electric grid, which is the next worst-case scenario, I want to discuss some of the other SHTF scenarios. A massive pandemic would be the third worst threat to our way of life after losing the grid and all out nuclear war. When I say "pandemic," I don't mean like the recent Ebola outbreaks around the world. I mean a weaponized version of swine flu or some other deadly virus with a low R-value. If a large enough outbreak were to occur, you would see society shut down pretty quickly. People would stop going to work, truckers would stop or be prevented from driving cross-country to deliver goods, police would stay home to protect their families from looters, and workers who service the electric grid wouldn't go into work for fear of catching the disease and bringing it home to their loved ones.

The state governments might actually shut down their borders and restrict travel to prevent the spread of the disease. Suddenly there is limited food at the supermarket, gas stations start running out of fuel and rationing, and rolling blackouts could occur. Our country's infrastructure is a finely tuned machine, and if a monkey wrench is thrown into the cogs, America could quickly grind to a halt. The positive side of this scenario is that it develops over time. If you see the writing on the wall, you may have enough time to stock up on some of the things you need before everything shuts down. You would also still have electricity (for a time at least) to receive radio and TV transmissions which the government and media will use to help quell the panic.

Fourth on my list of worst-case scenarios would be a total financial collapse. This is the other scenario that I am pretty confident we will see in our lifetime. Both parties in Washington, DC, continue to spend more money than they have. The stock market is at an all-time high, propped up by trillions of dollars in Federal Reserve funny money given to the big banks. The unemployment and inflation numbers are falsified by dirty politicians to help hide the rot festering in the wound. In my opinion, the only reason we haven't crashed yet is because everyone else's economies are worse than ours and there is no other stable currency in the world to replace the Dollar. Should that happen, "batten down the hatches," because the next collapse will make the 2008 crash look like child's play.

Now, I am not talking about a small stock market crash that is quickly papered over like in 2008. When I talk about financial collapse, I mean a total collapse in the value of the dollar. A lot of people, including the media, will point to the Great Depression and how we worked through things back then. The problem with that theory is that the American people today are fundamentally different than our great-grandparents who lived through the 1930s. Back then we had "working poor." The poor people were mostly small farmers in rural America who were able to still provide their own food. We didn't have the huge government-dependent, inner-city populations that we have today. Most people back then (even the city folk) knew how to grow victory gardens, preserve food, hunt, build fires, etc. Today, Americans have very little self-preservation skills, if any. When the welfare checks start shrinking or stop altogether, the poor (black, brown, and white alike) will burn the inner cities to the ground with rioting and looting.

Just look at what these inner-city populations do when their team loses a Super Bowl or Stanley Cup. Or look at how fast people panic when the EBT (food stamps) system goes down (like in Louisiana in 2013). There are videos showing long lines of people in the check-out lanes who have grocery carts overflowing with food, taking advantage of the situation. Could you imagine the same people when they are actually hungry, angry, and desperate? It is likely that the government would call in the National Guard to establish Martial Law and enforce curfews to quell the riots, which would only make matters worse. This would likely give the anti-government militias the excuse they need to start their fight against "the man." At the end of the day, it would be a big, scary, dangerous mess and your best bet would be to get as far away from large population centers as you could, be independent, and grow your own food.

There are multiple other SHTF scenarios that people fear, such as the earth's magnetic poles reversing, massive volcanoes and earthquakes, biological/chemical warfare, and global warming/cooling/weirding or whatever term the environmentalists are calling it these days. In the end, these are all scenarios that you have no control over even if you choose to drive a Toyota Prius. If your big fear is one of these other situations, that's fine. Just prepare for a grid-down scenario and tailor your preps toward what you fear and you'll still be covered.

Loss of the Electric Grid

So, aside from the unanticipated full-blown nuclear war, what is the most realistic, worst-case scenario that you should consider preparing for? Without a doubt, it is the electric grid going down for an extended period of time as a result of a massive solar flare, an EMP (electromagnetic pulse) attack, a physical attack on the electric grid, or a cyber attack on our infrastructure. Most Americans have never even heard of the EMP threat and almost every American assumes that electricity will magically flow into their houses without interruption forever. You can't really blame them; that's all they have ever known.

When Americans do lose electricity for an evening, it is an irritating adventure in most households with Mom and Dad scrambling to find a flashlight so they can find the candles packed away in some dingy box in the basement. The baby is crying because she is scared of the dark. Suzy is trying to comfort the baby but is irritated because she was in the middle of sending an email to her BFF. Little Johnny is angry because he didn't get a chance to save the video game he was playing. Dad curses as he stubs his toe on the bed looking for the flashlight. Eventually, things calm down and the family votes on a board game to play. Three hours later, the lights mysteriously come back on and the family scatters from the kitchen table. Mom heads back to the kitchen to finish the dishes while dad plops back down in front of the college football game. Suzy and Johnny run back to their rooms and zone out on their electronic devices, while the baby continues to play alone in her play pen. Sadly, the board game sits unfinished on the dining room table along with the first meaningful conversation the family has had in months. Unless you live in rural Alaska, this is probably your idea of "the grid going down."

When I tell people that we could easily lose the electric grid for more than a year, their eyes typically glaze over and they nod their head thinking back to the last time the power went out at their house. They have no clue that their ENTIRE life completely revolves around electricity. Most Americans have never contemplated what life would be like without electricity because it's always just been there. It's almost unfathomable. They don't realize the absolute death, destruction, mayhem, starvation, murder, looting, raping, and pillaging that would ensue within weeks after the grid going down.

The fact is, most Americans just can't connect the dots from Point A to Point C because they don't understand why this would be any different than 9/11, Hurricane Katrina, or the Great Depression. "This is America. We'll work together like we've always done!" That is typically true in a localized disaster when everyone's belly is full and FEMA is mobilizing and coming to the rescue. But if the national electric grid goes down, there is no one coming to help because the rescuers, government, and military are in the same boat as you with no electricity to function. Once the supermarkets have been emptied, true starvation sets in to the general population and with no help in sight, it will quickly become every man for himself. After presenting the evidence for losing the electric grid, I am going to try and paint a picture for you of what life would be like after the grid goes dark.

First, you need to understand why we could lose it so easily. The electric grid in this country is very vulnerable and its Achilles heel is the HV (High Voltage) Transformer. HV transformers are essential for the grid to operate because they are what step up and step down the power into usable loads. What this means is that you can't take your toaster oven and connect it directly to the large HV line exiting the Nuclear Power Plant because your toaster would literally explode into little pieces. The high voltages exiting power plants usually travel large distances to a HV transformer which steps down the power into usable loads. It is then stepped down again at a distribution substation before being sent on your local power lines, where it will be stepped down once more (by the smaller transformers you see on the power poles) and sent into your home at usable load. There are currently around 3,000 HV transformers across the United States.

The HV transformers are massive, typically <u>weighing between 200 and 400 tons each</u>. They are unique to each substation and must be custom-built to spec. Almost every HV transformers is made overseas and take between <u>6 to 18 months to build</u> and deliver, assuming there are no backorders on the raw materials they need to construct it. The transportation logistics once it reaches the coast are also extreme with special rail cars, cranes, and insanely long trailers needed to haul the heavy load. Power lines need to be moved and each bridge they cross has to be inspected before crossing. These <u>transportation logistics</u> can sometimes add months onto the lead time. Imagine the logistics of moving a transformer with no police escort, no one to inspect the bridges, and massive traffic jams of "out of gas" cars blocking the roads.

Why is this information important? This information is important because most of the threats to the electric grid could easily take out 300+ transformers at once. An EMP attack or massive solar flare would likely destroy all of them. If the electric grid were taken down in the US, then the few manufacturers in the continental United States that "technically could" produce the HV transformers wouldn't have electricity for their factories and all the transformers would still have to come from overseas. Even if those Chinese companies ramped up production, electricity wouldn't be restored before 6 months at the absolute earliest and the majority of the country would still be without power for more than a year.

Most government and media reports acknowledge that looting and rioting would be rampant but choose to focus on the "trillions" of dollars it would cost in commerce and repairs to the grid. The problem with this scenario is that social order would break down within a week of losing the grid and a total societal collapse would be inevitable within a month once people really started to starve. Most experts believe between 6 and 9 out of every ten Americans would die the first year due to starvation, murder, and sickness. America as we know it wouldn't survive six months without electricity, so who's going to be around to fix the grid and who are they fixing it for? I predict the government would focus on getting the power restored to important cities and military bases first, and most of rural America could go years before seeing power.

This is the threat that I prepare for and I recommend you do as well. If you are prepared for the electric grid going down long-term, then you are prepared for most anything that comes your way. The worst part? Losing the grid is a VERY likely scenario to take place in our lifetime as I'll present next.

"A massive and well-coordinated cyber attack on the electric grid could devastate the economy and cause a large-scale loss of life."

- Dr. Richard Andres, US National War College

Chapter 2
The Threat of Cyber Attack

One of the newest emerging threats to the United States is a cyber attack against our critical infrastructure. This is occasionally brought to the forefront of the news by stories like the Sony hacking attack by North Korea in 2014. What is surprising, though, is the lack of media attention on the likelihood of enemy nations taking down our entire electric grid and other critical infrastructure through cyber warfare. It is truly amazing when you research this, how our government is absolutely unprepared for, and I could say completely unable to stop, an attack against our electric grid and other critical infrastructure. Why are energy companies so vulnerable? One reason is that these industrial systems rely on 1970s-era electric grid technology and it's not getting upgraded, because doing so would interrupt service.

Do you want to stress yourself out and stay up late with nightmares? Go to *CSPAN.org* and watch some of the <u>congressional testimony</u> to the House Select Intelligence Committee by the experts on our vulnerability to Cyber Attacks. You will go crazy wondering how the government is doing virtually nothing to combat this threat when the consequences could mean 9-18 months without electricity.

To understand our vulnerability to cyber attack, I would first point you to an obscure and largely unreported test of our electric grid by the Department of Homeland Security, code-named the "Aurora Project". In 2007, the DHS (Department of Homeland Security) connected a diesel backup generator to an electrical substation (which is common for substations to have) and then attacked one of its control systems and breakers via the internet with an "out of phase" condition. In response, the generator started shaking and smoking and eventually tore itself apart and blew up (watch the video on my website). In response to the test, the Federal Energy Regulatory Commission (FERC) instructed utility companies to update them periodically for preparedness in combating an Aurora-style attack on their substation infrastructure. In an audit a year later, 23 of the 30 utility companies had failed to follow up and comply with FERC's directive. The Department of Defense has recently tried to offer shielding equipment to the utility companies for free to defend against an Aurora-type attack. The problem with this, according to industry expert Joe Weiss, is that "they couldn't give them to any of the utilities because any facility they put them in would become a 'critical facility' and the facility would be open to NERC-CIP audits." In other words, none of the utility companies want to open themselves up to federal oversight even if they could get the shielding equipment for free.

To make matters worse, in response to a FOIA request to the Department of Homeland Security in regards to the unrelated "Operation Aurora" cyber attack against Google, the DHS accidently responded with the wrong information and released to the public over 800 pages of highly classified data regarding the secret "Aurora Project" and their testing of the electric grid. The documents revealed names and locations of substations that are completely vulnerable to attack and could help any "interested parties" better understand where to strike to have maximum efficiency in taking down our electric grid.

The one big thing about the Aurora test is that it only tested A SINGLE control system in an electric grid composed of thousands of vulnerable, un-protected control systems and SCADA (Supervisory Control and Data Acquisition) systems. Even if every utility company protected itself against the Aurora threat, there are thousands of other unprotected control systems and ways an educated and informed hacker could shut down the electric grid in the US. To date, the utility companies feel uncompelled to address the problem, so they basically ignore it.

Joe Weiss is the managing Director of Applied Control Solutions and is the foremost expert in control systems engineering and vulnerabilities. He testified before Congress that, "The long-term ramifications of such an attack would be severe: If electrical equipment were destroyed, power could be lost for six to nine months because the replacement gear would take so long to manufacture."

As recently as Nov 20, 2014 (two weeks before the Sony cyber attack), the House Select Intelligence Committee held hearings on cybersecurity threats. One of the interviews was with Admiral Michael Rogers who is the Commander of US Cyber Command. He testified to some absolutely startling information about the likelihood of the US losing the electric grid in the near future. Unsurprisingly, it was barely covered by the main stream media.

While discussing the vulnerability of our control systems (commonly referred to as SCADA), he was asked if there are any hackers or nation states that currently have the ability to "flip the switch" and turn off our electric grid. Here is his response:

"There shouldn't be any doubt in our minds that there are nation states and groups out there that have the capability to do that. To enter our industrial control systems and to shut down and forestall our ability to operate our basic infrastructure: whether it's generating power across this nation, whether it's moving water or fuel... Once you're into the system, it enables you to do things like, If I want to tell power turbine systems to go offline and stop generating power, you can do that. If you wanted to segment the transmission systems so that you couldn't distribute the power that was coming out of power stations, this enables you to do that. It enables you to shut down very segmented, very tailored parts of our infrastructure that forestall the ability to provide those services to us as citizens... I think the industrial control systems and SCADA piece are big growth areas of vulnerability and action that we are going to see IN THE COMING TWELVE MONTHS and it's among the things that concern me the most, cause this would be truly destructive."

Admiral Rogers <u>was then asked</u> by the ranking member of the Congressional Intelligence Committee, Rep. Dutch Ruppersberger, about a recent report by technology experts that predicted a catastrophic cyber attack before 2025 that would cause significant loss of life and property. Rep. Ruppersberger asked if he shared this view along with the industry experts, and without even a second of hesitation, Admiral Rogers responded, "I do." He later said, "We see multiple nation states and in some cases, individuals and groups that have the capability to engage in this behavior.... It is only the **matter of when and not if** we are going to see something traumatic." <u>(The full interview is on my website)</u>.

Again, remember that this man is the COMMANDER of US Cyber Command and not just some conspiracy theorist. You are literally hearing it from the horse's mouth. I challenge you to do your own homework and watch the hour-long testimony yourself. If you don't want to, I can sum up Admiral Roger's testimony in a few short sentences. America's critical infrastructure (including the electric grid) is completely vulnerable to attack by multiple enemy nations and groups who currently have the knowledge and ability to literally "flip the switch" on our electric grid at any time. It is his biggest fear as the Commander of US Cyber Command and he fears a traumatic attack in the near future which will result in massive loss of life and property. Woohoo! Bring it on!

If you don't want to believe Admiral Rodgers or someone from inside the government, then how about Summer Fowler? Fowler, who is Deputy Technical Director for Cybersecurity Solutions at CERT, the nation's first Computer Emergency Response Team at Carnegie Mellon University's Software Engineering Institute. She is the front lines of defense against a cyber attack and works hand in hand with the Defense Department, Pentagon Cybersecurity soldiers, Intelligence Directors, and huge corporations to act as a first response team to combat a cyber attack. When asked about a devastating computer attack that unplugs the power grid, empties bank accounts and results in massive loss of life, her response to me is unsettling. "Ultimately, it absolutely could happen," Fowler said. "Yeah, that thought keeps me up at night, in terms of what portion of our critical infrastructure could be really brought to its knees."

According to an article from *CNN Money*, there were 79 significant cyber hacking incidents against energy companies investigated by CERT in fiscal year 2014, alone. Between April 2013 and 2014, hackers managed to break into 37% of energy companies, according to a survey by ThreatTrack Security. Cybersecurity firm FireEye (FEYE) identified nearly 50 types of malware that specifically targeted energy companies in 2013 alone, according to its annual report. In March, TrustedSec discovered spy malware in the software that a major U.S. energy provider uses to operate dozens of turbines, controllers and other industrial machinery. **It had been there for a year**, all because one employee clicked on a bad link in an email. Be sure to watch the video from USA Today on the vulnerability of our critical infrastructure.

Or you could listen to the advice of the former Director of Counterintelligence for the CIA, Barry Royden, who spent 40 years in the CIA and believes that cyber terrorism is the next big threat to America. He says, "The trouble is, it's extremely difficult, in fact, **it's impossible** — everyone is connected to everyone, and as long as you're connected you're vulnerable. And there are firewalls, but every firewall is potentially defeatable, so it's a nightmare in my mind. You have to think that other governments have the capability to bring down the main computer systems in this country, power grids, hospitals, or banking systems — things that could cause great economic upheaval and paralyze the country."

Also, even if you don't want to believe these experts and think they are just fear mongering, then why did the Defense Department recently announce nearly 1 billion dollars in upgrades they are working on at the previously decommissioned Cheyenne Mountain? Reports show that they are specifically trying to protect communications against an EMP attack or an attack on our electric grid which would take down communications for the rest of the civilian populations. Also please download and read the Congressional report to Congress "Cybersecurity Issues for the Bulk Power System" which was released on June 10, 2015. Don't read this report if you have your head in the sand and don't want it firmly pulled out. There is no disputing the absolute threat of losing our electric grid from a cyber attack in the near future. Please watch the news report video on Cheyenne Mountain Upgrades.

If you want to see a pretty accurate portrayal of the aftermath of a cyber attack on our electric grid, I would highly recommend you watch National Geographic's recent movie/documentary called "American Blackout". While I personally feel this movie is a very accurate depiction of how fast society would fall apart, I do strongly disagree with the ending. First off, most experts agree that a cyber attack could take down the grid for 6-18 months. Although it is probably possible, I have yet to see a report showing less than 6 months. This movie depicts the power being restored after only ten days. Secondly, when the power has finally been restored, it paints a picture that things may get back to normal fairly quickly. I strongly disagree. Once society goes over the edge of American killing fellow American over a can of peaches, it doesn't recover from that very quickly. It could take weeks or months to get an out-of-control populace functioning like normal again. But again, it is a pretty good movie and would be a great "ice-breaker" for someone to watch who has never considered what life would be like without the electric grid.

"Destroy nine interconnection substations and a transformer manufacturer and the entire United States grid would be down for at least 18 months, probably longer."

- Internal memo, Federal Energy Regulatory Commission

Chapter 3
The Threat from a Physical Attack on our Electric Grid

Did you hear about the terrorist attack on our electric grid on April 16, 2013, at the Metcalf substation in rural California? This attack could have brought down the electric grid for Silicon Valley and central California. To be fair, it hasn't been officially designated a terrorist attack yet by the FBI. At the same time, they are the ones who refuse to assign that designation to the Fort Hood shooting when Nadal Hasan (a self-proclaimed "Soldier of Allah" fighting for Jihad) shot up a military base while yelling "Allah Akbar" after discussing the potential attack online with a radical imam. That incident was clearly workplace violence in the eyes of the FBI. But I digress…. The Metcalf substation attack was originally reported as vandalism by the local media and most people moved on with their lives after getting the mental image of a couple good ol' boys in a pickup truck firing pot shots at a transformer after having a few too many drinks on a Saturday night. But that was never the case.

When Jon Wellinghoff, then chairman of FERC, heard of the attack on the Metcalf substation, he immediately flew to California, taking with him experts from the Joint Warfare Analysis Center in Dahlgren, VA. Months later, after their report was finished, a very different picture came to light. Even still, outside of *The Wall Street Journal* and a report on *Fox*, very few media outlets covered this attack.

Here is a short breakdown of what transpired on April 23, 2013 in rural California:

12:58 am - Some person(s) removes a 75-pound manhole cover and enters an underground vault cutting very specific fiber optic cables to shut down AT&T's telecommunication lines, effectively knocking out 911 service to the substation and the surrounding area. Next, they cut the cables in a different location for the internet service provider in the area, Level 3 Communications. They did this in such a manner as to prevent an easy repair, demonstrating a serious level of pre-planning and technical knowledge on the attacker's behalf.

1:31 am - Security cameras at the Metcalf power station picked up what investigators believe was the waving of a flashlight signaling the start of the attack. The security cameras show bullets hitting the chain link fence as the attackers fired AK-47 rifles at the large oil-filled cooling tanks designed to keep the transformers from overheating.

1:41 am - An employee at the nearby Metcalf power plant hears the gunfire and places a 911 call to police.

1:45 am - With over 52,000 gallons of oil leaking from their holding tanks, the transformers start to overheat. This sets off an alarm at PG&E's control center 90 miles away, allowing them to transfer and re-route power around the substation.

1:50 am - Another wave of a flashlight and the attack ceases.

1:51 am – Exactly one minute after the attack ends, police show up to investigate but find nothing out of the ordinary and can't gain access to the site, so they leave.

As of today, here is what we know of the attacks:

1. <u>17 mid-sized transformers were destroyed</u> and it took nearly <u>15 million dollars</u> and a month to repair the facility.
2. No one has ever been arrested and the FBI investigators don't have a single suspect.
3. The attackers used AK-47s and there wasn't a single fingerprint found on any of the shell casings left behind.
4. There was evidence that the location may have been scouted previously. Next to each pile of empty shell casings was a small, <u>triangular-shaped pile of rocks</u> similar to what Al Queda and the Taliban insurgents use for targeting packages and to show attackers where they can get the best shots for an ambush. On a side note, according to <u>State Department data</u>, between 1996 and 2006, terrorist organizations have been linked to 2,500 attacks on over 500 substations around the world. So let's not kid ourselves that the Metcalf attack is a one-off scenario and the bad guys don't have experience in knocking out power grids. Just look at how terrorists <u>took down the electric grid</u> for an entire country like Yemen.
5. If the attackers had chosen to <u>fire at a certain part of the transformers</u> instead of the cooling tanks or had lit the leaking oil on fire, the transformers could have arced and possibly exploded instead of slowly overheating. The specific location of what to aim for on the transformers to destroy them instantly has already been recklessly publicized in numerous articles online. This would have prevented the control center from having enough time to re-route the power around the failing substation and brought down the entire electric grid for Silicon Valley.

For almost a year after the attack, very little was reported or known about the investigation. Jon Wellinghoff continued his push to raise the alarm on this threat with the federal regulators, industry representatives, and Congress without much success. He ultimately resigned as Chairman of FERC later that year in frustration. Mr.

Wellinghoff described the attack as "the most significant incident of domestic terrorism involving the grid that has ever occurred." When speaking to the WSJ, he said, "What keeps me awake at night is a physical attack that could take down the grid…. This is a huge problem." In prophetic fashion, only five months before the Metcalf attack, Wellinghoff told Bloomberg that "a coordinated physical attack is a very, very unsettling thing to me," and "there are ways that a very few number of actors with very rudimentary equipment could take down large portions of our grid; I don't think we have the level of physical security we need."

Mark Johnson, former vice president of PG&E (the company that owns the Metcalf substation) reportedly told a private industry gathering in November 2013 that he believed this attack to be a dress-rehearsal for a larger attack. He said, "This wasn't an incident where Billy-Bob and Joe decided, after a few brewskis, to come in and shoot up a substation… This was an event that was well thought out, well planned and they targeted certain components." Under pressure from PG&E, he later refused to discuss his opinion on the matter further when confronted by journalists covering the story.

In February of 2014, after almost a year with no arrests, Mr. Wellinghoff grew frustrated that not enough was being done and contacted *The Wall Street Journal* with more details about the Metcalf attack and how vulnerable the electric grid was from a physical attack. He was concerned that a larger attack could be in the works and he decided to go public because he felt it was a matter of national security and our country's electrical substations were not being adequately protected.

Shortly after, an internal and confidential FERC analysis found its way into the hands of a reporter at *The Wall Street Journal* who was covering the story(for the record, I could not find any evidence that it was Mr. Wellinghoff who released it to them, but I have my suspicions). The WSJ reported that if as few as 9 of the larger, critical substations were attacked simultaneously, the entire Grid could be brought down for an extended period of time! Luckily, the

WSJ was responsible enough not to publish the actual locations of the many "critical" substation locations (but consider, how hard would it be for cyber hackers to get their hands on a document that has been shown and discussed at numerous conferences around the country, especially when even the WSJ can obtain a copy). The memo from FERC also noted, "Destroy nine interconnection substations and a transformer manufacturer and the entire United States grid would be down for at least 18 months, probably longer." What does 18 months without electricity look like to this country? I'll discuss that later.

Most everything else you want to know about the vulnerability of our substations and HV transformers can be found in this congressional report: "Physical Security of the US Power Grid: High Voltage Transformer Substations." I challenge you to read through it and you'll see how unprepared we are for a physical attack on the grid, how easily it could be pulled off with the right knowledge and rudimentary weapons, and how long it would take us to recover. To say that nothing is being done to protect us from a physical attack on the electric grid would be an understatement. Please be sure to also watch "One Year after Metcalf," a must-watch video on the follow-up of the Metcalf attack and where we stand today. I'll give you a clue; it's not good!

There have been multiple other physical attacks against our electric grid, but the Metcalf attack was definitely the most threatening. Especially since the perpetrators are still at large and possibly planning another, larger attack using the plethora of information, data, and reports that have come out in the aftermath of the Metcalf attack. To be honest, most of the vandalism against the electric grid involves scrappers stealing copper and disgruntled ex-employees. There was even a case a few years back of a disgruntled man trying to pull down a high voltage transmission line with his tractor. But with the amount of information we now know about the Metcalf attack, it shouldn't be lumped in with these vandalism cases. Even if the FBI refuses to label the Metcalf Attack as an official terrorist attack for political reasons, we Americans need to be aware of the threat and pressure Congress to act soon to harden the grid and protect the US from another, possibly larger, attack.

I'll leave you with one more thought. When asked by *The Blaze* magazine about the Metcalf substation attack, former CIA Director James Woosley, who had been trying to raise the alarm to Congress for years about the vulnerability of the electric grid, had this to say: "People have an almost infinite capacity for not wanting to think about ugly things, and the utilities and companies who could be affected have demonstrated an extraordinary capacity of ostrich-like behavior."

I couldn't have said it better myself!

"The vulnerability of America's electric grid is a ticking time-bomb. The government knows that if that vulnerability is exploited by enemies or afflicted by space weather, we could experience the end of our nation as we know it. Many of our foes are aware of both the grid's susceptibility to attack and the potentially catastrophic consequences for this country and its people should it happen... Only the public is still largely in the dark about these dangers. If something is not done promptly to rectify the situation, our countrymen and women risk being kept in the dark permanently. We must secure the grid now."
- Frank Gaffney, President of the Center for Security Policy

Chapter 4
The Threat of an EMP Attack or Solar Flare

I have thoroughly researched and studied the threat of EMP and Solar Flares for the last ten years and I DO believe it is hands down, the greatest threat against our way of life as Americans. I've even written about the threat in my Amazon Top Ten bestselling _EMP: Equipping Modern Patriots_ series. Especially when you combine the EMP/solar flare threat with the possibility of a cyber attack or a physical attack on the electric grid like we saw in California at the Metcalf Substation. I believe that we will lose the electric grid for an extended period of time within the next decade because there is just too much evidence showing this to be the case. An EMP attack is the absolute worst-case scenario though, because you don't just lose the electric grid, you lose most electronic devices as well. Even if you could eventually repair the electric grid, what is the point if most of the items you would connect to it are fried beyond repair?

What would you do if nearly every electronic device you can think of stopped functioning at the exact same instant? <u>Can you imagine</u> a world with no phones, no TV, no internet, and no way to access your bank account? Without the electric grid, there would be no lights, no heating or air conditioning in your house, your faucets stop producing water and the public sewer could back up into your home. There would be no gas for your car and no diesel for your generator. Without modern vehicles or interstate trucking, the supermarkets will quickly run out of food. How will you provide for and feed your family? Most people will have no clue what is happening and will expect the government and military to come to their rescue at some point. What if the majority of the military wasn't hardened and found themselves in the same boat as its citizens? What if the government had no plan in place to deal with the catastrophe? They don't, but I'll get to that in a moment.

So what exactly is an EMP? EMP stands for Electromagnetic Pulse and the technology has been around for over 60 years now. In a nutshell, an EMP is the result of detonating a nuclear warhead high above the atmosphere. As the gamma radiation from the blast passes through the upper atmosphere, it ionizes the atoms in what is called the "Compton Effect." Charged electrons then travel at nearly the speed of light across the affected area (line of site from the blast) in what is known as an Electromagnetic Pulse. The rapidly changing current, coupled with the earth's magnetic field, produces a damaging current and the resulting voltage surge would destroy our electric grid. There are typically three types of current produced by an EMP--E1, E2, and E3. Each current has different attributes and would affect electronics differently. Combined, they have the ability to destroy all but the hardiest electronic equipment, but that is also largely dependent on altitude of detonation, gamma ray output, energy yield, and other factors. At the end of the day you can make your eyes bleed reading all the technical aspects of the EMP threat. Suffice it to say that without a doubt, it would destroy the electric grid and some, most, or all (debatable) unprotected small electronics. Watch a short video montage on my website to get a better understanding about the EMP Threat.

In 1962, the US government exploded a nuclear warhead 250 miles above the Pacific Ocean in the "Starfish Prime" experiment to test the EMP theory. They vastly underestimated the results of the EMP surge and a lot of the test equipment failed as a result. They also didn't predict the effects it would have on Hawaii, over 900 miles away. Hawaii lost a third of its streetlights and experienced damages to other electronic equipment on the island as well. Remember to take into account that the electrical infrastructure of 1962 was very robust (compared to today) and repairs were easily made. Another unexpected by-product of the test was that one-third of the low-orbit satellites circling earth were crippled or disabled due to unexpected radiation belts that were formed around earth.

Around the same time, Russia conducted multiple high altitude nuclear tests called "Project K." These tests were much more damaging to infrastructure as they were done over more populated areas of Russia in an area with a stronger magnetic field than where the American Starfish Prime experiment had been conducted. It wasn't until after the Cold War ended that we were able to study some of the data from the Russian test results of Project K. One of the biggest damages was the literal destruction of a large power plant in Karaganda after the transformers caught on fire. In September of 1963, after the Project K and Starfish Prime tests and the realization of the potential damage that could be done via an EMP, the PTBT (Partial Test Ban Treaty) was signed by the US, Russia, and England to prohibit nuclear testing in the atmosphere or space. The reason EMP warfare never caught on in the early 60's is because it wasn't very effective against the older, hardy electrical infrastructure of the day. In today's world, where nearly everything we use has tiny internal circuit boards and microprocessors, an EMP pulse would be devastating to our infrastructure and our way of life.

Right now, every country that has even a single nuclear weapon also has the ability to take our country back to the dark ages. Why don't they? Again, mutually ensured destruction. The crack in that theory is the rise of radicalized terrorists. Do you seriously think ISIS or HAMAS would care if the Middle East economy crashed after taking America out with an EMP? Heck no! Most of their population already live in abject poverty. The same is true for Iran. In 2014, they test fired their new ballistic missile systems off a cargo ship in the Caspian Sea. Why wouldn't they just test fire their new missile system off solid ground? Worse yet, ask yourself, "Why the heck would they test fire it off a cargo ship and not off one of their naval ships?" We even had a secret agent in Iran's military who has warned us that an EMP attack is exactly what Iran is working on.

What about North Korea? They have nothing to lose as their country also lives in squalor, and due to existing sanctions the US economy collapsing would have little effect on their country. In fact, if you remember, they threatened us in 2003 with a nuclear attack. Because of those threats, DHS did a study to evaluate the risk of EMP from North Korea. That study was leaked to Dr. Vincent Pry and he said that it revealed North Korea **already has the technology and the ability to hit us with an EMP** in such a way that our missile defenses would be useless to stop it.

The EMP threat is so serious that Congress put together a commission to study it. They released their findings in 2004 and 2008 in two reports titled "Report of the Commission to Assess the Threat to the United States from EMP." Essentially what they found was that our country is completely vulnerable to this type of attack and the results of an attack would mean most Americans would die within a year. These two reports will teach you nearly everything you need to know about the threat from EMP. The question is, will you read them? At the end of the day, an EMP attack is hands down the worst-case SHTF for Americans, not just because it is a very realistic and imminent threat, but because the aftereffects would be so devastating.

Dr. Peter Pry, a member of the Congressional EMP Commission, testified to Congress that "Natural EMP from a geomagnetic super-storm, like the1859 Carrington Event or 1921 Railroad Storm, and nuclear EMP attack from terrorists or rogue states, as practiced by North Korea during the nuclear crisis of 2013, are both existential threats that could kill 9 of 10 Americans through starvation, disease, and societal collapse."

The reason I lumped the Solar Flare and EMP threats together is that a massive solar flare would have a similar impact on America as an EMP. A large solar flare would produce an E3 current which would geomagnetically induce currents that would travel down our long transmission lines and destroy every transformer in its path. Although most unplugged electronic equipment might survive, a massive solar flare could take down our electric grid for a very long time because it would likely destroy a good portion of our 3,000 HV (high voltage) transformers. Solar flares of varying size happen on a daily basis on the sun's surface and very seldom do they impact earth in any meaningful way. However, astrologists have been following the "sun's explosions" and "night time lights" for centuries, even though there was little effect to mankind before the modern electronic age. Science shows that, on average, earth gets hit by a massive Solar Flare about every 100 years with the last one over 150 years ago. Mathematically, we're due.

The last massive Solar Flare to hit the US was in 1859 and known as the "Carrington Event." It produced Aurora Borealis lights as far south as the Caribbean, even though those lights are rarely seen south of the northern hemisphere today. Newspapers of the day tell of people in New York and Colorado waking up to make breakfast in the middle of the night because it was so bright outside. Telegraph operators were shocked by their machines and there were reports of some telegraph offices actually catching on fire.

In 2014, two years after the fact, NASA released documentation that a Carrington-sized Solar Flare barely missed earth in 2012. Daniel Baker of the University of California was one of the researchers who studied it along with NASA researchers. He said, "If it had hit, we would still be picking up the pieces." One important thing to note in this revelation is the fact that the public wasn't made aware of the threat until **AFTER** it had passed. Take what conclusions you'd like from my last statement.

It's not just massive solar flares that are a threat, though. Lloyd's of London (the world's oldest insurance market) released a startling report in 2013 on the devastating impact even a smaller, more common solar flare would have on North America. The fact that the prestigious Lloyd's of London would spend millions of dollars <u>on a report like this</u> should prove to you that this is not an idle threat. Lloyd's states that even a smaller solar flare focused on just the Northeast could have a devastating effect on transformers and affect up to forty million people. Lloyd's predicts the blackout could last one to two years before the infrastructure could be repaired (and that is just a smaller localized solar flare, with the rest of the country being able to come to the aid of the affected region). They state the financial cost would be as high as 2.6 trillion dollars (compare that to Hurricane Sandy which only caused $65 billion in damage). After watching how long it took the government to respond to Hurricane Katrina and a single city in crisis, how well do you think they would respond to 40 million starving people spread across the entire Northeast?

An EMP would have a more devastating effect on the US because it would not only destroy the electric grid but would fry, at minimum, a high percentage of the electronic devices we rely on for day to day life. Even though a massive Solar Flare would only take down the electric grid and some non-surge-protected items plugged into the grid, the effects could be worldwide instead of line of site. This would dramatically decrease the chances of receiving assistance from other countries who are struggling to help themselves. Either event would lead to hundreds of millions of deaths and despair on a scale that has never been seen in the world's history.

I'll leave you with a short story about being ready for an EMP and whether or not you should take the threat seriously. <u>Roscoe Bartlett</u> was a twenty-year Congressman from Maryland's 6th Congressional District who sat on the Armed Services Committee and the Committee on Science, Space, and Technology. When he left congress at the ripe old age of 86, Mr. Bartlett did not move to the sunny beaches of Florida or California for his retirement. He moved to a piece of property in rural West Virginia and built a completely off-grid cabin for his entire family. When asked why, he explains that between his Top Secret meetings with Russian Intelligence officers and his confidential back door meetings with experts on the threat from an EMP attack, solar flare, or cyber attack, Mr. Bartlett believes the grid will come down in the near future and likely in his lifetime. I personally hope Mr. Bartlett lives a lot longer; as of 2015 he was 90 years old.

*"The Congressional EMP Commission on which I served
calculated that within a year of a blackout that knocks out the
national grid, we would probably lose up to 9 out of 10 Americans
through starvation, disease, and societal collapse.... The only reason
we can sustain a population of 310 million Americans is technology.
If you take that away, we don't have any way of feeding, providing
water or even providing communications and government for an
orderly society that is going to sustain 310 million Americans."*
**- Dr. Peter Pry, Executive Director for the Task Force
on National and Homeland Security Policy**

Chapter 5
Life after Losing the Electric Grid

The severity of what life would look like after a grid-down scenario depends on which scenario was the culprit. A cyber attack or physical attack on our infrastructure could leave the electric grid down for months and in some rural locations, years. A massive solar storm or small EMP would leave the grid down for six to eighteen months in most locations, but a Super EMP could cripple the grid for many years and fry most of the electronics we depend on. When dealing with a Super EMP attack, scientists have varying views on what percentage of small electronics would be affected. Either way, any national blackout, regardless of the reason for it, lasting for more than a week will result in major metropolitan areas descending into utter chaos and total anarchy. Anything longer than a few weeks and, in my opinion, this country will never fully recover. It will be survival of the fittest from that point forward.

Before we get into how losing the grid would affect you personally, let's consider how it would affect the country as a whole. Today, America is the richest country in the world and every other industrialized nation leans on the US for our buying power. Since 1944, the US Dollar has been the world's reserve currency and is what the central banks use to set exchange rates and the price of oil and other commodities. In recent years (due to irresponsible financial policies by our government) countries like China, Russia, and others have been working to replace the dollar on the world stage, which would have disastrous consequences for the US. The only reason they haven't been successful to date is because they can't offer a more viable alternative.

I believe the US Dollar would be replaced as the world's currency very soon if not immediately following a national grid-down scenario. Think about it: no American has the ability to buy anything from stores or the internet without their credit cards and the stores can't be restocked due to lack of transportation. Essentially, this shuts down all our imports from overseas. Our Stock Market would unofficially crash (unofficially because it would be closed for business without electricity). This would crash every other market around the globe, and Asian countries would especially nose dive without Americans being able to buy their exports for the foreseeable future. Many overseas factories would be forced to shut down, putting their employees out on the street without jobs, further exacerbating their own countries' woes. Mere weeks after the grid goes down, your dollar bills won't be worth the paper they are printed on.

In contrast to other "experts" who have written about the aftermath of a SHTF scenario in America, I believe the ensuing global financial collapse would seriously hamper the ability of our UN partners from coming to our aid in the aftermath. I'm sure some European countries and maybe even Russia and China would pitch in for a short while, sending us some cargo ships with food...but for how long? They are going to be experiencing their own financial collapses, record unemployment, and likely social unrest. They are going to need to focus their resources on helping their own populace. Even if they did send large amounts of food for an extended period of time, how would that food get distributed? We would have 300+

MILLION starving Americans scattered across an enormous land mass with no infrastructure or way to transport food throughout the country! You've seen the movies and videos depicting when we deliver food to starving refugees in developing nations. It's total mayhem with the stronger men beating up women and children to get a small bag of rice. Could you imagine a container ship of food arriving in New York City's harbor with TEN MILLION angry and starving people stampeding the docks? Again, it would be total mayhem, and my suggestion is to stay far away from these types of scenarios because they will be absolutely deadly environments!

In a nutshell, I believe our country would cease to exist in any realistic fashion shortly after losing the grid. The EMP Commission Report and Lloyd's of London talk about how it would cause trillions of dollars in damage to our economy. With half the US population dead from starvation, sickness and murder after six months and eighty to ninety percent dead after the first year, why would you even fix the grid? And who's going to accept our worthless dollars? EMP Commissioner Lowell Wood calls an EMP attack a "giant continental time machine that would move us back more than a century in technology to the late 1800s." The problem is that is our infrastructure is completely different than it was in the 1800's. We aren't set up to live like the people did 150 years ago. It's not like you could open up a Sears and Roebuck catalog and order a horse drawn plow from your local general store like they do in Western movies. Today, it's nearly impossible to find the tools and supplies that were needed to live before electricity! In fact, most of those pre-electric tools aren't even in circulation anymore.

Most people expect to see the US government step in during a national crisis like this, but don't hedge your bets on that because it CAN'T happen. The Department of Homeland Security (DHS) is responsible for taking control in the case of national disasters. They have plans in place for all types of scenarios; however, as of today, they have not put together a plan for feeding 300+ million starving Americans following an EMP attack, solar flare, or long-term loss of the electric grid. I predict they never will put forth a plan because it is an impossible undertaking. What you have to realize is that FEMA was only designed for localized tragedies and disasters like hurricanes, not for a national scenario like a grid-down event. Right now the US government only has 6 million MREs (emergency meals) stockpiled for just such emergencies. Now here is a simple math question for you: How long do you think 6 million MREs are going to feed a country of over 300 million people? Not even a single day. "What about the military?" you ask. Most people are unaware that 99% of the US military is completely reliant on the civilian electric grid. Most bases have diesel generators for backup that would only last a few hours to a day at most. Please read the Department of Defense report titled "Small Nuclear Reactors for Military Installations: Capabilities, Costs, and Technological Implications" in which the US military is trying to get mini nuclear reactors for each base to make themselves self-reliant. Hint: it's not going to happen in the next decade at best. In fact, the report states:

"DOD is unable to provide its bases with electricity when the civilian electrical grid is offline for an extended period of time. Currently, domestic military installations receive 99 percent of their electricity from the civilian power grid…. Most military bases currently have backup power that allows them to function for a period of hours or, at most, a few days on their own. If power were not restored after this amount of time, the results could be disastrous. First, military assets taken offline by the crisis would not be available to help with disaster relief. Second, during an extended blackout, global military operations could be seriously compromised…. During the Cold War, this type of event was far less likely because the United States and Soviet Union shared the common understanding that blinding an opponent with a grid blackout could escalate to nuclear war. America's current opponents, however, may not share this fear or be deterred by this possibility…. Even with massive investment in efficiency and renewables, most bases would not be able to function for more than a few days after the civilian grid went offline."

So you think the US government is going to step in and save you? They are not going to help you in a grid-down scenario because they are in the same boat as you. The government CAN NOT feed 300+ million Americans without our critical infrastructure intact. Please realize right now that you are on your own! My bet is that politicians will be shipped to some underground mountain to ride out the storm while you and I figure out how to survive on our own. When the grid goes dark and you start picking up government reports on your battery-powered radio telling you that all is well and help is on the way, do not believe them! I have just given you the concrete evidence that they can't help and they are lying to you. Those messages will be designed to try and keep people calm and they will lie as long as they can to prevent panic.

Lastly, if you have any survival skills whatsoever, the absolute WORST thing you can do is go to a government camp or specific location where they promise food and safety. These "Green Zones" will quickly become overcrowded and rife with disease and violence. If you have no other options, then go ahead and roll the dice, but when the people there start to starve and realize the government lied to them and can't feed them, it's going to get really ugly at those locations. Look at the Super Dome after Hurricane Katrina with the violence, theft, rapes, murders, and overflowing unsanitary conditions. It's an ugly scenario but one that was only a localized disaster and it only lasted for a few days! Could you imagine weeks and months of living like that? Most people who go there will eventually die or flee the horrible living conditions and disease.

Chapter 6
How Would a Grid-Down Scenario Affect you Personally?

How long do you suppose the food in your pantry will last? Most Americans go to the grocery store every three days. Let's assume you eventually eat the boxes of uncooked food raw (you will once you're hungry enough). With rationing, most households might have enough food for one to two weeks. A tiny minority may have canned food to last them a bit longer or have looted their local grocery store before the masses arrived (within 48-72 hours) to clean it out. Only ma and pa stores may open their doors and then they will only take cash (for a few days, or until they realize the power isn't coming back on). Unlike some popular post-apocalypse books on the subject, major supermarket chains will not be open for business. The managers have no vested interest in the stores, which are owned by some vast, faceless corporation in another state. Employees aren't going to show up for work without lighting in the windowless stores and the cash registers not functioning. Once the food is looted, there is no resupply coming.

Most people don't realize how the food supply in this country has radically changed over the last 100 years (especially in the last 10 years). A century ago, most people, even "city folk," grew and preserved a good portion of their daily food. Today, very few people garden and the ones who do consume it as it grows. Very few Americans know how to can or preserve fruits and vegetables to last through a winter. With the introduction of electricity and food on demand at your supermarket, the skills needed to live without electricity have been completely lost to 99.9% of Americans. Even most of today's older generations grew up with electricity. With the help of computers we now have a "just in time" delivery system. In other words, food is grown, canned, and resupplied to the grocery shelves as fast as it is taken off. There are no great towers of grain like in ancient Egyptian days. If you stop the growth, canning, and resupply, it won't be long till ALL the food in this country is completely gone.

Most supermarkets don't operate storerooms anymore or stock much in the back room like they did 20 years ago. Have you ever asked your local supermarket employee to check the back room for something they are out of? They look at you like you're stupid and then pretend to go in the back only to return a minute later and tell you "it's all out on the shelves." Most supermarkets get two to three truck deliveries per week to keep their shelves stocked. In the modern world (with electricity and computers), when you buy a can of beans at your local store, the checkout computer tells the warehouse to put another can of beans on the next truck. The warehouse's computer then tells the distribution center's computer that they need another can of beans on the next truck. The distribution center's computer tells the canning factory's computer they need another can of beans to be sent on the next truck delivery. The canning facility computer then emails the farm in Mexico that it needs more raw beans on the next available truck. What are the two common denominators in all those steps? The computers can't communicate with each other and the trucks can't drive across the country because of traffic jams and the gas stations don't have electricity to run their pumps. This is true with every item you buy at every store you visit. Interstate commerce completely shuts down and you will not be able to buy ANYTHING you need to survive once the store's current supply runs out or gets looted.

You would have no money outside of what is in your wallet or safe. Our entire finance industry is run by electricity. Most people have no clue that the average bank branch has less than $10,000 on hand at a given time. I wanted to pay cash ($9,000) for an older EMP-proof Jeep a while back and my bank told me I would have to schedule that size withdrawal in advance and it would take the bank three days to get it. If you can't get quick access to your money at the bank pre-SHTF, what makes you think you're going to get your money out after things have fallen apart? My bet is that the banks aren't even going to open their doors once the grid goes down. They know people are panicking and they don't have the cash on hand to give to them (most of whom will want to drain their accounts). Besides, every bank I know of uses computers and electricity to perform bank transactions. There is no electricity, remember? You were a millionaire before the crash? Not anymore. Don't bet on a single bank opening its doors for business. Also, don't rely on storing up large amounts of gold and silver for a grid-down scenario. No one is going to trade you precious food for your gold or silver coins. It will be years before there is any semblance of normal commerce where you can use precious metals to barter for tools or food. I would recommend spending whatever cash on hand you have in the first few days getting as much food as possible. Within a week, once store owners (the very few with heavy security that haven't been looted already) figure out that the power isn't coming back on, your money is worthless. A hungry person isn't going to trade you a can of beans for a thousand dollars.

There would be no communication with those who live farther away from you than earshot. In other words: no phones, no emails, no mail delivery, no Facebook, and no Twitter. Are you getting the picture? Think about all the family and loved ones that have moved away. Do you have a sibling in California? Do you have a son or daughter at college in Texas? You'll probably never see them or speak to them again. If someone breaks into your house looking for food, how are you going to call for help (not that the police would be able respond anyway)?

There will be no emergency services. Police, firefighters, and the National Guard will all be in the same scenario as you are. There will be no way to contact them, their vehicles will quickly run out of fuel and the traffic jams will pen them in just like you. They are just everyday people like you and me. Once the looting begins, most will rush home to be with their families and protect them from the rioters and home invasions. Very few will show up to work on day three. Some of the more honorable, single men may stay at their post for a while and try to help out, but within days of the grid going down, don't expect to see any emergency services. You will likely see the same result with National Guardsmen who are typically activated via a phone roster. Most will not be reached and most will not report for duty or will go AWOL to protect their family once things go south. Again, in a crisis situation, they will put the safety of their family before orders from their superiors. Even active duty military will experience a huge amount of AWOL soldiers heading home to protect loved ones and family. However, a good portion of their families live on base and they will be available for duty. Even so, as I explained earlier, the military bases WILL NOT be able to perform disaster relief because the military is dependent on the civilian electric grid. While they may have a few thousand MRE's on hand, their food situation is the same as yours. It's eventually going to run out. Law and order may last a while longer on military bases with possible C130 shipments of food from international aid, but eventually the big bases will dissolve into rioting and looting just like the big cities.

There are no hospitals or medicine. Most hospitals are only required to have a one or two day supply of backup electricity. Once they run out, loved ones on life support will die. Hospitals will be flooded with emergencies and injuries related to people doing stupid things out of their normal routine. How many nurses and doctors will stay more than a few days without going home to check on their families and protect them from the looters? Without the ability to get resupplied, the hospitals will soon run out of bandages and the like. How long before the doctors and nurses throw up their hands in despair with their inability to help an ever increasing number of patients and head home?

You need a prescription to survive? Guess what, almost twenty percent of America's population do as well. This includes everyone who suffers from asthma to diabetes. The drug stores will be closed because they have no way to verify prescriptions or check you out with non-functioning cash registers. How long before the tweekers and heroin addicts raid your local pharmacy because there are no security cameras and no way for the police to respond? How long will the vials of medicine you so desperately need last without refrigeration once the electric grid goes down? If your child requires medication and you haven't stockpiled or are unwilling to risk looting your local pharmacy, then you will know exactly when that child will die....shortly after his or her current supply of medicine runs out.

Your house will not protect you like it has in the past. There will be no A/C or heat in your home. If you live in an area of the country that has cold winters or hot summers, life will become very uncomfortable and deadly in some cases. A lot of malnutritioned people, not thinking clearly, will resort to doing incredibly stupid things to get warm, like start a fire in their house or burn a charcoal grill indoors. In urban areas with row houses and large apartment buildings, you will likely see large out-of-control fires burning whole city blocks because one person does something dumb and there are no fire trucks (out of gas) to come and put the fires out. Besides there's going to be no water pressure at the fire hydrants even if they could get there. You could actually see whole sections of large cities burn to the ground with no way to stop the flames. Do you know how to stay warm in your home once the thermostat drops below freezing? Many people will go to bed and not wake up the next morning. Also, a lot of people watch action movies and think they can hide behind a door or wall to be protected from someone who is shooting at them. This is not accurate. Most bullets will travel through multiple walls until they hit a stud or two. Your home is NOT bulletproof! Ducking down below your window in a firefight with your starving neighbors will not protect you from their bullets.

If you rely on city sewage, it will likely back up into your home over time. Raw sewage could start bubbling out of your sinks and tubs as people continue to use toilets and sinks even though the sewage facility isn't operating. This will create dangerously high levels of methane in your home that could make you very sick. Because of poor sanitary conditions around the country and most people not cleaning their hands properly before cooking due to lack of water, Dysentery and Cholera will become major pandemics in this country with a lot of people getting sick and dying. Regular baths will become a thing of the past, and many people will start bathing in their local creek or water source, causing dangerous bacteria to float downstream where other families rely on the same water source for drinking.

Don't rely on your vehicle getting you out of Dodge. In the event of a Super EMP, a large number of cars will come to a stop in the middle of the street. Even if they don't, a lot of people will try to flee the cities on empty gas tanks causing massive traffic jams. It only takes a handful of cars to run out of gas on the roadways to completely block traffic. If you do not flee town within 24 hours of the grid going down, you are likely to find yourself penned in. If you have a vehicle that is running, it will only run if you can get fuel for it. Most gas stations don't have back-up generators. The ones that do will be quickly overrun and emptied. There is no way to resupply them because the trucks rely on the gas stations to get the fuel to other gas stations. Even if they could be rigged to resupply from their own tanks, don't forget that there are massive traffic jams all over the country. Even if they could work out the details, very few truckers are going to leave their families behind unprotected while they travel across the country with rioters and looters everywhere.

Oil refineries take massive amounts of electricity to operate and will not be operational any time soon. What about the nation's precious fuel reserves? If you don't think the government is going to confiscate that for military and government use, I have oceanfront property in Arizona I'd like to sell you. There will be no refueling shortly after the grid goes down. If you were a forward thinker and have a large supply of fuel for your vehicle, I would only recommend using it the first few days. After a week, most cars will be out of gas and people will be desperate for a running vehicle to get them where they need to go. If you are driving one of the few cars on the roadways, YOU ARE A TARGET. I wouldn't start using the vehicle again for a full year (after most of the starving masses are dead).

You will not have lights once it grows dark outside. I understand that you may have a flashlight and some candles at your house, but honestly, how long will your batteries and candles last? I would use them very sparingly for a couple reasons. With no streetlights or ambient light in the cities, nighttime will become a very dark and dangerous place to find yourself outdoors, and light attracts attention. If you do have a large supply of batteries or candles, use them very carefully. Two weeks in, once people start getting hungry and desperate, lights coming from a house will be a huge beacon for looters and home invaders who will use the cover of darkness for their nefarious activities. Most people have never been to the mountains on a backpacking trip. On a cloudy dark night, you can see someone smoking a cigarette on the next mountain over. In a perfectly dark city, light escaping from around the edge of your blinds or curtains will be seen from a long way off. In a grid-down situation, you want to rise with the sun and go to bed once it gets dark, utilizing natural light and conserving flashlights and candles for emergencies.

These are just a FEW of the ways your life would be impacted by the electric grid going dark.

Next, let me paint a picture for you on how difficult it would be to just procure water.

For the last seventy-five years, you turn a faucet and a seemingly endless supply of crystal clear water comes pouring out to drink, cook, and bath with. It's always been that way and that's all contemporary Americans have ever known. Most Americans don't even realize that half of the world's population will never enjoy that luxury…but I digress. That endless water supply stops within hours of the grid going down, and I'd guess many of you've probably never pondered the logistics behind gathering and purifying your own water. Please don't get lazy when it comes to purifying your water. If you do, you will eventually get sick or die from waterborne viruses, bacteria, or parasites. It's only a matter of time.

Depending on your home's location in relevance to your local water tower, your house could lose water pressure within minutes or hours. Due to the extreme amounts of electricity used to process and pump water into the water tower for the average town, most cities do not have backup generators for this. The ones that do will only last for a few hours to a day at most. If you live in the country and have a well, did you know that typically your well pump operates on 220 amp electricity? Your water stops instantly unless you are one of the lucky few who have a backup diesel generator or similar power source.

Now, how much fuel do you have stored? FEMA estimates that the average person with a backup generator has less than 5 gallons of fuel on hand at a given time. Even if you have more, you're going to run out at some point. Also, gas and diesel generators are extremely noisy, letting every starving person within a mile know you have electricity. What if you live in the Southwest? To put it politely, you're probably going to be dead soon. Deserts were never meant to be inhabited for obvious reasons and only electricity and our modern infrastructure allowed us to live there in comfort. The Nomads throughout the centuries who traveled the world's deserts had life skills available to them that we both know you don't possess.

For those of you who live in areas where you have nearby streams or other water sources, do you know how to purify your water? Let's assume you do. You are going to soon run out of bleach drops and Iodine tablets or your purification cartridge will eventually get clogged. You are now a week or more into a grid-down situation and you are going to have to boil your water just like everyone else did for the last 3,000 years. How far away do you think starving and desperate people can see and smell your fire? Farther than you think. On the plus side, your shoulder muscles are going to be huge from carrying five gallon buckets of water from the nearest stream back to your home. Sounds like fun, right? You are eventually going to need to take a bath. How many five gallon buckets does it take to fill up a bath for each member of your family? Think about it.

Next, do you know how to start a fire in the rain to boil the water? You do… great! How much firewood do you need to have on hand to build a fire and boil water twice each day? If you have any firewood at all, it will probably be gone faster than you think. Do you have a large saw or ax to cut down a dead tree and how many dead trees do you think you have close by your home? How far will you eventually have to travel to find firewood? Can you physically cut the tree down and then bolt it up into six foot sections and then carry the logs long distances back to your house only to cut the long logs into sixteen inch lengths? You are still not done. Have you ever split wood before? Are you proficient enough to do it without sticking the ax in your shin when you miss the log you are aiming at because you are physically exhausted and weak from hunger? Hospitals will be overrun and most won't be operating without electricity or supplies after day five or six. I hope that deep cut doesn't get infected or you'll lose the leg and you'll probably die from infection. But again, I digress....

So far, we have only been discussing water. Let's add in the fact that you were a bargain shopper and have a stockpile of canned goods from Costco in your basement. Maybe you were really prepared and had some long-term food storage for your family. What happens when you spend a lot of time being noisy and walking around your neighborhood procuring firewood to boil your water, and cook your food? What happens when your sick neighbors see you and show up for some heat by your fire and begging for water because they don't have the tools, energy, or ability to purify it on their own? Okay, it's only water, so you help them out and give them some because you are a nice human. Good for you; you have now guaranteed that they will be back the next day probably with a couple other loved ones or neighbors from down the street who saw the smoke plume from your fire. I'm also willing to bet those same people weren't forward thinkers like yourself and they have long ago run out of food. They are literally eating pine cones from their driveway at this point (no joke).

With no chances of getting resupplied, are you going to give your hungry neighbor some of your child's food? That was nice of you. I guarantee they are coming back for more water and food every single day until you run out of supplies or the energy to help them. If you refuse them from the get go, they will probably beg and cry for help. They will even use their sick baby or elderly mother to play on your heart strings. How heartless are you? If you still refuse, that neighbor (who you've had a beer with on multiple occasions and borrowed a mower from a time or two) with a hungry and thirsty family down the street will get mad and demand you help them. He may even try to fight you. So you scare or beat him off with a piece of log you were just splitting.

How long do you think it will be until your neighbor is sick and desperate enough to return with his Pappy's shotgun to take your water and food by force because his kids are literally starving and dying before his eyes? In his weak mental state, he will resent you for not suffering like he is and would rather kill you than watch his family starve to death. Oh…so you have a battle rifle and you defend yourself, killing your neighbor and leaving his sick and starving wife and kids (your son's best friend) without someone to protect them. It was justified. He pointed the gun at you first...I understand. Good luck sleeping for the next month with those images floating around in your head.

Now the rest of your neighbors are ticked off at your "selfishness" and gang up on you with multiple handguns and rifles. Okay, so you are John Rambo incarnate with an arsenal that would make a militia proud and you fight them all off without getting shot a single time. Good for you. More sleepless nights full of nightmares (ask any soldier). How many people do you think heard that gunfight? Take out a map and make a one mile circle around your location point. What percentage of those starving people might think that someone with a gun has something that is valuable and worth protecting? How many of those starving people will eventually come for your stuff hoping to take you off guard at some point? Can you stay awake every waking hour to protect your family? You have to sleep sometime or you won't have energy to chop more wood tomorrow.

What happens when the bad guys show up while you are out cutting wood? Is your wife just as John Rambo as you are with an AR-15? Did you ever buy her the Tacticool plate carrier with ballistic plates that you wear when you are out of the house? Could she fight off a dozen rednecks with deer rifles without getting shot in the melee? Let's be honest, probably not. Instead of killing your wife, maybe they just watch you each morning till you head down to the creek for more water. Maybe they post up in your dead neighbor's house waiting for you to step outside and weed your garden in the back yard. You are hungry, sore, and exhausted at this point. Are you alert enough to see that man with the deer rifle a hundred yards away hidden under some garbage bags? Probably not. What becomes of your beautiful wife and daughter then? What will their life resort to after their food is gone? What will they have to do to survive? Do you think I'm being vulgar or gross? If so, I'd say you are being naive. Outside of the GI Jane types, most women without protection in this type of society will use what they have to survive.

Look at history and some of the horrific things done to women by the Russians and Germans during World War II. Those are events that people don't usually discuss in history class or make movies about, but they still happened.

What I'm trying to show you here is how impossible it will be to survive in a suburban area after the grid goes down. Even if you are in a smaller suburb of thirty thousand upscale people, how many rounds of ammunition do you have? Ninety five percent of the country will soon be starving, sick, and desperate. They will resent anybody who is not suffering with them. It's just human nature. PLEASE do not listen to the survival experts who will try and help you "fortify" your home or apartment and show you how to successfully ride out the storm in town. If you follow their advice, I can almost guarantee you will be dead within a month. I would also be very leery of the same type of survival experts who recommend you band together with your neighbors and fortify your cul-de-sac. Here is why. Most likely, even with all their big talk, your neighbors haven't taken the threat nearly as serious as you have. Most of them won't have nearly the supplies and long term food that they brag about.

What about all the other neighbors who weren't part of your planning group but live on your street? You're going to need their help to protect the cul-de-sac and work together for food gathering missions, growing crops, security, wood gathering, etc. Guess what? You are feeding them now as well. If you have $100k in long-term food reserves, then this scenario may work out for you. But in all likelihood, your neighbors will help you eat your family's food supply in a month and then you will starve to death through the first winter just like they do. Do you seriously think you are going to keep your food from them because it's "yours" and you paid for it before the collapse? You may for a short while. Eventually, they will be starving and your family won't be. THEY WILL NOTICE AND THEY WILL COME FOR YOUR FOOD EVENTUALLY. I don't care how close you are to them or what kind of "agreements" your little band of survivors has in place. All that goes out the window when blue-collar Jerry watches one of his little girls die of starvation. Blue-collar, church elder, and your fun-loving neighbor, Jerry has just become a starving, desperate, irrational, natural born killer and you are going to take the brunt of his anger before he watches his other child die a slow and painful death. DO NOT under-estimate a starving and desperate person regardless of his personality before the collapse. Hungry people make absolutely crazy and un-characteristic choices. Trust me; I've seen it firsthand with highly-trained soldiers in the field who have gone only days without food. We are talking about civilians with no training and no food for weeks or months. Most will literally become half-crazed walking zombies with one mission...food.

A lot of the "experts" will say I am fear mongering or exaggerating how bad it will be. They say Americans will work together and will get through it. They do not understand human suffering and have no experience dealing with starving people. Starving Americans will act no different than starving people in the Congo or Mogadishu. In fact, they will likely act much worse. Americans (even the poor) have never seen true hunger or been actively starving regardless of how the media portray them. America's "poor" eat better than 80% of the world's population. They didn't grow up without food like people in certain parts of Africa or China. Americans and their entitlement mentalities will be VICIOUSLY ANGRY when they get hungry. They will have no experience or idea how to deal with the mental hallucinations brought on by hunger pains and most will resort to anger and violence. Looting, raping, and pillaging will become the norm. It will be straight *Mad Max: Beyond Thunderdome* and eventually like the movie *The Postman*. I don't care if they fix the electric grid a year later. Most Americans will be dead and the only ones left will be the survivalists, the extremely lucky, the larger well-organized gangs of looters, and the strongest and most brutal of men who left their souls at the gate and did horrible things to survive. Who are they going to fix the grid for? Are we all going to forget what has transpired and go back to driving our Priuses to work at Starbucks? Are you going to get the warlords to give up their positions of power among their men and their harems of sexual slave girls? The day the electric grid goes down, America as a civilized nation ceases to exist.

You need to understand that life after the grid going dark will probably be **ten times worse than I am describing**. There will be 300+ million Americans facing the same horrific questions as you. Where do I go? What do I do? It is vital that you understand and accept that the following is true: A few weeks after a grid-down scenario, there will be hundreds of millions of starving people wandering around the country desperately fighting over every last scrap of food. A month or two after the grid going down, most Americans will be violently sick from food deprivation and other illnesses. THE AVERAGE DESPERATE AND STARVING AMERICAN WILL KILL YOU IF YOU HAVE FOOD AND THEY FIND YOU. I don't care how protected you think your home is. You will eventually be overrun!

There are very specific things you can do to survive this scenario. If you have the financial resources, you MUST hire an Emergency Preparedness Consultant like myself to help develop your family's plan of action following a total collapse scenario. There are a million details I can't fit into the pages of this book and every family's situation is different. Don't spend a bunch of money on a rural cabin that has serious OPSEC issues before getting professional survival retreat advice. Also, don't just buy two years of food supply and put it in your basement in town thinking you're covered. You will only be feeding the looters who will eventually scramble over your dead body to take YOUR food and haul off your beautiful wife and daughter to God knows where.

Chapter 7
So the SHTF... What do I do now?

Lots of "experts" have covered this subject and depending on which survival forum you frequent, it will result in completely different and sometimes opposite advice. In my opinion, some of the advice will prove deadly to most preppers. So if the SHTF, there is no easy answer and there are too many variables to give you a definite, "Hey, go do this!" First I'd like to get you thinking and to show you what NOT to do. You will have to come up with your own game plan for your family depending on where you live. I am also going to address some ideas for those of you with minimal preparations. Now remember, every family's situation is different and there is no one-size-fits-all advice or recommendation.

The first thing that you need to realize is that your plan of action will be different depending on what type of SHTF scenario you encounter. As preppers, we know that things in this country are not as they seem. We know that the stock market hitting all-time highs, while at the same time having a record percentage of Americans out of work, spells trouble. Fairly soon we will have a nuclear Iran and combined with the threat of North Korea, we face a realistic and imminent threat of an EMP attack. The pharmaceutical companies are no longer developing antibiotics and with the over-prescription of them by doctors, a nationwide or global pandemic could certainly be in our future. With a porous southern border and verified terrorists entering our country at an alarming rate, a physical attack on the electric grid could be in the works. My recommendation to "prepare for the worst and hope for the best" applies here; prepare for a long-term loss of the electric grid.

So what should you do and where should you go? First off I'm going to tell you what not to do. The #1, absolute, positive, you're-going-to-die mistake is to take the "Lone Wolf" approach. You know who I'm talking about. The guy on the prepping forum that plans to move out to the national forest and "live off the land" like the Legend of Mick Dodge. I would guesstimate that only 30% of those individuals actually believe they have the necessary skills to pull it off, while the other 70% are too lazy to actually make long-term preparations and they've just convinced themselves that if Grizzly Adams can do it, then they can too. Either way, none of them have ever stopped to actually consider what surviving in the wild looks like AFTER YOU FACTOR IN A SHTF SCENARIO. While a small percentage of the 30% might make it through the winter in normal times, only a small fraction could do it during a SHTF scenario.

First off, I'm speaking from experience. I've actually done it. I've spent an entire month in the mountains of Washington State during January with six feet of snow on the ground, almost no food, and very limited supplies during my training to become a SERE Instructor. During that month I lost over fifteen pounds (for a 6' 4", 190lb, 19 year old in peak physical shape…that is a lot!). I can make a solid prediction that 99% of people that go this route will not make it through the first winter. I can already see those of you who disagree. You are sharpening your hypothetical knives and getting ready to crucify me in the comments section on Amazon telling me about your amazing prowess as a half-man and half-wildling creature that was raised by a pack of wolves in the forest. Please read through my rationale before you keyboard commandos comment.

To begin with, living in the wild during peak conditions is hard enough. Very few Lone Wolf types have actually done it during the dead of winter for any extended period of time. Hiking-in your Mountain House freeze-dried food doesn't count and won't get you far. I'm talking about actually foraging for your food when there's two feet of snow on the ground. There are no berries to save the day and no dandelion salads to be scavenged. During my training to become a SERE Instructor, we literally spent as much time during the day chopping and splitting firewood as we did training and instruction. It takes an incredible amount of time, energy, and calories to maintain a fire in the winter. It's not like you can take a chainsaw with you. Where are you going to get more gas? Besides, the sound from using a chainsaw will bring in other hungry Lone Wolves from miles around. Even an axe will bring in unwanted guests from long distances. Okay, so you're going to use a handsaw…good luck with that. You'll never be able to maintain the calories needed to use it long term. So you have a magic supply of firewood stashed in the woods somewhere, pre-planned for this scenario…good for you. It will run out much faster than you think.

All this talk of procuring firewood doesn't really matter anyway, because the second you light a fire, you are attracting attention from a long way off. All the other thousands of Lone Wolves and the locals who are hunting the big forests will be drawn to your camp like moths to the flame. And the locals probably won't take too kindly to you infringing on their favorite hunting spot. How do you plan to warm yourself, dry your sleeping bag, boil your water, or cook your meat without a fire? Some will try to convince me by telling me they'll use a Dakota fire hole or a rock ledge overhang etc. to hide their smoke and flame, but that doesn't work either. Those methods only minimize a fire's signature, not eliminate it. When we train pilots who might get shot down behind enemy lines, we teach them that a fire is only acceptable in a life and death situation (i.e., you fall in a frozen lake during an evasion scenario). Living as a Lone Wolf after the SHTF definitely qualifies as an evasion scenario. The less people you encounter in the woods, the better your chances of survival. I vividly remember during one of my trips to the mountains noticing a strange, slow pulsing orange glow about a half mile away on the next mountain over. I asked the instructor what I was seeing and I learned that another element of trainees was on that hillside. One of them was breaking the rules of evasion, and smoking a cigarette! In the dark cloudy night, the tree canopy around the person smoking lit up faintly each time he pulled in a puff. Don't try to convince me how you're going to hide a campsite, your fire, the smoke and the smell of fresh meat from hundreds or thousands of other Lone Wolves wandering around the mountains.

"Meat!" That is the number one thing I hear from the Lone Wolves on how they will survive: by hunting. What they don't understand is that with thousands of other Lone Wolves roaming the forests, combined with all the other locals who are also going to be out hunting for their family's sustenance the first few months, THERE WON'T BE A SINGLE DEER OR OTHER BIG GAME ALIVE within a month of the SHTF. You might be able to survive off game during normal times, but not during a SHTF scenario. You'll be lucky to shoot a squirrel or a rabbit a month. There are hunting seasons for a reason: to maintain the game populations. Factor in 350 million starving Americans and no game wardens, and you're going to find a hunter behind every tree and in every small patch of woods throughout this country during the first couple months following the collapse. Let's say you get lucky and shoot a deer. Guess what? You're more than likely to have a dozen starving hunters who heard your shot show up while you're gutting it. I hope you intend to share your prize or be ready to kill a fellow human being to keep what's yours.

I could go on for ten more pages on the reasons why you don't want to Lone Wolf your way through a SHTF scenario. But for now, I will add one more reason, and it's the biggest one: desperate, starving people! A very small percentage of you reading this MIGHT be able to convince me of your wilderness scavenging skills.

However, what you will never convince me of is the other 99% of Lone Wolves who don't have our skill sets. Even though you might be able to survive the cold, the hunger, the loneliness, and the depression, you'll never convince me that you'll survive the other desperate and hungry Lone Wolves who are not making it: the ones who have decided they'd rather kill you for your food then to passively die of starvation on their own. It only takes one starving Lone Wolf to creep up on you at night (don't forget you are a Lone Wolf so nighttime security details don't exist and you have to sleep sometime) and shoot you from 100 yards away with their Pappy's 30-06. I don't care about your security measures or your hidden trip lines. It's just a matter of time till someone pops you off from a distance on the hope you "might" have something in your pack that they can eat. Every second of every day in the forest you run the risk of being shot from a distance. All the tactical training in the world won't save you from stumbling upon a hunter who is in a tree stand or hidden in some brush. If you Lone Wolf it through the SHTF, you will die!

The next type of survival strategy I would shy away from would be the "Taker" or "Looter" theology. These people are too lazy to prepare ahead of time and they plan to just take what they need from those of us planning for hard times. Do not underestimate this type! This is another reason why it is so critical to keep your preparations private. Even when sharing information with your closest friend, you can't be sure who he is talking to about your plans. Even in an innocent conversation, it only takes one looter to hear your name and the fact that you have plans laid out. They will eventually show up to take your food when the SHTF. These types of survival scum will become ruthless, and with no moral compass and no police to stop them, they will be the ones committing some of the greatest atrocities. If you are a prepper, steer clear of these types on the forums and message boards and especially in real life. Don't engage them or try to change their thinking. You want them to know as little about yourself and your plans as possible. Matthew 26:52 (the

Voice) clearly spells out a warning to these types: "People who live by the sword will die by the sword." Even if you aren't "into religion," there is karma that is going to catch up to you. Again, don't underestimate these types. The "looters" who survive the first couple months without getting shot will have figured out a pretty good game plan on how to assault even the most protected retreats.

The next segment of preppers would be what I call the "Roamers." These are the people who plan to pack up their RV and hit the open road headed for some campsite or some remote area of Canada hundreds of miles away. First off, if we are hit by a Super EMP, there is a good chance your RV may not even run. Assuming it does, there are going to be traffic jams from people running out of gas all over this country which you will have to bypass. Unless you have a custom built 4WD rig with a winch and reinforced bumper, you may be driving hundreds of extra miles out of your way which takes extra gas (which you have to have in advance and haul with you) and extra time (which you don't have). Again, during a grid-down scenario, it is vital that you leave town immediately and you'll only have two to three days before total panic develops in the bigger cities and four to five days before things fall apart in the small towns. The last place you want to be is out on the open road with tens of millions of people fleeing the big cities. If you are driving around in a big vehicle laden with food and supplies, you are a target. I hope your vehicle is protected with AR500 steel plating because you are now a bullet magnet.

Another bad idea I find more typically with wealthy people is the plan to build bunkers in their back yards in suburbia. Now, I am not against bunkers in general, just the ones in town. If your only fear is a short-term disaster like a tornado or localized disaster, then a bunker is fine for short term survival. For a long-term SHTF scenario, you are in trouble if you stay in town! Let me be clear here: cabin fever is a real thing. While it may not be as crazy as "Here's Johnny!" from *The Shining*, it will still make you go crazy. This is compounded if you have multiple family members and small children cooped up in a small space underground. Humans were never meant to live underground in tight spaces. While a good bunker is a great short-term fall back plan or storage location for your supplies, don't plan to live there long-term. You will get claustrophobic and start coming up more and more often for sunshine and fresh air. Besides, your supplies will run out at some point and you're going to have to grow a garden and/or hunt for sustenance. At this point you become a target and it's just a matter of time before you are discovered. Eventually you'll get caught. Living in a bunker isn't living, it's marinating.

The next group I want to discuss is what I call the "Pacifists." These are the *Mother Earth News* types (don't get me wrong—I love that magazine). These are the Preppers you often see on Doomsday Preppers who are building a sustainable off grid homestead in conjunction with the small town they live near. They are the ones who actually have the skills in place beforehand and you would think they would have the best chance of survival. Similar to the Amish, they grow their own food and maybe even operate a small farm stand in town selling and trading free-range eggs and grass fed beef. The problem is that MOST of these types suffer from two fatal flaws. One, they operate out in the open and the entire town knows where they operate from and what resources they own. Unfortunately, once those townspeople who absolutely loved you beforehand start to starve to death, THEY ARE COMING FOR YOUR FOOD. You can't keep everyone in town fed no matter how large your homestead is and how badly you want to help people. They will either consume all your winter stores from your charity or they will take them by force. Either way, you don't make it through the first winter. Two, "Pacifists" are typically the hippie types who don't believe in guns and believe in the overall goodness of mankind's human nature. They are the ones you see on Doomsday Preppers running around with Super Soakers filled with pepper spray…clown shoes!

If you are faced with a starving and desperate mob of locals or transients and you bust out your Super Soaker, you are going to get shot and killed. You can't bring a knife to a gunfight and expect to live. You can have all the skills and preparations in place, but if you are unwilling or unable to defend them with force when necessary, you will lose everything…guaranteed! The hippie commune philosophy of "everyone works together and shares" ONLY WORKS if everyone has enough food to eat. Once people start to starve to death, that philosophy goes right out the window and there is no such thing as sharing.

Okay, I'm taking a big breath here and exhaling slowly. For all those Lone Wolves who are going to react negatively to what I've said, there are going to be ten times more people that disagree with my next section. I am probably speaking to the largest segment of preppers out there: the "Bug-in" or "Survive in Place" preppers. These are the honorable middle-class people who live in cities and small towns all across this great country and can't afford to build a remote off-grid retreat to bug out to. I get it! I was actually one of you at one point myself. Most of the people that fall into this category are there because there are tons of prepping "experts" telling them they'll be okay boarding up their windows in town and they don't see another reasonable way out. You know the city around you is going to explode, but what else can you do and where else can you go? This is the most frustrating part for most preppers, and to some, it makes the point of prepping almost hopeless. I know there are a lot of people who are storing up hundreds of gallons of water and hundreds, if not thousands, of pounds of survival gear and food in their basement in downtown suburbia. Now, I am going to throw you "Survive in Placers" a bone here. If your only fear is a short-term disaster, hurricane, or small financial collapse then you will likely be okay. For anything long-term where we lose the electric grid, there is limited or no rule of law, or there is a total collapse and mass panic for a long period of time, you are screwed.

Unfortunately, instead of thinking and planning your way through it, there are tons of prepper "experts" out there that stroke your hopelessness and write books and articles explaining how to take the easy road and "hide in plain sight." They teach you things like "build a tall fence around your backyard for your garden." Yeah...like your neighbors aren't going to hear you hoeing and digging up your backyard for a garden. Also, the looters and raiders roaming around will be trained to notice a high fence right off the bat. You might as well hang a sign on your fence that reads "Garden Full of Food." These so-called experts teach you how to turn your suburban home into a "fortress." Please, catch me while I fall over laughing.

Your average home CAN NOT be made into a fortress. Regardless of the action movies you've seen, walls do not stop bullets! Your house is not fire-proof! You are not Rambo! And boarding up your windows or installing steel grates or shutters over them will only draw attention to your home. These groups of looters and raiders are quickly going to become very, very proficient at assaulting homes. If they can't force you out because every family member in the house was prior Seal Team 6, then they'll wait you out with superior numbers. How do you plan on stepping outside to maintain your garden? You have just become a prisoner in your own home. If you do go through the enormous expense to turn your home into a fortress, then you should have just bought a few remote acres and built a small off grid cabin!

The other thing you need to be aware of are "firestorms." A lot of the big cities are going to burn down to the ground, especially the older ones and city centers where houses are built close together. It only takes one idiot trying to warm their home with a charcoal grill to set fire to entire city blocks. If it's a windy day, and with no firefighters to stop the blaze, the fires could grow enormous and spread to the suburbs. These so called "Bug-In Experts" are going to be responsible for the deaths of thousands or millions of American preppers because they don't understand the concept that a desperate and starving neighbor will eventually kill you for a can of peas. They have probably never been to a third world country or studied human desperation.

The same philosophy of the "Survive in Place" crowd also spills into what I call the "Fortify My Street" preppers, similar to the book *Lights Out* by David Crawford. While it is an entertaining read with a few hidden gems of wisdom, they don't realistically explain how they feed all those people on a daily basis. This is an area where a lot of preppers aren't prepared at all. Most preppers buy a year's worth of freeze dried food not realizing that they are actually only getting about five to six months of actual calories (barely enough to make it through a single winter). Very few preppers, aside from those that homestead already and are currently living off grid, have a clue how much food is actually needed to feed their family through a winter. And I don't mean make it until the first rays of springtime, but until your crops start actually producing a harvest and you can replenish your food stores. That's also assuming you understand how root cellars work and how to properly store your fruits and vegetables. If you plan to fortify your suburban cul-de-sac, you better be 100% sure that EVERY SINGLE PERSON on your block has the exact same amount of food, ammo, and seeds as your family does. What is most likely going to happen is everyone is going to talk the talk but very few of them are going to actually put their money where their mouth is and buy enough long-term food.

At the end of the day, YOUR FAMILY'S FOOD is going to be distributed among the group once they figure out that you aren't starving like everyone else. The group WILL confiscate your food eventually...guaranteed! Granted, as a group you have some strength in numbers, but that also plays against you when your entire street is starving to death and they decide to come for your food. If your cul-de-sac is on the outskirts of town, I can assure you that eventually there will be raiding parties much bigger than your band of merry men. The moral of the story is if you stay in or near the city, you will be overrun eventually.

The overwhelming truth in all these scenarios, once again, comes down to a single focus. It's not the EMP, the cyber attack, or the solar flare that is going to kill you. Your plans MUST include staying as far away from the starving masses as possible. Aside from the resurgence of long forgotten diseases like cholera and dysentery from poor sanitation and hygiene, the starving and desperate masses (even the everyday Joes) are going to be the real killers. So maybe I've convinced you to re-think some of your plans. Now what? Back to square one? Not quite. All the supplies and food you've already attained are still needed. You just need to stage them far away from the population centers and you can actually do this on a budget. Don't bank on the fact that you are going to have a running vehicle or clear roads to load up all your gear and bug out of town. Regardless, you must get out of town which means bugging out. To do so requires a pre-organized plan of action. Below are my recommendations.

Where to Go...

Some would say to find an existing survival group on a prepping forum, especially if you have some sort of skill or expertise to bring to the table. That may work out for you if you're a doctor or surgeon and I am not discounting the idea. Just be careful. The TV show *Doomsday Preppers* is a perfect example of how bats**t crazy some preppers are. By the way, if you are getting the bulk of your prepping advice from the aforementioned TV show...you are doing it wrong! There are hidden gems of information in that program, but the experts are the same ones I've already discussed numerous times: they have no understanding or experience with societal breakdowns and the dangerous side of human desperation. A lot of the "suburban" preppers they give good ratings to wouldn't last three weeks in a grid down scenario.

If you can't afford a bug-out retreat location, I would first point you to family members (even extended family, like second cousins) who live well away from the city. If you think discussing the whole prepping idea with them will make you the "crazy nephew" at family get-togethers, then just rent a storage unit close to where they live and cache your supplies there. Once the SHTF is in full effect and you show up at their doorstep with boxes of food, your former preparations will make you out to be a genius and a forward thinker.

If you don't have rural relatives, then I would suggest you take up renting cabins in the mountains for weekend vacations pre-SHTF. Do your research and make sure the cabins fit within proper retreat location parameters. Also, try to find rentals that are corporate owned and not a cabin that some family rents when they are not using it. A carefully worded casual conversation with the management company or the person renting you the cabin can go a long way to getting an answer to that question. This is a time-consuming process and it may take you multiple weekends to find the right cabin, but it is a lot better option than staying in town. Again, cache your supplies in a storage unit near that cabin. To be clear, you are NOT taking that cabin from someone else; you are hoping it will stay abandoned. If the owners do show up, please realize that YOU are the intruder, not them. However, if you have any savvy whatsoever, you should be able to explain the SHTF scenario to the owners and explain the benefits of joining forces with them for security purposes, as well as extra manpower for growing and harvesting a large garden.

Lastly, if you procrastinated your preps and the SHTF before you are ready, follow the advice I lay out to my co-workers in chapter three of my first book, *EMP: Equipping Modern Patriots, A Story of Survival*. It is risky, but it is still realistic and far better than hanging out in town waiting to get over-run. Knowledge is power, and if you can articulate well what the future holds after a grid-down situation, you WILL EVENTUALLY be able to find a rural elderly farmer to take you in. The key here is having something to trade for room and board, and it doesn't have to cost a lot. You need to have a pre-planned bug-out strategy with paper maps of the rural area you are headed for. Your area should be away from a major city by at least 100 miles. If you live in New Jersey or Washington, DC, you may have to travel much further to get away from the sprawling cities and population centers.

Locate a rural, preferably elderly farmer or couple. Explain to them what is going on in the world and persuade him that he needs you and your family's help to survive the coming apocalypse. The best way to get room and board from them is to have something they need in trade. This goes back to your basic survival gear, having weapons and ammo to help protect his farm and to hunt with, offering you and your family's younger muscles to plant and harvest (this will need to be done by hand, because a tractor will attract too much attention after the SHTF), offering to help keep 24-hour surveillance over the farm and crops, and most importantly having seed to plant the next harvest. I grew up on a small farm and every farmer I know buys his seed two days before planting.

If you did stash food in a storage unit down the road, it will make this conversation MUCH easier (but keep this information as a last resort, your ace card). Also, this recommendation is ideally for the first week after the SHTF. After that, people will be really on edge and approaching multiple farms and knocking on doors will be far more dangerous. I realize that this is a scary scenario, and the perceived safety and comfort of staying in your own home is hard to let go of, especially when you have lots of "experts" telling you that you'll be just fine in town. You won't! Please head my advice and get out of the cities IMMEDIATELY! The uncomfortable nature of this plan is sure better than figuring out three weeks into the SHTF that your decision to board up the windows in your duplex was a very bad decision, and by then it has become far too dangerous to travel on the open road.

All the recommendations I have laid out in this article are still SITUATIONAL dependent. Every person's geographic location and circumstances are different. If you live in Las Vegas and you're surrounded by desert for hundreds of miles, bugging-out by foot would be extremely difficult, almost impossible, without caches of water and supplies stored along your route (hint, hint). Having a classic 4WD pickup to get out of the city in this scenario would be almost vital and at the top of the list for your survival needs. Maybe

you do have an old RV that will get you where you need to go...
great! Then utilize it. Maybe you're a "Pacifist Homesteader" but at
the same time you've negotiated with a "security team" to come help
you protect your farm after the SHTF...that may work for you (make
sure they're trustworthy people). What I'm saying is to stay adaptable
and flexible, but at the same time, never underestimate the starving
masses or what your next door neighbor is capable of once his
children start dying from starvation. Regardless of your
circumstances, please don't make the mistake of thinking that you
can "hide in plain sight" in a big city. You can't! It's just a matter of
time till they find you and your food.

Chapter 8
Bugging Out

Okay, so the SHTF and you've decided your family's safety is more important than the comfort and falsely-perceived safety of staying in your suburban home. You have a location pre-planned to bug out to and it's now time to hit the open road. Once again, you've revolved your plans around a worst-case scenario and you're all ready to head out on foot.

Let's first assume it's a massive financial collapse or pandemic that you're fleeing. You need to be out the door and travelling as soon as things start going south. With the electric grid still operating, you'll still have access to radio and TV news reports, the internet, stores and gas stations. The question then becomes, "When do we actually leave town?" That is difficult to answer, because likely you have a job that will still expect you to come in to work. Your kids may still have school and other commitments. At what point do you say, "Okay, things have gotten completely out of hand and I need to get my family out of here." Every situation is different. If you leave too soon and things settle down, you may end up coming back to town without a job. If you leave too late, you may get boxed in on the highway leaving town. There is no black and white answer here.

My recommendation would be to err on the side of caution and leave earlier as opposed to later.

There are a few things you will want to be aware of. Pay attention to your town's supermarkets, banks, gas stations, and any excessive looting of stores. When things really start spiraling out of control, these places are going to be hit soonest and the hardest. If you are hearing and seeing news reports of massive panic, you need to leave. Especially when facing a pandemic, while living in a ground zero city or one of the original towns facing a high percentage of infected, you need to leave sooner rather than later. It is quite possible that local or federal governments will declare martial law and quarantine your town. Even if that happens I would still try to bug out, but it would be on foot through the woods and late at night as opposed to driving a vehicle. It may not be as easy as you think, though. You won't just be evading patrols of soldiers on foot; the military will likely be using Night Vision, Thermal, and FLIR from helicopters and drones to prevent people from leaving. Don't underestimate the Army's ability to set up a very secure perimeter! Getting in and out of town won't be as easy as it was for the kids in the classic action movie, *Red Dawn*. In the case of a pandemic, it's best to get out as soon as possible.

So the financial collapse or pandemic has gotten really bad and you've decided to get out of Dodge. You have a pre-planned location you are bugging out to, with your SHTF food and supplies staged at that location or a storage unit in the area. Great, but if you are leaving in a vehicle, don't forget to spend a good portion of time scouring your house for anything you might possibly need and everything you can reasonably fit in your vehicle. I would put the highest priority on cleaning out my kitchen pantry and fridge and taking every extra scrap of food that I could find while eating the refrigerated items first. Also, be careful when packing your vehicle that you don't have cases of food pressed up against the window where any passerby can see them. Try not to stack supplies four feet high on your roof racks like you are headed on a safari. These are things that will draw unnecessary attention to your particular vehicle. Use a tarp or blanket to cover and hide your supplies.

When fleeing by vehicle, the first thing I would do is make sure each member of my family had an EASILY ACCESSIBLE bug-out-bag (BOB), which I'll discuss in a later article. Should you get stranded, find yourself boxed in on the freeway, or get held up by someone demanding the use of your vehicle, you need to have your primary survival supplies in manageable packs that you can quickly grab when ditching or surrendering your car. Don't fight to the death defending "extra" supplies from your house. It's better to walk away unscathed from a standoff with a group of desperate people than to lose your life or a family member over "stuff." You can always scavenge, beg or plead for replacement supplies, but you can never replace the life of a child or spouse lost in an unnecessary firefight.

If you followed my recommendation and your primary supplies are at your bug-out location, it will make walking away from your "extra" household supplies a lot easier to stomach. I am not insinuating you leave your vehicle and extra supplies on a whim. If you can gain a tactical advantage and you are sure you can overwhelm your opponent easily, then do so; just don't take unnecessary risks over "extra" stuff. Don't let your ego and pride overwhelm your common sense, either. Gunfights are horrible things, and having all your family members walk away unscathed is unlikely. Also, if you stayed in town till the last minute, you may want to avoid the highways altogether and use secondary roads. Make sure you have multiple avenues of escape PRE-PLANNED on a PAPER map in case one of them doesn't pan out.

There are pros and cons to taking freeways out of town. If traffic is moving at a good pace, you can make better time leaving. If you have a 4WD vehicle, you can even run along the grass or berm if traffic stops (be aware that this draws negative attention to your vehicle by people frustrated and trapped in the same traffic jam). If secondary roads clog up, you may not have the extra space along the edges of the roads to get by. Every city and town's road systems are different and you'll need to weigh the pros and cons of your escape routes on an individual basis. If you are single or married without children, an older, kick-start dual purpose motorcycle with a small travel trailer could also make a great bug-out vehicle.

When I lived in Pittsburgh, my plans were to take the highway north out of town because it was three lanes wide in each direction with a ton of open grass on both sides of the road which could accommodate my 4WD Jeep if needed. However, if I needed to go south, east, or west out of the city, I would NOT have taken the main highways, because even though they were three lanes wide, they have concrete barriers on both sides, preventing a driver from four wheeling out of a traffic jam or bad situation when needed. Also, all three of those directions required passing through long tunnels leading out of town. I recommend avoiding tunnels like the plague! Even in normal traffic, they are the first to jam up. Maybe I've seen too many scary movies, but the last place I want to get stranded is in a potentially pitch-black tunnel with no easy avenue of escape by foot. If this is your scenario, you may need to leave town in an opposite direction and circle around the city on more rural highways and secondary roads. Just stay flexible. Getting from point A to C doesn't mean you absolutely have to go through point B.

Bugging Out in a Grid Down Scenario

Now let's assume that the worst has come to pass and the national electric grid has gone dark for whatever reason. The first thing to do, which may be difficult, is to determine whether or not it is a national or local outage. It would be embarrassing to start bugging out and get a few miles up the road only to discover the street lights working and people looking at you funny. If it's a super EMP attack, it should be easier to determine as a lot of your small battery-operated electronic devices won't be working either. There has been a lot of research and debate on this matter and there are a lot of factors on how severely an EMP will affect different electronics.

There is no guarantee that EVERY electronic device will fail. But it's safe to assume that after an EMP attack you will have multiple devices that won't work. In the case of a cyber attack or physical attack on the grid and possibly even a solar flare (depending on its severity), you should be able to use your cell phone or battery-operated radio to get some updates. Most radio and cell towers are backed up by diesel generators for around 24 hours. Your first order of business would be to call a family member out of town to see if they have electricity and listen to the radio to determine the breadth of the outage. If the solar flare hits only a portion of the country, I would still bug out. If you read the Lloyd's of London report on the scenario of a small solar flare hitting the Northeast, then you know they estimate power being out for as long as a year in most areas. Remember Katrina and how long it took the country to get aid to one city? Trying to get supplies to forty million people in the Northeast would take ten times as long and probably wouldn't be very successful.

Once you've established that the national grid is probably down, now what? This is the worst case scenario and it will likely be TEOTWAWKI (The End of the World as We Know It) within a few short days. If I have access to a running vehicle, I recommend taking the remainder of the first day to score extra supplies or acquire things that I'd never had the money to acquire beforehand. Some stores could still be open (taking cash) and most people wouldn't yet realize the magnitude of what's going on. Most grocery stores have electronic registers and you are unlikely to be able to barter with the manager of a large corporate grocery store. Shoot for the smaller mom and pop stores. Go home and find the smallest, most valuable items you can find, such as jewelry and anything of value in your house that you can easily trade or barter. Having a couple hundred or a thousand dollars in a safe at home would really go a long way in this situation. Go to the mom and pop stores, gas stations and mini marts and barter with an employee or manager for as much food as you can. Try to get primarily canned goods, but anything is better than nothing. Try to procure a grocery cart for each member of the family old enough to push it while you travel. The major looting of grocery stores will probably start within two to three days. You do not want to wait till then or be anywhere near these places when order falls apart. The looting will turn violent very quickly as desperate people fight over a single can of soup.

If your kids are at school, I would consider getting them right away. I would also walk the kids past the local library on their way home and check out as many books as they can on subjects like survival, wilderness medical, canning, farming, and homesteading (unless you have procured a small library on those subjects already at your retreat location). Less than one percent of our population has the knowledge needed to survive the next couple years. Make yourself part of that one percent. Also, if you have a family member who is diabetic or needs some kind of maintenance medicine to live, I would add that to the top of my list for day one. After two to three days, when the drug stores are looted (primarily for their Percocet and Oxycodone), you will likely not be able to locate the medicine you need. Again, make sure you take a couple grocery carts home with you unless you have a better system to travel with supplies.

Spend the rest of that first evening and night cataloging and prioritizing what you can fit into your grocery carts or bug-out vehicle. Be sure to get a good night's sleep because you will want to head out at first light the next day, and that may be the last long night of sleep you get for a while. You've got roughly seventy-two hours before REAL panic sets in. Most people don't have more than four or five days' worth of food in their house. What do you think is going to happen within two weeks? Desperate people are the most dangerous kind. With no police, military, or rule of law, there will be looting, rioting, and violent atrocities on a scale that has never been seen before in this country. Within a month, major cities will burn to the ground. Please trust me on this. You have to get out of the urban areas! This is especially true for those of you who live in upscale neighborhoods. Most inner city people are headed to your neighborhoods first. Rich people have tons of food in their house, right?

Next, let's talk about protection. This includes protection from the elements as well as other people who may try and take what you have. I'll get more in depth on different clothing options later, but for now make sure you dress in layers. Be sure to take an extra pair of socks and a fresh under shirt with you. Wet socks will cause blisters as well as prevent your feet from staying warm. In cold weather, a sweaty or wet undershirt will make you cold. Make sure you change your undershirt before you go to sleep if it's wet; the same applies to your blankets or sleeping bag. In cold weather, do not go to bed with wet clothes, blankets, or sleeping bags as most insulating fabrics lose a majority of their insulation properties when wet. If they are wet from the night before, you need to fully dry them by a fire before sleeping in them or you may not wake up.

If you are travelling, take a tent or a tarp with you. Don't plan on sleeping under the stars. If the weather gets really serious, you may think it's a good idea to find a barn or vacant building to hold up for the night like you've seen them do on *The Walking Dead*. Be very, very careful with that. If you absolutely have to take refuge from a monster storm, make sure you knock and be as non-threatening as possible and explain your intentions. Say something like "I'm just trying to take shelter from the storm with my family. We don't want any trouble, do you mind if we crash in your barn?" Just be very careful. If no one answers the door, it does not mean that no one is there; they may be just hiding and scared. You need to make sure they don't perceive you as a threat.

After protection from the weather, you need to consider protection from other people and that means weapons. I'll discuss weapons much more in depth later but for now, if you don't own a gun, make sure you at least carry some kind of weapon on you. I would keep them hidden for the first day or two, but after that carry a baseball bat, hammer, or fireplace poker. Make sure you carry it in your hand at all times and when you cross paths with other people, be sure to stare them down. Do not be taken off guard by getting into a conversation with some nice older woman only to have it turn into an ambush. The only conversation you offer is an authoritative "Back off!" and "Get away from my family!" You need to pretend you are the baddest gangster on the block. Puff up your chest, walk with a purpose, and stare people down like a professional fighter would. If you act timid or scared, you are portraying an easy target and you are setting yourself and your family up to get ambushed.

Again, make sure you get everything together the first night and start out at first light of day two. Travelling on the first two or three days after a grid-down scenario should be relatively safe. Most people are just going to be confused or scared. If you try and stick it out at your house and realize two weeks later that things are ten times worse than I described they would be, you are screwed. If you are pushing grocery carts full of supplies through the city two weeks after the grid came down, you best be prepared to shoot your way out. Heaven forbid you wait two weeks and decide to leave town without a gun or two, because someone else WILL have a gun and they will take everything you own including the baseball bat they pry out of your cold, dead fingers. Who knows what they might do with your wife and kids. I truly hope I am painting a bleak enough picture for you. With no police, military or law and order, it is going to be survival of the fittest. The biggest meanest man with the biggest meanest gun will be the last one standing at the end of the day.

If you're bugging out on foot, stay on the major highways for the first couple of days for easiest travel and avoidance of the smaller towns and cities along the way. Major highways tend to go through smaller hills and you will experience much less elevation gain and loss than secondary roads, making travelling by foot much easier and faster. Also, highways typically go around smaller towns, which is what you want. Don't get off any exits or enter the towns for any reason! Your grocery carts full of supplies will definitely make you a target. If you cross paths with others on the highway, remember what I said: don't engage in conversation, look as menacing as possible and give them a wide birth. Aside from those of you who live in remote desert areas, it should only take you a couple days to get where you are going. If it takes you longer than a week, you will probably start encountering a lot more desperate people travelling. That is one of the reasons why I recommend your pre-planned area should only be 150 miles outside of town instead of 250-500 like some experts suggest.

If it's taking you longer than four or five days to get where you are going or you start to experience more people on the highways "eyeballing" your gear, I would start travelling secondary highways or roads to avoid the growing hordes of people travelling the highways and interstates. Just be aware that these roads have more houses in view of the road and a tendency to pass through towns instead of around them. This will also be a good time to start travelling at night. I don't care how tired you are at this point, YOU DO NOT ENTER THE TOWNS for any reason! If you have to back track until you find a cross road and work your way around the town using your paper maps, then do so. You need to get AT LEAST a hundred miles from a major city before approaching farmers (if that is your plan). Once the gangs of looters have cleaned out the big cities within a couple months, they will start raiding the smaller surrounding towns and suburbs. You do not want to be caught in their path. I would also try and find a farmer at least five to ten miles away from the small rural towns and preferably at the end of a dead end lane.

While travelling the first few days, be sure to find a good spot to camp well before dusk. If you wait till it's too late, you may end up on a section of the highway that is too populated. You also want to have plenty of time to gather firewood, eat, set up camp and be in your blankets JUST AS it gets dark. You need to conserve your flashlight batteries for emergency use only. When your batteries run out, you have no more light. If you wait too long to leave or it takes you longer to get to your bug-out location, seriously consider travelling at night…but don't use your flashlight. You're night vision will adjust and you'll be just fine walking on the roads. A flashlight will just make you visible from a long way off to potential looters.

Make sure you pick a campsite well out of sight from the road. Yes, I realize this means that you will have to pack your gear in and out to the highway from your grocery carts every evening and every morning. But don't get lazy in this area. If someone travelling your road in the evening sees or smells a fire or hears you through the trees, you may end up with an unwanted guest eating your food or, worse yet, stealing it. I would even go as far as to take shifts throughout the night keeping watch. Spouses and older children are perfectly capable of taking shifts as well. You cannot allow yourself to get burned out by trying to watch over your family day and night and not getting any rest.

Keep an eye on your water while you travel. Never, ever, pass up a water source unless you are sure there is another one up the road. Don't wait till you run out before you start looking for a new water source. Also, don't conserve your water. The last thing you want to do is end up dehydrated. Don't forget to purify the water with drops of bleach or purification tablets. If you have enough good water to get you through until evening time, wait till you can boil it that evening over a fire and conserve the bleach for emergencies. Don't forget to pack the largest pot you have for boiling water.

I would only utilize a fire if you really need it to boil water, cook, dry your clothes and sleeping bags, or to warm up if you're absolutely freezing. In those cases, I would build the fire as small as possible while it is still light out, letting it die down before dark. A fire can be seen from a long way off at night. I would only build a fire at night in the case of an emergency. When the sun goes down, you need to be ready to climb into the sack. Go to sleep early and be up at first light to utilize as much daylight as you can. Again, it is very important to be at least a hundred yards off the road. It will suck lugging your supplies through the woods every morning and evening but it may save your life. Also, make sure no one is around when you leave the road. You don't want anyone seeing you leave the road or where you're planning to spend the night.

These are some things you should consider when bugging out of a big city. Don't get sloppy or lazy and don't hesitate in your actions. Be decisive and follow through. Your family members, especially small children, will probably be scared and worried about the circumstances. Being a voice of confidence and assurance will really help them through the stressful situation.

Chapter 9
Finding New Members for your Retreat

So you've decided to make plans to leave town and bug out in the event of a SHTF scenario or a societal collapse and either buy/build a retreat or move in with a rural relative. You have a plan of action and the financial resources to accomplish your plan, yet you are only one person or single family unit. The list of items to be accomplished in order to provide a safe haven for yourself or your family is endless. Even if you hired a preparedness consultant to organize and guide you through the process, you would quickly find yourself overwhelmed. You cannot reasonably become an expert on "all things prepping" without decades of research, education, and most importantly, experience.

The reason I emphasize *experience* is because there is a huge learning curve in gaining the skills to survive on your own. You can own and read all the best books on homesteading, gardening, OPSEC (Operational Security), food preservation, medical, energy production, etc., but until you have implemented those skills and worked through the nuts and bolts, you cannot rely on that knowledge to sustain you or your family. You cannot wait until the SHTF and then expect "book knowledge" to guide you through.

That knowledge should be cultivated over time through hands-on experience. Preparedness is a long-term, constantly evolving process that happens over months and years. The longer you prepare, the more prepared you will become.

The more areas of prepping that you need to become proficient in, the longer it will take you to prepare. Once you gain some experience in these subjects, you will quickly find that it would be nearly impossible to do them all as a single person or family unit. For instance, you will have to spend countless hours per day gardening, splitting firewood, gathering water, hunting, preserving food, and many other daily tasks, all while keeping a 24-hour watch over your livelihood. You are only one person. When do you plan on sleeping?

In most cases it will be more efficient to team up with others who already have experience in those skills that you lack. At the same time, while there is strength in numbers, there are also huge logistical and OPSEC concerns with larger groups. Having fifty like-minded people living and working together after the SHTF would give you a huge security advantage against roaming bands of looters, but it will also make it very difficult to feed that many mouths in one location. Fifty people will eat an astonishing amount of food on a daily basis; this is food that must entirely be grown, harvested, stored, protected and prepared each day. Short of having a multi-million dollar retreat and the proper infrastructure in place, a group that large would be very difficult to sustain. In my opinion, the sweet spot for a survival retreat group that doesn't have a wealthy benefactor is between 10 and 16 adult members. With this size group, you can buy/build an average size home or cabin and have enough personnel to rotate through security and physical labor duties without overwhelming the members of your group.

So how can you grow to a full retreat when it's just you and your family right now? Very carefully! When looking to form a retreat group or MAG (Mutual Assistance Group), your first priority should ALWAYS be OPSEC. Who can you trust these days? The more people you discuss or share your plans with, the more people are likely to show up at your retreat once they are hungry and desperate. My first recommendation would be to reach out to blood relatives. Having a majority of your group made up of family members will likely prevent disagreements in a SHTF situation from growing into full-fledged feuds and fracturing the group. (However, there are exceptions, such as a very dysfunctional or estranged family.)

I realize that reaching out to siblings and other family members can be quite intimidating when they don't see the world the same way you do. If your extended family members aren't concerned about the direction of our country or don't believe that hard times are coming, then it's because of ignorance. I am not using that word in a derogatory way; I just mean they are uneducated on the subject. It's not like you woke up one day, your head flew off the pillow and you said, "Holy cow! I've got to buy a year's worth of freeze-dried food for my family!" That would make you slightly crazy. You arrived at that point from information you have heard or read through books, internet blogs, and news stories on the subject over the course of months or years. If your other relatives aren't preparing, it's because they haven't had the same information that you've had and you can't expect to have a realistic conversation on preparedness without educating them first.

Educating your family on the threat of hard times doesn't mean you buy them a copy of James Wesley Rawles' *How to Survive the End of the World as We Know It* and expect them to jump on board. Even though there is some good prepping information in it, they will likely never crack the cover of a manual like that. You have to start slowly by forwarding them articles on the threat you are preparing for. On my website, *GridDownConsulting.com*, I have links to literally dozens of convincing articles from reputable news sources on the threat of losing the electric grid. Once they show a little more interest but are still skeptical, you can share the dozens of links to official government and intelligence reports I have there as well. If they like to read novels, I would highly recommend William Forstchen's *One Second After*, an entertaining read from a very accomplished author which paints a bleak picture of how a grid-down scenario would affect everyday life. If they enjoy watching movies, buy a copy of *Electric Armageddon* produced by National Geographic and let them borrow it. That movie depicts how fast society would collapse after the loss of the electric grid due to a cyber attack. While I disagree with how the end insinuates that normal life will quickly resume after society has completely fallen apart, it does present some very good visuals of how fast social order would collapse without electricity.

Unfortunately, it is highly unlikely that your group would be made up strictly of extended family members. Since living with another person or family relies heavily on mutual trust and friendship, the next obvious people to approach would be existing friends. But not any friend will do. Unlike the responsibility you have to help family members during a crisis, your friends should have some sort of survival-related skill they can bring to the table. Don't approach your accountant friend who hates the outdoors just because he's your friend and it's easier than approaching a stranger. When seeking people outside your family to join your group, it's important that you are looking to fill specific roles for your group. You should approach friends who are doctors, mechanics, farmers, hunters, and those with tactical experience and other skills that would be needed in a SHTF scenario.

Even after you have arranged a group with a few family members and friends with specific skills, you will likely still have need for a member or two to fill a specific missing role. Having a rural retreat or MAG that doesn't have members with gardening, medical, or tactical experience would be an enormous mistake! If you can't gain those skills from people inside your immediate sphere of friends and family, you will need to reach out to people you don't know. Randomly approaching your family doctor or the person who works on your car would not be very effective (and likely very awkward) unless you have reason to believe they have similar views as yourself. A better strategy would be to join online preparedness forums and prepping groups that meet to hone their skills. One website to check is *Meetup.com* for groups in your area.

One benefit to reaching out online rather than approaching people you already know is your ability to maintain anonymity. You can easily create a separate email account for such activity while operating under a fake name. Your objective here is to eventually meet and interview someone to join your group, not to brag about or discuss your current preparations! You wouldn't discuss your life insurance policy or the status of your bank account with a complete stranger; keep your preparations just as private. Beware! There are dishonorable individuals who are too lazy to prepare themselves and troll those websites to gain intel on locations to loot after the SHTF. The only information you need to disclose is that you have a retreat group or MAG that is looking for someone to fill _____ role.

Just like any job search engine, you will likely get people who respond, desperate to join a group, who will lie or exaggerate their qualifications for the position. Be sure they know up front that you will require proof of their experience if you meet them in person. When you do find a couple people who may fit the role, be sure that you use a false name and only meet them in a public place—NEVER at your home or your retreat! They will likely have lots of questions about your group, but it is important that you resist the urge to share any specific information and politely let them know that you will be happy to share more information only after they have been chosen. If they are serious about their preparations, they will understand your need to keep things private. Some people may not like that, and if that's the case, let them leave. Just because they have a skill you really need, don't relent and share private information with them until you are absolutely 100% sure they are a good fit for your group.

The one exception to this rule is in the area of security. Without giving specifics, I wouldn't hesitate to really talk up the group's tactical training and your airtight retreat security. In case the individual finds out who you really are or where your retreat is, you'll want them to have some healthy fear of your group and really think twice about trying to approach your retreat after the SHTF. I wouldn't outright lie about your security, though. If you eventually end up choosing them to join your group and they realize you lied to them, it could ruin your trustworthiness.

Don't just improvise these interviews either. Think long and hard about specific questions you want to ask and write them down, like an employer would. Ask them what they are preparing for and be sure it lines up with your group's approach to a SHTF. If they fear an alien invasion and start talking about the mothership, you need to move on! Ask about their work experience, family life, criminal history, current preparation level, religious beliefs, etc. Ask them to give you an example of a stressful situation they have been in and how they overcame it. Be sure to take notes during these interviews so you can compare them with different applicants. Once you make a decision, you MUST perform a background check on the individual. Do not skip this step! If you find any negative information or find that they have lied about their past, you must move on to the next applicant. If they lie to you in their first meeting, they'll likely lie to you in the future and you need to be sure you can trust the people you are bringing into your group and around your family.

Don't be in a hurry and just accept anyone. Follow your gut instincts. Unlike a job position where you can simply fire someone if they don't work out, this relationship will be closer to a marriage. If things don't work out over time, the situation could get messy, especially if they have invested time and money helping you build your retreat and formed emotional ties and relationships with the other retreat members. Potentially, you could end up spending decades living with this person and their family and it's important they are a good match for your group. That not only goes for the men, who typically get along easily, it also goes for the many spouses involved. Remember, it's much easier to invite someone into your group than it is to get rid of them.

Once you have found someone you like, the next step would be to gather with other retreat members so everyone can become acquainted. I still wouldn't have them over to your house or retreat yet. Consider organizing a picnic or barbeque at a park or something similar where everyone can interact. Once you have the other retreat members' blessings, pull them into the group a little at a time and slowly dispense your retreat information as they get more involved. After they start attending meetings and retreat work weekends, I recommend having them invest more sweat equity at first rather than financial resources. That way, if a couple months down the road you are forced to remove them from the group for any reason, you won't have to pay them back to get them to go quietly.

When accepting outsiders into your group, it is imperative that they understand and agree to several things. The first is that they will be required to attend your group's meetings and monthly work/training weekends at the retreat. Secondly, I would insist that they store their 1-year food supply at the retreat location to demonstrate that they are serious. A lot of people talk a big game where prepping is concerned but hesitate to put their money where their mouth is. If they haven't invested in a year's worth of food yet, I would put a timeline on it. Never bring in someone who promises to buy their long-term food "in the future" or insists they want to store it at home, because they may end up showing up after the SHTF with their hat in hand expecting you to feed them. I am not insinuating that you don't return their food if the relationship doesn't work out, I'm just saying that having their food stored at your retreat shows they are committed to showing up when things go south.

The third requirement should be for them to be willing to cross-train into other areas as well. As a retreat group, it's important that everyone has at least a little experience in each area of survival. Every adult member must be willing to learn about the safe operation and handling of firearms, learn to garden, learn to can, learn to take care of animals, learn emergency medical, learn how to walk a patrol, etc.... The person you interviewed may be a doctor first, but he must be willing and eager to learn other aspects of survival as well. Just because he's a surgeon doesn't mean he isn't going to need to pitch in and get his hands dirty in the garden or take a watch at a lookout post after the SHTF.

It's also vitally important that your potential group member's morals and values line up with your existing group's. That's not to say that Christians and someone from the Jewish faith can't live and work together in harmony. However, a person's views on life and morality do matter. I would find out their thoughts on taking lives in a SHTF scenario, looting, and other hot button topics related to survival. What holds them to their morals and values? Their responses can give you a pretty good snapshot about the type of person they are.

The problem is that most people tend to lose values in desperate situations, and the less morals they start out with the faster they lose them. If you don't believe me, read *The Lucifer Effect* by Stanford Professor Philip Zimbardo. While I don't completely agree with him theologically, his book is definitely eye-opening. He is one of the professors who performed the Stanford Prison Experiment in the early 1970s. If you don't know about this, be sure to Google it. His life's research revolved around how good people can do horrific things. He has studied how the German populace so easily went along with genocide, to how regular soldiers do terrible things in wartime, to how normal everyday people can sometimes do horrendous deeds when they are in a stressful environment with little oversight. A person's personality type and religious beliefs matter!

Hands down, the most important thing you need to stress to a potential group member is the need to keep your group's plans completely private! This is absolutely non-negotiable. In your first meeting warn them that if they are caught discussing your groups plans outside the group, it is just cause for immediate removal. I realize that every situation is different and should it ever come to pass, your group can make a judgement call at that time whether to remove them or give them a warning based on the severity of the information leaked. However, as far as they need to know, any discussion of the group to outsiders will result in their immediate removal.

In addition, make it clear that they CAN NOT under any circumstances bring anyone else to the retreat when they arrive after the SHTF. This is a controversial topic and one that very rarely gets brought up when discussing retreat groups and MAGs. However, in my opinion, this is an essential item to discuss when planning a retreat. Between their first meeting with you and their second, you need to insist that they have a discussion with their spouse about the other members of their extended family. Are they seriously prepared to leave their siblings, parents, and grandparents behind to fend for themselves? This is a controversial subject, but if every member of your group showed up with just a single loved one that they couldn't leave behind, your food storage will never get you through the first winter. Even if the majority of your group is related, when the food runs out and people start to starve, your group will fall apart and turn on itself. It is human nature…; it is the Lucifer Effect! Honestly, I suspect this will be the downfall of many prepper retreats when the SHTF. The number one threat to a retreat is running out of long-term food storage too soon!

Every member of your group must understand that if they show up with outsiders after the SHTF, you will politely turn over their food storage and ask them all to leave. Whether or not you actually do this when the time comes is another story, but they must not doubt your resolve to turn anyone away when needed. The ONE exception to this rule is if the individual had stored extra food for the person(s) he planned to bring with him (without hiding his intentions from the group). For example, retreat member "Joe" has discussed the threat of a collapse with his elderly parents numerous times and they just refuse to see the light. He can't stomach the thought of leaving them behind so he buys a year's worth of extra food for both his mom and dad and plans to just show up at their house on day 1 post-SHTF and drag them along to the retreat. At the planning point, it would need to be discussed and voted on within the group. I am not against it as long as it doesn't get too far out of control. If every member does the same thing, you need to be sure you have the proper facilities to house everyone and enough garden space and livestock to support the extra members. The member must also make sure the individuals they are bringing are kept in the dark until the day comes to grab them on their way out of town. Without the ability of the group to vet the newcomers, it is too risky for them to know anything about the retreat. If this is unacceptable to the person trying to join your group, you need to advise them to start their own group for their own family.

Once your group is established, it's very important that you set up a community structure on how things are going to operate. This is not the time and place for a Democracy. Democracy is essentially mob rule (which is why the U.S. is actually a Republic and not a Democracy). If every single person had a chance to vote on every line item that needed accomplished, you would end up with bad decisions being made by well-intentioned members who have little knowledge on the line item in question. This would result in very long argumentative daily meetings which would slow progress on your retreat's work load, as well as squabbling over minor issues with different factions joining together and splitting the fabric of your group. On the flip-side, you can't have a king and serf type of command structure either. Even if it is "your" property and you are the natural leader pre-SHTF, if you try to lord over your group, you will eventually find yourself kicked off your own property weeks or months after the SHTF. Trust me on this! It's not like you can call the police and have them come in and remove the now trespassers that have taken over your property.

The best way to set up your group structure is to have a committee system similar to a small town government. The committee should meet each morning and go over the day's goals and any issues that may need to be discussed. These committee members would make the bulk of the daily decisions for the group.

Major decisions for the group can be scheduled to be voted on at a weekly meeting of all retreat members (other than those on security who could be approached individually for an absentee vote). My recommendation would be to have a five-member committee (unless you have a very large group with numerous departments, thus requiring seven or nine members) with the following structure:

1. An executive leadership position that guides the direction of the committee but still only counts as one vote. This would be the best leader of your group and likely the person who owns and operates the actual retreat property.

2. A food production committee member that is in charge of all things related to growing, harvesting, and storing food.

3. A committee member in charge of security. It is important that this member have real world combat and tactical experience and not just be a local police officer or someone who likes to shoot guns.

4. A logistics committee member who would oversee storerooms and supplies as well as mechanical systems of the retreat.

5. A health and sanitation committee member that is in charge of food preparation, medical, and water supply.

These are not set in stone and you could decide to split up the group's various responsibilities under different committee members. There are also numerous other areas that you will need people to be in charge of but only have limited committee positions. For instance, you will need someone in charge of communications and they could make their recommendations and report directly to the committee member in charge of security. Maybe the person in charge of the hunting parties reports to the logistics committee member, or maybe you'll have him report to the committee member in charge of security. Each group is different and you'll have to decide how to organize your committees and what each member is in charge of.

Your designated committee members must be effective and organized leaders, not necessarily the most knowledgeable person on the subject. For instance, let's say farmer John in your group has the most knowledge on how to grow and store crops but he is also a soft-spoken individual who isn't very organized. In that case, you may want to have someone else sitting in that committee spot that John reports to. The point is, put qualified, educated, and moral individuals in positions to make the important decisions for your group.

It is also essential that you discuss how this committee system will operate and put it on paper so there are no misunderstandings later. I would recommend writing a set of by-laws for your group. People need to understand that in a lawless society there are still rules that will need to be followed. Within these by-laws I would include a list of serious offenses that would result in expulsion from the retreat. To enforce these laws, I would recommend electing a "judge" that would be in charge of settling any minor disputes that are sure to arise between members living in close proximity to each other. This should be an older member of your group that is a moral individual and a person that the other members respect. For major disagreements that can't be resolved by the judge, they could be brought before the committee members to discuss and vote on a solution to the disagreement.

Even with the best laid plans, you can never know how things will end up after a societal collapse. Each person is different and they all have their own way with dealing with stressful situations. You may end up with members who close up emotionally and just sit in a corner in despair. You may have members who become agitated, angry, or even violent. Some of the people planning to come to the retreat may not leave in time and never show up. You never know how people are going to react. If you don't have an agreed upon leadership structure for your group in place before the SHTF, you are asking for bedlam. It's best to make these decisions about who to let into your group and how it will be structured before the SHTF and while everyone still has their sanity.

Chapter 10
Bug-Out Bags

Every prepper's website has articles on bug-out bags (BOB) and every survival forum has threads on the subject as well. If you were to line them up side by side, you'd be hard pressed to find two alike. But that is okay. There are multiple reasons for a BOB and there are lots of reasons why Jim's BOB from Arizona will be considerably different from Craig's BOB in Illinois. Regardless, some individuals get very passionate when defending "what's important" in a BOB. Before we even start discussing my opinions on the subject, we need to clarify: what exactly is a bug-out bag? Part of the reason why many people argue over a BOB's contents is because they're not even talking about the same thing. In prepper's lingo, any fabric sack that you put survival items into could be considered a BOB. I am going to break BOBs down into four categories to remove some of the confusion.

First would be what I, and most others, refer to as a "Get Home Bag." This is a bag that you have in the trunk of your car consisting of the bare essentials to get you home should a catastrophe strike while you are away from home, such as at work. The second category would be what I like to call an "Assault Pack." This bag is lean and mean, containing the minimal survival items you will need if you get stuck out away from your retreat for a day or two. This is also what you would carry on a day hike in the forest pre-SHTF, or while walking patrols around your retreat at night post-SHTF. The third category would be your actual "Bug-Out Bag," sometimes referred to as a "3-day BOB." This bag is intended with just enough supplies to get you from your home to your retreat location while still staying as light and lean as humanly possible. The common misconception is typically found when comparing a 3-day BOB with what I consider a "Lone Wolf Pack," the final category. Now you all know where I stand on the Lone Wolf survival approach, but that doesn't mean you don't need a pack designed for a Lone Wolf. A Lone Wolf Pack is a very large pack with everything you may need to survive for an extended period of time on the road or in the forest. After reaching your retreat or bug-out location, you should repack your 3-day BOB into a larger Lone Wolf pack and place it near your back door, ready to go at all times, in case your retreat gets overrun or a chimney fire breaks out which you can't control.

Here are the five core essentials that ALL of these packs MUST have (these will be discussed in detail in the next chapter):

1. Water canteen and purification system or tablets
2. A fire-starting kit
3. Knife and multi-tool
4. Flashlight
5. First Aid kit

The Get Home Bag

Let's start with the smallest of the four packs and work our way up. A Get Home Bag is very important to have in your vehicle at all times as you never know when things may fall apart. The importance of it increases the further you travel from home. If you work less than a mile from home, it may not seem that important to you. But what about those instances where you go to visit your Aunt Martha an hour away? If we experience a grid-down scenario when you're 45 miles from home, you will regret not having one. In truth, it doesn't really need to be that extravagant or large. In fact, mine fits in a Camelbak MULE ($115) or Condor Fuel ($50) hydration pack. At the bare minimum, you need to have the items listed above.

As far as proper clothing for a get home bag, you need to use common sense here. If you work in an office where you need to wear dress shoes, I would highly recommend you have a pair of sneakers in your trunk (or waterproof boots in the winter). If you get a massive blister from your dress shoes walking the twelve miles home from work, you are going to hate life the next day when you lace up your hiking boots, throw on a pack, and start your 100-mile hike to your retreat. Don't start your bug out on the wrong foot (pun intended). If you are a female who regularly wears skirts to the office and it's winter, consider carrying a pair of sweat pants or even insulated snow pants in your trunk. Even you guys may appreciate a pair of sweats under your dress pants if it's really cold out. Obviously, having a spare heavy winter coat, warm gloves and hat in your trunk is good advice regardless of your preparedness mindset.

If it's summer, I would consider having a light waterproof jacket in case it takes you longer to get home for whatever reason and you get stuck walking home in the rain at night. You can figure it out; just use common sense and take some time to actually think through your personal travel habits. Also, don't get complacent about switching out your summer clothes/shoes with your winter coats/boots when the weather changes. The last thing you'll want is to find is a spare t-shirt and a pair of running shoes in your trunk when there's six inches of snow on the ground. Most smart phones have calendars with reminders that pop up on your phone. Just set a reminder for October 1st and April 1st each year, or whatever dates the weather changes in your area.

Another consideration for a get home bag would be a pistol with a couple spare mags. Again, in most catastrophes like a grid-down situation you shouldn't have any looting and rioting on day one while you're walking home. However, it never hurts to have some protection on you, even in normal times. There is no reason why you need to carry an AR-15 or AK-47 in the trunk of your car unless you are travelling far from home and things will deteriorate before you can get back there. It's just an extra 8 pounds you will need to carry home from work, and it will earn you sideways glances. You'll get plenty of practice carrying around the extra weight of that weapon in the near future, I assure you.

All that being said, please check your local laws about keeping handguns in your trunk and FOLLOW THEM. If you live in a place like Maryland or New Jersey, which outlaw the practice, don't be stupid. Follow the law. Four days after the SHTF when the police are staying home to protect their loved ones from the looters, THAT is when these types of laws go out the window. Don't get arrested and lose your future rights to own guns over something stupid. Personally, I have a conceal carry permit and you would be hard-pressed to find me out in public without a concealed Glock 19 and a spare Glock 17 +2 magazine. I'm not paranoid or trying to be a hero, but every victim of a violent crime probably thought at one point, "It won't happen to me." I have a wife and a three-year-old boy to protect, and I refuse to let them be victims!

The Assault Pack

The other small sized BOB you should have is what I call an Assault Pack. My personal assault bag is the Voodoo Tactical *Praetorian Lite* pack ($100). The reason I love this pack is because it is extremely streamlined and only extends off your back about 6 inches while also offering a built-in scabbard system for carrying a rifle. Another great assault pack is the Camelbak Coronado ($130) which is also an exceptionally streamlined pack. On a budget, you could feasibly dual-purpose your get home and assault packs and buy something that serves both purposes. Just remember that you will want this pack to be as compact as possible so as not to interfere with your weapon sling or plate carrier. This pack will be primarily used to carry your survival essentials, a single MRE, and extra magazines of ammo. You'll be using this pack the most once you are established at your retreat. This is the pack you will take with you if you need to leave the retreat to go out hunting, gather firewood, set an ambush, or while walking a patrol of your property. It will provide enough supplies to get you by if you get stranded out for a day or two away from home.

The Bug-Out Bag

Next comes your actual 3-day Bug Out Bag. In previous years, my BOB resembled more of a Lone Wolf Pack and it wasn't until after an extended backpacking trip that I realized there is no reason to carry half the crap I was carrying with me to my retreat. Over the course of three days in the forest, I hadn't used half of the items I had brought with me. So why was I carrying it? Each item had seemed like a good idea at the time.

Some of the stuff you plan to take with you should probably be staged at your retreat location. Why would you want to burden yourself with a 70-lb pack when you could just as easily reach your destination while keeping your BOB to under 30 pounds (in the summer)? There is no need to carry a bulky hand-crank radio as you can easily go three days without outside information. There is no reason to carry a survival fishing kit as you're going to be walking the whole time and you don't have the time to stop, drop a line in the water, and wait for the fish to bite. Your priority is reaching your bug-out location as quickly as possible. You don't need soap, toothpaste, or a change of clothes (other than spare t-shirt and socks). You might get a little funky, but who hasn't gone three days without a shower before? Why carry the extra weight?

As I went on and on, pulling items out of my pack, I realized that I was going to need to buy a smaller pack! This is going to be a very stressful time for you and your family. You can't really make it an enjoyable trip, but you can make it suck a whole lot less by carrying half the weight. Plus, you will get to your destination much faster with fewer breaks.

One of the big things I look for when purchasing a pack, besides the overall quality, is whether its hip belt rides fairly high. I want it to circumvent the lower part of my stomach so I can effectively wear a Battle Belt around my hips at the same time without the pack getting in the way of my pistol draw. Luckily, I am 6' 4" and most average-sized packs fit me that way anyhow. My personal BOB is the Eberlestock Little Brother with the separate hip belt attachment and internal frame (unfortunately, they are sold separately). All were bought for around $225. I realize this may be a lot of money for some people, but if you've ever handled or used an Eberlestock Pack, you will understand. They are the gold standard in tactical packs and well worth the money. If you are on a budget, I would recommend the Drago Assault pack which can be bought for around $60 or a medium-sized military surplus Alice pack, which you can find on eBay in good condition for around $40. Just be sure you get an Alice pack that includes the frame. I used an Alice pack for many years while I was in the military and they are extremely durable and capable packs.

As subsets of the BOB, you can have what I consider a spouse BOB and a BOB for a child. Your spouse's BOB will closely resemble your own, but there are multiple items you can easily remove and share items from the main pack. One of these shared items is your first aid kit. However, I would still want my spouse to have a Trauma kit on her battle belt at all times. Spend some time and really ponder what items you could possibly share with your spouse and eliminate anything that is not mandatory.

A child's BOB is totally dependent on their age and size. At the very least, a young child's backpack should have his/her own food and water in it. I would be sure it includes a small Camelbak bladder as staying on top of children to drink and stay hydrated may be difficult. For kids, Camelbak makes a smaller 70-ounce bladder. One of the big considerations you'll need to consider is sleeping bag arrangements. I have yet to find a good quality, reasonably priced, toddler-sized sleeping bag. Also, in winter time, I'm not so sure I'd want to put my small child in his own sleeping bag since I wouldn't be able to monitor how cold he is getting throughout the night. You may need to consider a double sleeping bag for you, your spouse, and your child. If that is the case, finding a Gore-Tex bivy sack for a double sleeping bag could be tough. In this situation, you may need to carry some sort of waterproof tent, once again increasing the weight of your main pack.

The older a child gets, AND THE MORE YOU TRAIN him/her on the use of various survival tools like the ferro rod, the more you can expect them to carry. Teenagers' packs could resemble your spouse's BOB. After looking at numerous packs for my short wife, I settled on the Drago Scout pack ($45). Since your children won't be carrying very much weight, almost any small school backpack will work unless you can afford to splurge on them. Buying cheaper packs for your wife and children is one area where you could cut costs if you don't expect the packs to get regular use. If you plan to go on numerous backpacking trips before the SHTF, then get them something better quality like a Kelty brand pack.

The Lone Wolf Pack

The Lone Wolf Pack is the largest of the four packs and totally dependent on your particular circumstances and the geographical area into which you will be bugging out. Again, I am staunchly against the Lone Wolf approach as a bug-out strategy, but once you are at your bug-out location, you need to put together a lone wolf type of pack just in case you get overrun or need to flee at a moment's notice. This is a very tough pack to nail down as there are SO MANY things you are going to need for living off the land until you are able to find a new retreat location. As a human, you can only carry so much weight and your individual body shape, size and condition will determine the best pack to carry this weight.

When I was in my early twenties, I regularly carried over 100 pounds in a Kelty pack during my SERE days in Washington State. Today, I wouldn't make it two miles with a pack like that. You need to pack your lone wolf pack with as much gear as possible, yet still remain mobile. My personal preference for a lone wolf pack on a budget would be the ALPS OutdoorZ Commander Freighter Pack with frame ($110). I must admit that I have yet to purchase this pack, but the features are exactly what I'd want in a lone wolf pack and the reviews on Amazon are pretty stellar. The other option would be to purchase a quality Kelty or Eberlestock Pack. Unfortunately, most large Kelty packs don't come in earth tone colors and they don't have molle webbing or options for attaching a rifle scabbard. A close friend of mine has the Eberlestock Terminator ($499) and it's one of the coolest and most comfortable packs for carrying a lot of weight. Unfortunately, spending $500 on a seldom-used pack is out of the question for a mere mortal such as myself. On a budget, purchase a large-sized ALICE pack with frame which can be purchased on eBay for around $45.

Most of my suggested pack recommendations in this chapter were geared towards a summer bug out in a temperate environment. When choosing the correct BOB for your specific situation, remember there are multiple things that you will want to consider, like the time of year you are travelling and the geographical area where you live. My recommendations may not work for you. In the following chapters, I'll go in depth on the actual items to carry in your various packs and explain the pros and cons of each item.

* Check the back of the book for multiple BOB checklists...

Chapter 11
The Five Core BOB Essentials

Of all the things you may consider stuffing into your BOB or get home bag, there are five things that you MUST have in each of these bags. Everyone knows you need water to survive. The problem with that is the same water that keeps you alive could also make you deathly ill or worse if you don't purify it first. In all the areas of your preparing, this is one area where you can NEVER cheat. I have seen first-hand the high velocity puking and diarrhea brought on by Giardia in a SERE classmate of mine. Trust me when I say you NEVER want to catch Giardia!

There are pros and cons to different types of water purification methods. The most effective method is to boil your water for a full two minutes to be safe. Unfortunately, boiling water takes significant time and effort, not to mention you need a fire which isn't prudent in most evasion or bug-out scenarios. Therefore, you need to choose an alternative, faster solution. In the tablet form, Chlorine Dioxide and Iodine tablets are the most common. They are also the lightest weight of any purification method. Be sure to follow the tablet's instructions precisely and allow plenty of time for the tablets to take effect.

On the flipside are the pump filters that you can buy. Be aware that most filters don't protect against viruses. This may not be a huge issue for you unless you are gathering water in developing countries or where there may be factories near the water source and high agricultural runoff areas. This is something you should research for your bug-out location and your route there beforehand. The other drawback is that pump filters are typically heavier and they require maintenance to keep them working properly.

My personal water kit in all my bags works like this: I carry both tablets and a Sawer Mini Purifier ($20) in each of my bags. The Sawer Mini is very lightweight (only 2 ounces) and it's my go to means of purification, with the tablets as a backup. The Mini is rated for over 100,000 gallons. Once clogged it can be back flushed and still retain 98% of its flow rate. Even so, it is important to screen out any large sediments when gathering water out of a stream or open water source by placing a section of thin T-shirt material over the opening of your canteen (or in the case of the Sawer Mini, the enclosed water pouch). This will drastically extend the life of your purifier as it will get clogged much faster by the numerous floaties in unscreened water. I carry a 6"x6" piece of t-shirt fabric used solely for this purpose, as well as for a sound cushion between my canteen cup and stainless water bottle to prevent them from rattling.

Something else to remember: never use your canteen to draw water from a stream and then place the purified water back into the same container. Even small amounts of residual unpurified water in the bottom of your canteen can contaminate the purified water and make you sick. I always draw my water with the flexible water pouch that came with the Sawer Mini, and then slowly squirt it into my Nalgene Backpacker 32-ounce Stainless Steel Bottle ($25). Instead of carrying a typical plastic canteen or water bottle, it's better to get a single wall stainless or titanium water bottle which will allow you to boil the water in your bottle just in case your purification pump fails or you run out of tablets (redundancy is our friend). If you're not on a budget, I would recommend the HealthPro Titanium 24 ounce water bottle which weighs only 40% of the Nalgene Bottle but also costs a hefty $50.

Once the water is purified by the tablets or it has cooled down (in the case of boiling water in my canteen), I add it directly to my 100-ounce Camelbak bladder in my pack to drink from. I almost never drink straight from my canteen (not that you couldn't or shouldn't); I primarily use the stainless canteen in the purification process and for carrying extra water. In my opinion, owning and using a 100oz Camelbak bladder it is an ABSOLUTE must. Dehydration is extremely common when hiking and doing physical exertion that is outside your normal daily routine. Having water bottles that are strapped to the back of your pack that you drink from when taking a break is unacceptable! You need to be drinking water constantly and twice as much as you think you need. The Camelbak is the perfect solution as the tube rests on your shoulder ready to go. There is no excuse to get dehydrated when the obvious cure for your ailment is four inches from your mouth.

When buying a Camelbak bladder, it is very important to buy the actual Camelbak brand. They are 30% more than the off brands but well worth the extra ten bucks. I learned my lesson as I've now bought two other brands and their seals have either dry rotted or they began leaking at one of the connection points with the tube, soaking my entire pack. I'm not saying that every brand is junk, but I still have my original Camelbak bladder from my SERE Days (almost twenty years ago); it is stained and old but still functions perfectly. I keep it as a backup at my retreat (never throw away old survival items that can still function; store them at your retreat as a backup).

As far as purification tablets, I always carry them as a backup to my Sawer Mini. The best thing about tablets is they are fool proof and you can never break them on accident like your plastic water purifier. For example, you lean against a tree to rest and hear the sound of plastic cracking... (yes, I've done this). I personally prefer the Katadyn Micropur MP1 Purification Tablets as, in my opinion, they have the least aftertaste. At the same time, I practically lived off the cheaper Iodine tablets during my SERE days with no ill effects. Try some different reputable brands and make your own decision. One tablet typically purifies one liter or quart with most brands taking between a half hour to an hour to fully kill most bacteria and viruses in the water. Make sure you follow the instructions precisely and don't shortchange the purification time.

The number of tablets you carry depends on how long you will be out, always adding an extra couple days' worth, just in case. These tablets are extremely lightweight, so the more the merrier in my opinion. In my get home bag and assault pack, I typically carry a dozen tablets as I don't travel more than a day's walk away from home or my retreat. In my bug-out bag, I carry a 60-pack as backup to my filter, but also realize that my trip is less than five days by foot. In a lone wolf pack, I would carry at least ninety (this won't last you as long as you think it will). In that circumstance I would also use boiling any chance I got. Only use the tablets when absolutely necessary like travelling abroad from your static camp.

Another great item I have discovered recently is the Vapur Eclipse water bottle/bladder which I recently purchased on eBay. This is a very lightweight and flexible 1-liter bladder that is BPA free and stands on its own when full of water. It has a screw off lid as well as a pop top for drinking out of it directly. On the lid is a plastic carabineer, allowing you to hang it from the outside of your pack. In addition, when it's empty, you can roll it up and slide the carabineer around itself so it stays very compact. I have not had them long enough to torture test them, but they seem to be decent quality. Instead of carrying the weight and bulk of the stainless water bottle in my get home and assault bags, I'll use the Vapur bottle to hold my water during the purification process before adding it to my Camelbak bladder. The other great use for these would be if you live in a desert environment and have to carry extreme amounts of water with you. As you use them, thy can be rolled up and stashed away in a pocket as opposed to heavier and bulkier bottles.

I will make one more point on hydration. Most people don't realize that hydration should start 24 hours before your physical activity. If you are already dehydrated as you walk out the door to begin your long hike to your retreat, no amount of water pounding is going to help you on your trip. Once you are dehydrated, it is next to impossible to rehydrate while at the same time exerting yourself physically. I mentioned bugging out of town the first morning after the lights go out. Do yourself a huge favor and drink A LOT of water all day and evening the night before you head out. It will honestly make a HUGE difference in your energy level while you're on the road the following day. A simplistic rule of thumb is to pay attention to your urine color. If you are hydrating correctly, your urine should look almost clear. Even if it is light yellow, you are still dehydrated to a degree! If it is dark orange, you are very dehydrated. Most Americans drink a fraction of the recommended daily water intake and unknowingly live in a constant state of dehydration.

Fire Starting Kit

The next vital piece of survival gear that you need to have in every type of BOB is a fire-starting kit. Again, this is an area where people have very strong opinions on the subject. As long as you practice with it and can get a fire going in the rain, then I am okay with what you've got. Here is what I keep in my fire-starting kit and why. First is the most obvious: Bic lighters. I actually carry two, brand-new, full-sized Bic brand lighters and while backpacking I typically start most of my fires with them for speed. Don't buy knock-off brand lighters at the gas station as they typically break much easier (advice from a former smoker). I don't recommend Zippos as the fuel tends to evaporate when it's sitting in the trunk of a hot car for a long period of time before use. If you want to carry an extra 12 ounces of lighter fluid and wicks to keep the thing going, then go ahead. My recommendation would be to buy some extra Bics and have the redundancy. I would consider Zippos more for a retreat as they are higher quality and can be refilled. Butane lighters are even heavier than Zippos and you run into the same problem of needing to carry extra fuel...more weight. At the same time, they are great for starting fire in the driving wind and rain. However, if you know what you are doing, you can work around the wind and start a fire with a single match. Now, my recommendation for a SHTF scenario would be to use the lighters only as needed or when you are in a rush to get a fire going. Once they run out, they are gone for good. Lighters are a luxury.

The most important part of your fire-starting kit would be a quality Metal Match or ferro rod. Yes, you can buy these for three or four dollars on eBay, but please don't skimp here. This is going to be your go to for starting fires. Your life will be much easier if you spend the extra $10 and buy a thicker 6" model like the one by World of Fire on Amazon. You will get a much larger spark throw and you can flip it over and use the other side once you've built a thousand fires with the first end. Don't get the gimmicky all-in-one push rod style devices like the Blastmatch as they don't work well at all and typically scatter your tinder as you use it. If you have never used a metal match to start a fire, I would highly recommend using it exclusively for a while pre-SHTF because they do take a little practice to master. Use them when camping and even when lighting your fireplace in your home. The last place you want to master a needed skill is AFTER the SHTF and your body and mind are running on low batteries. Save yourself the frustration...practice now. As far as matches are concerned, I am not a big fan. The worthwhile ones are large and bulky and you can't carry that many of them while trying to keep your fire kit as compact as possible, but they would be better than nothing.

One of the more debatable aspects of the fire kit is what to use for tinder. You've probably read the forums and the recommendations for using dryer lint, cotton balls and vaseline, and numerous other do-it yourself ideas. Here's my caveat on those methods: if you know how to do it AND PRACTICE WITH THEM beforehand, then by all means use them. For the beginner or those who don't build fires on a regular basis with these methods, I recommend using tried and proven commercial methods. My personal favorite is a tube of Coghlan's Fire Paste. It is not the lightest method, but a single tube can last a very long time. Picture a tube of toothpaste with fire gel inside. A little goes a long way and it will even work when raining and in quite windy conditions. I also carry a couple WetFire tinder cubes for emergency situations or when it's raining and I'm in a big hurry. I would carry two or three in a get home bag and an assault pack, ten in a BOB, and a couple dozen or more in a lone wolf pack. As a back-up, I also carry military-surplus Trioxane Tablets for my Esbit travel stove using them for heating water for coffee and Mountain House Meals. Esbit tablets for your stove are another option. In my opinion the Esbit Tablets produce a brighter flame and more light than the purplish flame of Trioxane Tablets.

To heat and boil water for my meals and coffee, I carry the Esbit CS585HA 3-Piece Lightweight (only 6.9 ounces) Camping Cook Set ($25). It has a little burner cup to offer wind protection to the tablets, as well as a 16-ounce lightweight canteen cup with a lid. It all packs down neatly into the canteen cup. You can use this with any type of fire cubes/tablets. I do recommend surrounding an actively flaming kit with large rocks or digging a small hole to place this in to prevent as much light output as possible, especially when using the Esbit Cubes. I don't carry this in my assault pack or my get home bag as there is no need for the extra weight and I typically only carry a single military surplus MRE which contains its own heater pack. I know some people choose to carry other types of camp stoves with most of them using various types of fuel canisters. In my opinion, they are overkill and this is one area where you can cut weight in your 3-day BOB.

Knives
The third core essential for your various BOBs is quality steel. This is another area where I don't recommend skimping even when

you are working on a budget. There are thousands of knife manufacturers in this world and many options can be purchased for ten or fifteen bucks. But this is a tool your life is going to depend on and one that is going to get a ton of use and abuse. You will want to carry a smaller folding blade in your pocket which can be quickly opened with one hand, a larger fixed blade knife, and a quality multi tool.

When looking for a fixed blade, stay away from the cheaper "survival" knives. You know the ones I'm talking about with the hollow handles and a compass on the bottom. "Survival" is the very last thing they are good for. I don't care if it's made by Benchmade, do not buy one of those knives. It is critical that your fixed blade knife has a full tang design (the blade and handle is one continuous piece of steel) for durability. The knives with the hollow handles typically have blades which are glued, pinned, or otherwise attached to the handle. With the type of harsh treatment your fixed blade knife will receive, it is not a matter of if but WHEN those hollow-handled survival knives will break!

You are looking for a blade length in the neighborhood of 6 inches. Some people want to carry large bowie knives to double as a machete or to be used to chop down small limbs like an axe. Please don't do this. There is no need for the extra weight, and it won't function nearly as well as an axe for chopping or a machete for brush cutting. Don't dual purpose your knives! If you need a machete for your geographical area, then just carry a machete. Another thing to avoid on both your knives is partially serrated blades. Serrations dull quickly and are much harder to sharpen in the field, essentially shrinking the useable portion of your blade in half. A well-sharpened blade will cut items just as well as, if not better than, serrations. If you need to saw through something, use the saw on your multi tool or your Silky hand saw which we'll discuss later. Again, don't try to dual purpose your knives.

Another factor to consider when buying a knife is the blade's contour or shape. For both of your knives, you're going to want a clip point, drop point, or straight back shaped blade for ease of sharpening. Specialty blades like the tanto will just make your life more difficult when it comes time for sharpening while out in the field. Also for both knives, you'll want a good high-carbon steel which will hold an edge as well as be sharpened quickly when needed.

The gold standard steel you can buy for a survival knife is S30V steel, but it is also hard to find in a blade for under $100. If you don't have a tight budget, I would highly recommend the Benchmade Bushcrafter knife which runs around $165. For most people, spending $165 on a single knife is not an option and I realize that. My personal favorite fixed blade carry knife is the Cold Steel SRK which can be found for around $70 on Amazon. It is a very durable, quality knife; just watch Cold Steel's YouTube advertisement on the knife where the employee punches it through oil barrels, car hoods, and slices a pig in half while swinging it like a sword. I've never (and never would) used my SRK for those purposes, but it has held up flawlessly while I've used and abused it in the field for years.

The other major reason why I chose the Cold Steel SRK is the adaptability of the factory sheath. The Kydex sheath has good positive retention even when not utilizing the safety snap. The sheath has multiple slots and holes around the edges, allowing it to be mounted in the horizontal or vertical position on the molle webbing of your pack, plate carrier, or battle belt. If you are really working on a budget, I would then recommend the USAF Survival Knife which I carried for many years and it served me well through an enormous amount of use and abuse. Beware of cheap knock offs by Rothco and others. If you buy a military surplus knife or the USAF Survival Knife by Ontario, either should cost you around $40-45. If you are paying less, it is probably a knock-off and doesn't have the high carbon steel.

While your fixed blade knife is used for larger cutting jobs and splitting firewood, your personal Every Day Carry (EDC) pocket knife is for smaller jobs like cutting 550 cord. One of the more important things to me when considering an EDC knife is whether it is easily opened with one hand. This is the knife that will get the most use and typically you are going to be holding the item you need to cut in your other hand. Being able to reach down into your pocket and open the blade with a flick of your finger is important. For this reason, I prefer an assisted opening blade, though you should check your local laws for what's legal in your state or city.

For an EDC knife, I would steer clear of automatic, button-operated or switchblade style knives as there are more moving parts that could break over time. As with most things survival or prepping, we want our tools to be durable and stand the test of time. I also don't prefer butterfly-type knives. While fun and unique, they are typically heavier and don't come with a belt clip to keep it easily accessible at the top of your front pocket. Your EDC blade should be somewhere between 3 and 3 1/2 inches in length. Again, you can't have the best of both worlds here and your EDC pocket knife can't be multiple tools. If you need a bigger knife, just grab your fixed blade knife. If you carry too big of a pocket knife, it will make doing some of the smaller, more precise cutting jobs difficult. Size is only important in certain aspects of life....

In my opinion, one of the best EDC pocket knives on the market is the Zero Tolerance (ZT) model 0350 which uses S30V steel and Speed Safe opening for around $150. If that is too rich for your blood, reach for the Kershaw 1678 Camber folding knife which is a terrific value and my personal EDC. At only $70 on Amazon, it surprisingly still utilizes S30V steel and has lightning-quick assisted opening. If you are working on a very slim budget, you have a ton of options to consider but remember that you get what you pay for. I wouldn't go too cheap on a tool you will be using multiple times a day. My original EDC, which I carried for years and still use as a backup is the Kershaw Clash which utilizes fairly decent steel, has assisted opening, yet only costs around $30. Just make sure you get the model without the serrations!

There are also a few optional knives you may want to consider like a push knife or a "necker." A push knife is a compact tactical knife/dagger for hand-to-hand combat. This is something you would have mounted easily accessible by your strong side hand on a battle belt or plate carrier. They almost always come in a compact Kydex sheath to make mounting on molle webbing a snap. A couple models to consider are the Benchmade Adamas CBK for $95 or its cheaper cousin the Gerber Uppercut Knife for $35. This is one area where even a cheaper knife would serve the purpose just fine. Realistically, how many hand-to-hand combat situations are you going to find yourself in where you need to stab someone in the throat? If you answer that with "often," then you are doing something wrong and you need to re-evaluate your protection strategy and stop letting potential threats get within your personal space.

The other knife I would consider would be a "necker" knife. A necker knife is a lightweight, very compact knife that you carry on a chain around your neck. I personally don't care for having that extra weight around my neck, but I can still see the usefulness of having one. Let's say you get captured and they have your hands zip-tied. Having a tiny blade hanging over your heart could easily be missed in a pat down allowing you to get free at some point. My only qualification for this knife would be that it is as small and thin as possible. You may also want to consider throwing your BOB on and making adjustments to the chain so your knife isn't resting underneath the sternum strap of your pack. That would be *no bueno, amigo.*

Staying in the category of knives, another must-have in all your BOB's would be a quality Multi-Tool. Even in the name, "multi," it explains how this tool can be used for multiple projects. I don't have any serious objections to whichever brand you buy except 1) don't go cheap and 2) don't get crazy! Don't go cheap is self-explanatory; you should expect to pay at least $40 to get a quality tool that will last you for years. What I mean by don't go crazy is to keep your multi-tool practical. You don't need a million useless gadgets on the thing, half of which barely work for their intended purpose. You don't need a pair of miniature scissors, mini wrenches, ice pick, or an eyebrow brush on your multi-tool. Here is what I want in a multi-tool:

- A straight blade knife to act as a backup to my EDC
- A small aggressive toothed saw for a backup to my Silky saw
- A straight tip screwdriver and a Phillips head that is somewhat pointy for multiple screw heads
- A can-opener as a backup to my p38
- A file to sharpen the serrations on my sawblade if needed
- The back section of the pliers to act as wire cutters

Everything else is superficial and extra weight. In my opinion, the perfect combination is the Leatherman Sidekick for around $45. You can get much more expensive multi-tools if you'd like, but that is up to you.

Flashlight

Believe it or not, the fourth essential is going to be the one that I highly recommend NOT using, or at least using sparingly: a flashlight. Once again I trek across the sacred grass of some people's addiction. I admit freely and my wife can attest to the fact that, "I, Jonathan Hollerman, am a flashlight addict." There is just something about bright lights that makes me feel all warm and fuzzy inside like a gremlin. That being said, brightness IS NOT your main concern for a survival flashlight. Let me repeat that....brightness is not your main concern for a survival flashlight! It's funny to think back to only a decade ago where you had one gold standard for flashlights and that was Maglite. If you wanted a brighter light all you did was get bigger batteries until your flashlight resembled a baseball bat. Even the biggest Maglite of the day couldn't hold a candle to one of today's compact LED flashlights. With the invention of the high intensity, nearly indestructible LEDs and more powerful batteries, flashlights have been getting brighter and brighter. Brighter is NOT always better though. In a tactical flashlight on the end of my Glock or attached to the rail of my AR-15, you can't be too bright. If they made a tactical flashlight that would blind my opponent a mile away, I would probably stand in line on Black Friday to get one. In a BOB flashlight, there are other things that are more important to me and to be honest, I'm not trying to announce to the whole world where I am.

When picking a BOB flashlight the first thing I think of is batteries. Not only what is the battery life like, but what type of batteries does it take. Again, planning for a long-term grid-down scenario with no electricity, what type of battery do think is going to be easiest to scavenge for: AA batteries, a CR123 battery, or heaven forbid an 18650 battery? You will see that flashlights transition from AA to CR123 and even the newer 18650 whenever you cross over about 300 lumens. While you can argue that the efficiency of the newer CR123 and 18650 batteries is better than the efficiency out of AA or AAA batteries, you can't convince me that AA batteries aren't going to be far easier to find if you're ever forced to scavenge for batteries. Trying to scavenge rechargeable CR123 batteries would be next to impossible (this will probably change in the future).

Currently, AA and AAA batteries are also much easier to recharge with a small solar kit. Yes, yes, I know…some off brand companies are now making rechargeable CR123 batteries. Unfortunately, if you do some research, you'll find that they are unreliable at best…and complete crap at worst. With 18650 batteries, they come in two types of voltages and about a dozen levels of Mah. With the same research, you'll also find that if you put the wrong Mah 18650 or CR123 battery into your bazillion lumen flashlight, you could possibly melt the circuitry and LED in your flashlight, leaving you with an expensive paper weight. Now, I'm not saying that the technology won't come around in the near future, but for 2016, I'm saying you should stick with a rechargeable battery in a standard size. Years ago, I used Sanyo Eneloop AA rechargeable batteries for XBox controllers. They must have gone through a hundred cycles on the recharger with no observable difference in how long they would keep a charge. I highly recommend Sanyo Eneloop batteries for your retreat.

Pausing for my personal flashlight rant.... A big pet peeve of mine where flashlights are concerned is that every company wants to compete for the most annoying flashlight in the world by adding multiple flashing options. It's next to impossible today to find a modern flashlight with only high and low beam features. Every time you turn it on, it's like spinning the big wheel on The Price is Right to see what mode comes on. And if you click past the light mode you want, you need an abacus to count the modes until you get back to the one you want. Heaven forbid you click quickly because you are frustrated and click past the mode you want a second time. I have nearly thrown a flashlight in a river before. Who the heck needs an SOS light on their stinking flashlight?

Don't even get me started on the uselessness of a strobe light (which I'll discuss later when I cover tactical gear). I'd like to find the boy genius who decided that every flashlight in the world needs a strobe light, dig him up at the graveyard, and kick his carcass in the jingle bells. Are there way more people having techno rave parties in their living rooms than I think there are? Maybe I'm just not getting invited to the parties...who knows.

I can already hear Tacticool Bobby instructing me, "The strobe feature on your flashlight is meant to disorient an attacker...." *Really*? I didn't know that, Tacticool Bobby. Guess what, it also disorients the user and any team mates nearby and makes it much harder to make a split second, life or death decision on whether or not to pull that trigger! The 500+ lumen tactical lights offered today are more than sufficient to disorient an attacker in a dark room and cause him to divert his eyes, THERE IS NO NEED TO HANG A DISCO BALL IN FRONT OF IT! In the days of 100 lumen flashlights, you could potentially make the case (BARELY) that there was a practical application for a strobe feature as 100 lumens doesn't really disorient someone or cause temporary blindness. But with the super bright flashlights available today, there are zero, zilch, nada reasons to have a strobe feature on a standard flashlight regardless of what some keyboard commando on the Intraweb tells you. Okay. Personal flashlight rant over, I'll continue....

There are a bunch of really reliable flashlight companies out there like Streamlight, Surefire, Fenix, Olight, just to name a few. I am not here to force you into one brand or the other. For your BOB, my recommendation is to buy a 200-300 lumen flashlight, with a low power mode, that takes AA batteries, has a sturdy aluminum construction and o-rings, is decently waterproof, and comes from a reputable manufacturer. The manufacturer doesn't matter to me unless you are buying cheap knock offs from China (not that I don't have a few of those lying around as well). Once again, do not try and dual purpose your survival flashlight and turn it into a tactical light or the other way around. There is no reason to have 600 lumens bouncing off the trees around you while setting up camp and announcing to everyone else in the forest where you are.

My recommendation if you can afford it is the nearly indestructible Surefire E2L Outdoorsman ($225). If that is too steep for you, my personal favorite (even over my Olight and Streamlight) is my Nightcore MT2A which throws out 345 lumens on two AA batteries. The most important reason I like the Nightcore is the switching mechanism. Even though it has all the crazy SOS and strobe features, I have the ability to program them out and never, ever, ever have to see them again. Basically, every time I turn the MT2A on (tail switch), it starts on high every time. I then have the ability to quickly switch between low and high as I'd like with a slight turn of the bezel. I am not trying to badmouth anyone's brand of flashlight, I am just saying that Nightcore is my personal favorite when working on a budget.

One flashlight is not enough for a BOB though. Redundancy is our friend and not being able to see in the dark if needed could be bad. Now, I will concede that if you are trying to keep your pack as light as possible, you could always use your battle rifle's tactical light as a backup, but that goes back to not wanting to use a super bright light in an evasion situation. As a backup light (camp light) I like to use the cheap 5 LED lights that clip on to your hat bill. Typically they run on the common CR2032 batteries which surprisingly last a long time due to the efficiency out of the small LEDs. They are extremely lightweight and allow you the freedom to use your hands. They are bright enough to do close tasks with your hands around your campsite but not so bright that they blind someone if you turn your head towards them to speak. Even though I have been using the same one for many years during numerous hunting seasons, they are not bulletproof and I typically buy them by the 5-pack. Having a new one in your BOB should more than get you where you need to go without needing to carry an extra battery (though it's never a bad idea).

Another option, especially if you don't wear ball caps like I do, is the headlamp design which attaches around your head with an elastic band. Once again, there is no need to go crazy here. You do not need a super bright 1,000 lumen headlamp for this use. Typically, you are going to be looking down at your hands or camp stove and there is no need for 500 lumens to glare back at you. If you are going to be mountain biking through the forest at night, then yes, you may need the 500 lumens. Get a headlamp that uses the same batteries (AA or AAA) as your survival flashlight. You don't need to go super expensive here if you don't have the funds, but don't get the super cheap China knock offs either. A Rayovak or Coleman brand headlamp will do the trick. While I own a couple different styles of these headlamps, I don't typically carry them in my BOB as they are much bulkier and heavier than a hat bill light. A third option for hands-free lighting, besides a hat bill light or headlamp, would be to just get a cheap elastic headband that would hold your primary BOB flashlight.

BOB flashlights should only be used for a few minutes per night, such as if you wake up to use the restroom. Like I've mentioned before, while bugging out, you need to have already eaten, built camp, and be climbing into your sleeping bag shortly after the sun sets and rising at first light. The exception to that rule would be if you have somewhere really far to bug out to by foot or you are travelling after the first 4 or 5 days after the collapse. At that point, I would recommend travelling at night. THAT DOESN'T MEAN YOU NEED A FLASHLIGHT THOUGH! Especially in circumstances where your travel is closer to an evasion scenario, the less light you make the better. If you are walking or pushing a grocery cart down the open road at night, there will be plenty enough ambient light to keep you on the road, even on the most cloudy of nights.

Even if you are travelling through the woods at night, you still don't NEED a flashlight. During the Evasion section of my SERE training, I don't remember using a flashlight a single time. Wear a hat bill, hold a two foot long (skinny) twig vertically in front of your face while you walk slowly. It will let you know if you are about to walk into a branch. Your concentration should be down at your feet placement and the bill of your hat will protect your eyes. You will surprise yourself at how well your night vision adapts and allows you to move (slowly) about a dark forest.

First Aid Kits

The last item on the survival list would be a first aid kit. Before I begin, it is important to inform you that I am not a doctor, nor do I have any formal medical training other than Emergency First Aid training when I was a SERE instructor. All of the information below was gained through personal experience, conversations with professionals, and research. Do your own research and consult a doctor. You cannot hold me liable for any information or misinformation below.

I actually have my first aid kit broken into two. I carry a very compact Bleeder/Trauma kit on my battle belt which is always accessible no matter where I am, and a larger first aid kit on my BOB. Whether it's two years later and I am hoeing in my garden, going to get firewood for my cabin, or stepping out into the woods away from my campsite to relieve myself, I always have my battle belt and trauma kit within reach. We'll discuss the battle belt later when I go through tactical gear.

Essentially, the trauma kit I carry on my person is enough to stop massive bleeding and get me back to my retreat or campsite where my BOB and larger Med Kit awaits. Again, minimalistic is the key here because this is something you will be wearing 24 hours a day. The best system I've found for this is using the HSGI Bleeder pouch which is just the right size to hold the bare essentials. What I carry in this compact trauma kit is:

- 1 - Pair of nitrile gloves
- 1 - Pair of Hyfin Vent chest seals
- 1 - Israeli 4" battle dressing or a 4" flat fold H-battle dressing
- 1 - Z-fold Celox impregnated gauze
- 1 - Celox granule plunger
- 1 - Combat application tourniquet (CAT) attached to the side of the pouch.

That's it. No Band-Aids, no Tylenol or anything else; just the bare essentials to stop massive bleeding most likely brought on by a gunshot wound.

The reason I picked the HSGI Bleeder pouch is because it's streamlined and just big enough to fit the bare essentials. It is small enough that when mounted in front of my pistol holster, it doesn't get in the way of my draw stroke or bunch up when I sit down in a chair or in a vehicle. When you pull the flap up on the HSGI Bleeder pouch, you are greeted by a plastic ring attached to a red piece of webbing that loops down through the bottom of the pouch. With a light pull, you can slowly pull the contents of the pouch out one by one. In an emergency, you can give the webbing a harder pull and it will spill the contents on the ground next to you where you lay bleeding. I really like the system and highly recommend it.

It is important to wear gloves when working on yourself to keep any bacteria that may be on your hands from infecting the wound. When working on someone else, you should also wear gloves as you may not know what disease or virus they may be carrying at the time. I'll leave it up to you what type of gloves to carry. Where the Israeli and H-bandage Battle Dressings stand apart from other common battle dressings is they both have a plastic clip on the dressing itself which allows you to wrap the wound one handed. This system allows you to put considerable pressure directly overtop the wound even with the use of a single hand.

The next item in the trauma kit is the Hyfin Vent chest seals. One of the more serious combat injuries is a gunshot wound to the lung. What happens in this situation is that the chest cavity is no longer a sealed system and air rushes in through the wound causing the lung to collapse. This prevents the lung from introducing fresh oxygen into your blood stream and in a lot of cases it only takes the patient a few minutes to go into irreversible shock, causing them to quickly die. It is important to react quickly in this situation. The reason I chose the Hyfin Vent chest seals is that they contain a proprietary valve built into the seal which allows blood and fluid to escape the wound yet still prevents air from entering the wound. Don't forget to search for an exit wound in the back of the patient as that would obviously need sealed as well. Using a chest seal does not fix the problem permanently but will buy you some time to get back to your retreat and locate a surgeon.

One of the most important items in your trauma kit are the Celox gauze bandage and plunger. Celox is a blood clotting agent designed to stop the flow of massive bleeding from injuries like a gunshot wound or a chainsaw accident. Before I begin, it's important for you to know that this is a last resort item. You need to try stopping the blood flow first with direct pressure and utilizing pressure points; only use this when other options have failed. While an amazing, life-saving product, it can be difficult to clean out of the wound once you've reached professional help. With the introduction of Celox onto the battlefield less than a decade ago, soldiers are now surviving wounds that would have most-assuredly killed them before Celox was invented. Previously, you would need to take the Celox gauze and use your figure to press it deep into the wound channel and then apply pressure. With the recent introduction of the Celox plunger (which resembles a large syringe), you can now inject Celox granules deep into a wound to reach internal bleeding or a partially severed artery which may have been hard to reach with the Celox gauze.

I highly recommend carrying both and only using the plunger as a very last resort. Whenever the patient reaches professional medical help, the surgeon will need to remove the majority of the clotting agent before closing up the wound. It is much simpler if the surgeon can slowly pull a piece of gauze out of a wound as opposed to a bunch of loose granules which have spread internally throughout the wound area. This is where the Celox brand over the Quick Clot brand is vital. I have read articles online where doctors have said that removing Quick Clot from a wound is much harder than removing Celox and in a lot of cases requires scrubbing, which often re-opens the wound. In a hospital setting, this may be okay, but if you are operating on your retreat's kitchen table out of a medical journal, you may have a much harder time removing the granules while controlling excess blood loss. The other reason is that, to my understanding, you need to remove almost all traces of Quick Clot before closing up a wound whereas Celox is a more natural-based formula and if there is some small residual left behind, the body can absorb it. Now, I have read this in two locations from reputable sources. However, I cannot vouch for its accuracy. Once again do your own research on the subject.

The last item in your trauma kit doesn't actually go in the bleeder pouch but gets attached to the side of the HSGI Bleeder pouch. The Combat Application Tourniquet, otherwise known as a CAT, is absolutely vital to have on you at all times to stop massive blood loss from an injury to one of your extremities. After the invention of prefabricated tourniquets and their full implementation into the military in 2005, studies showed an 85% decrease in mortality from extremity exsanguination in injured soldiers on the battlefields in the Middle East. The effectiveness of the CAT was so dramatic that in 2005, the Combat Application Tourniquet was selected as one of the Army's top 10 greatest inventions. However, along with all the items in your trauma kit and first aid kit, it is not a matter of just having it on you, but knowing how to use the item when the time comes. There are numerous instructional videos on YouTube for each of these products I've mentioned and it's absolutely vital that you educate yourself on their use. You don't want to be bleeding out on the ground while trying to read the fine print on the back of your Celox Plunger or tourniquet!

The trauma kit is something you carry on you every day, all day. Your actual first aid kit is something that stays with whatever BOB you are currently utilizing. You can include everything including the kitchen sink in a first aid kit, and there are a hundred different configurations and recommendations on the different survival forums. You don't need a field surgeon's backpack-sized first aid kit for a four-day bug out. My personal opinion is to keep your bug-out bag's first aid kit lightweight and easily accessible. This is where having molle webbing on the outside of each of your packs comes into play. There are innumerable prepackaged first aid kits out there, but most are cookie cutter and use cheap nylon pouches which don't allow you to attach it to the outside of your pack and typically don't include Celox. They also include tons of things you're never going to need, or items you can do without on a four-day journey. The exception to this rule are companies like *ChinookMed.com* and *TacMedSolutions.com* which make stellar tactical first aid kits, but expect to pay a couple hundred dollars to get a kit with everything you need.

I highly recommend building your own for a couple reasons. One, you can tailor it to your family's specific medical needs without carrying excess items. Two, the experience of building your own kit will make sure you know exactly what you have in your first aid kit and where it is in the pouch. If you buy one off the shelf, you will probably never open it and study it. When the emergency happens, you are going to be fumbling through the unfamiliar first aid kit and pulling everything out onto the ground to find what you need. Three, you will end up with extra supplies for your retreat's first aid kit. For instance, you'll buy a box of various size Band-Aids but only throw a handful in your first aid kit keeping the rest for your retreat.

For my first aid kit, I use a Condor First Response Pouch which allows you to quickly tear it off your pack in an emergency. It is around 5"x7" and about 3" deep. Remember, you can't bring everything, so consider what is most important and pack the items you can't do without. Tailor your first aid kit to your family and the size of pouch you will be using. You don't need a full bottle of anti-diarrheal medicine for a short bug out. Just bring a couple doses of each type of medicine you may need and put the rest with your retreat's first aid kit. The other thing I would recommend is when you actually assemble your first aid kit, make it a fun family event some evening. This will ensure that all the family members know what's in it and where to find it, in case you're not around when the need arises.

* Check the back of the book for multiple BOB checklists…

Chapter 12
Bug-out Bag Supplies

In the next two chapters I am going to break down the rest of the supplies you may be carrying in your pack and discuss the pros and cons of each, as well as my own personal recommendations. Aside from the five core essentials I laid out in the last chapter, food would be the next item on my list. The only reason it didn't make it into the top five is that it may not be necessary in the get home bag or the assault bag; you can easily last a day without food. After that, you can only go so long without food until your body starts to shut down. In the high stress, high energy activity of bugging out of a city, your body is going to need plenty of calories or you're going to crash.

In recent years, there have been some new high tech survival bars, otherwise known as Emergency Food Rations, that can give you between 2400 and 3600 calories in a small lightweight package. I do not recommend them for bugging out though, and would only purchase them to use as a last resort when all your long-term food is depleted at your retreat. Regardless of how prepared you may be, a SHTF scenario where you are forced to leave home is going to be a very stressful situation with the potential to push you beyond your mental limits. Even the most "normal" people can be pushed too far to the point of insanity and deep depression. I am not kidding when I say that having good-tasting food to eat after a stressful and physically demanding day can REALLY lift your spirits. If you spend an entire day struggling to push yourself and your family, and then sit down to eat a survival bar that tastes like cardboard, you are going to want to slit your wrists. I know I would. Even if it requires carrying a little extra weight, give yourself something tasty to look forward to after a long day.

If you are forced to walk to your retreat carrying a pack or pushing a grocery cart, you need to realize that your body is burning double or triple the amount of calories you would be burning in a normal day sitting at your cubicle. Plan accordingly! Just because the Mountain House package says two servings on it, doesn't mean it's actually two servings for most of us. In fact, a typical serving of Mountain House only has around 240 calories in it! With the large amount of food necessary to get you through three days' worth of hiking, you need to be mindful of weight. The answer for most preppers is freeze-dried food. I always chuckle when I hear the survival "experts" mention this rationale. The one thing you need to remember is freeze-dried food requires water to prepare it. If you have to carry that water on your person, then it's not saving you weight. If you are travelling where water is scarce, that means you'll need to carry extra water with you to make your meals. Technically, you can eat freeze-dried foods without adding water, but it will literally suck the water right out of your body like a sponge, forcing you to drink extra water to rehydrate. At the end of the day, freeze-dried foods don't really weigh less because the water to reconstitute them has to come from somewhere, typically from the water bladder you are carrying in your pack.

Once again, I am not going to tell you what type or brand of food to carry. This is an area where every individual's taste buds are different. Make sure you try each flavor at home before you stuff them into your BOB. You don't want to discover that you absolutely despise Mountain House Lasagna (one of my favorites) and be forced with the realization that you only have that to eat the next three nights. Talk about a depressing thought. I personally have yet to try a Mountain House meal that I don't like or couldn't stomach. On the other hand, EVERY SINGLE knock-off brand of MREs has caused me to want to gag.

If you are going to go the route of MREs, I highly recommend you buy ACTUAL military surplus MREs. Especially when buying on eBay, beware of false advertising as a lot of manufacturers of fake MREs use terms like "military contracted," "military approved," "Mil-spec," and other terms that may be confusing. Make sure they are official military surplus cases, which will be labeled Menu A or Menu B. Also pay attention to the dates as some unscrupulous sellers will try and sell MREs close to or past their expiration date. The other reason why real military surplus MREs are superior is they come with the heater packets to warm your entrée whereas the knock-off brands typically don't. Being able to eat a hot meal with no fire, flame, smell, or smoke is obviously beneficial over a meal where a flame is required to heat water. Perform a simple Google search and you will find multiple online guides for buying surplus MREs.

In my opinion, and what I personally carry in my BOBs, is a mixture of Mountain House Pro-pack (vacuum packed) meals, MREs, and cold weather MREs otherwise known as LRP (Long Range Patrol) Rations. They are harder to find but can sometimes be found on eBay. LRPs are obvious as the outer wrapper is white instead of tan. LRP rations have all the same features as normal MREs except that most of the items are freeze-dried. This means the LRPs have a much longer shelf life than normal MREs. While I like Mountain House meals, they don't give you near the variety or calories as a full MRE. You are essentially stuck with one item. In an MRE, you get extra side items like crackers and cheese, pound cake, brownies, drink mixes, and candy. It is a much more pleasant meal than simply eating a single pouch of food.

With either type of MRE, I recommend removing the outer bag and repacking them in zipper-seal bags to save space while removing items you don't need. I have no use for six bottles of Tabasco Sauce, three dozen creamer and salt packets, or six plastic spoons, and therefore no need to carry the extra weight. Only remove the outer pouches on MREs that you are actually placing in your BOB. For the best long-term storage purposes at your retreat location, always leave the outer pouch intact.

In my get home bag and assault pack, I will typically carry a single MRE and a handful of Clif bars. In both those situations, I am carrying limited water and no steel canteen or the Esbit cup kit for heating water. In both those situations, I am also probably eating on the move and not in a stationary camp. In my main three day BOB, I carry two LRP MREs, three Mountain House breakfast meals, two regular MREs, and a dozen Clif bars for a four-day trip. If you leave late, or plan to travel longer, I would carry regular MREs for the extra days so you won't need to build a fire to heat the food like you would with the Mountain House Meals (after day three, you need to adopt more evasion-based travel and eating habits). In a lone wolf pack, I'm going to jam every spare square inch of the pack with food and Clif bars after I have my other supplies packed. In this situation, I only recommend MREs for the evasion properties of the meal and the flameless heater packet. This is also one of the few times I would recommend taking as many of the high calorie survival bars as you can. Life as a lone wolf is going to suck anyway and the survival bars could extend your life expectancy dramatically.

After food, one of the most universal survival essentials that you need is a good portion of 550 cord. Otherwise known as para cord (parachute cord), the unique properties that make up 550 cord can be used for many things related to your survival. While first introduced and applied in parachute construction during WWII, it was quickly found to be useful for many other tasks like building shelters, snaring game, lashing items to your pack, replacing busted boot laces, and fishing or sewing with the inner cord. Unfortunately, today you have a lot of companies making fake 550 cord and passing it off as "mil-spec."

True Mil-Spec (MIL-C-5040H Type 3) cord will have at least 7 core strands, each of which is three ply, and if made by an actual military manufacturer, one of the seven strands will have a colored cord woven into it, symbolizing which manufacture it came from. Authentic 550 cord is made from a specific type of Nylon which is abrasion resistant, kink proof, water resistant and mold proof. It has also undergone rigorous testing to ensure it supports at least 550 pounds (in most cases it will hold up to 700 pounds). "Real" military para cord can be quite hard to find in long lengths. On eBay, look for the 550 cord that has been cut out of military parachutes; unfortunately, they typically only come in 20 to 30-foot lengths. If you can find a 1000-foot spool of the real stuff from a trusted source, get it!

I have bought numerous off brands before and you can obviously tell they are not mil-spec. One of the easiest ways to tell is if they use 7 strands, but only 2-ply inner cords. What you will also find is that the sheathing on the outside of the cord will be kind of sloppy and loose over the inner strands, causing it to kink fairly easily which mil-spec cord is tested against. The commercial stuff will also hold 550 pounds, but once you've used the real thing, it's hard to go back. I highly recommend at least 100 feet in each of your BOBs. The best way to carry your 550 cord is in a daisy chain. If you daisy chain your 550 cord, you can ball it up and stuff it in any pocket in your BOB and it will never get knotted up or twisted. If you don't know how to daisy chain 550 cord, look it up on YouTube (just be sure to watch the daisy chain of a single cord and not a grouping of multiple cords).

The next item on the list would be a military surplus poncho; actually, two of them. A military poncho is cut extra large in the back to fit over top of your pack as well as your person, unlike most civilian models which are designed just to cover a person. The reason for my recommendation of a military poncho is that they can also be used as shelter with a little 550 cord. Snap two together and you have a large enough shelter for two to three people. Your spouse should carry a poncho as well, which can be used for a ground blanket under your sleeping bags. This is one area of gear that I do recommend dual purposing. When used with a Gore-Tex bivy sack over your sleeping bag, it completely eliminates the need for carrying the extra weight and bulk of an actual tent. In an evasion situation, you can even curl up under the bottom bows of a large pine tree and drape the poncho over you for extra protection from a hard rain while still staying hidden.

Now, I cannot stress this recommendation enough: only buy military surplus ponchos that have the light rubberized coating on one side. Never, ever buy "mil-spec" ponchos from Rothco or any other commercial source that now makes them. Regardless of what they say, they are nowhere near mil-spec. They are made from completely inferior products, cheap plastic buttons, easily torn grommets, and they don't even shed water. Imagine my surprise, when I bought two of these knock-offs and on my first use, water soaked through them, drenching my shoulders and my pack completely. The best place to find military surplus ponchos is eBay. Almost all of them come in the older Woodland BDU camo with a few coming in the original Army digital (skip these unless you are trying to hide on your grandma's flower patterned couch; Army Digital has almost zero camouflage properties).

The next item I carry is what I call my accessory pouch. It is a 6"x9" OD fabric pouch that I use to keep various items in. By using a pouch like this for accessories, it keeps things organized in your pack and you have fewer singular items floating around in different pockets to dig through. It is also easy to pull out of your BOB and throw in your assault pack, get home bag, or lone wolf pack. This is the pouch that changes the most depending on how long I plan to be away from civilization. First thing in the pouch is TP (toilet paper) wipes or "Wet Ones." I'm not sure how fully I need to explain this supply item, but for sanitation purposes, it goes on the top of my list.

I can go three days without a shower or brushing my teeth, but not without TP wipes. Yes, I know that I could probably shave 6 ounces off my pack by using leaves and vegetation to wipe, but no thank you. If at some point you run out of wipes or are forced to use "other" methods, be sure you are cleaning your hands well afterward and using anti-bacterial hand sanitizer. Dysentery and Cholera are outbreaks that will be common in a post-SHTF scenario and are typically caused by poor hygiene conditions and bacteria that are prevalent in feces.

The next item in my accessory pouch goes hand-in-hand with the last item: a travel-size bottle of hand sanitizer. Again, this item is to protect you from the many diseases floating around post-SHTF. Be sure to use it each time you use the restroom and before you eat. An item in my accessory pouch that is optional is a travel-sized deodorant stick. I have found that Axe makes an extremely lightweight (a couple ounces) travel stick which I picked up at Walmart. If you are trying to shave off every ounce, then this may be an item you cut out. Personally, when I climb into a tight sleeping bag after a long day of sweaty hiking, I would prefer to sleep soundly as opposed to wallowing in my own stench...but maybe that's just me.

Two other small Items I carry in my accessory pouch are a small bit of moleskin and a couple dozen ibuprofen (or other pain-killer of your choice). If you skip the first item, the moleskin, you will probably need to pack more of the second. Even if you are regularly on your feet all day for work, having an extra thirty pound BOB on your back may cause blisters on your feet you weren't expecting. If you start feeling hot spots in your shoes, stop immediately and use the moleskin! Don't just push through, expecting to deal with it later. Stop travelling, use some moleskin and change your sweaty socks.

The reason for the pain-killers is obvious. While carrying a heavy pack, you are going to be using muscles in places you didn't know you had muscles. Your shoulders, especially, are going to be very sore for the first few days. If you are travelling in a lot of pain, it makes it much harder to focus on your surroundings and locate potential threats. I carry the moleskin and pain pills in my accessory pouch instead of my first aid kit so they are easily accessible and I don't have to dig through my tightly-packed med kit. Feel free to put those items in your med kit if you choose and if you have the extra room in it. My accessory pouch is also where I carry the extra batteries for my flashlight. Typically, I tape them together with a bit of masking tape to keep them together.

In my accessory pouch I also carry a long-handled Titanium spork and discard the plastic forks that come with the MREs. Be sure you get the long-handled version as otherwise your knuckles will be coated with food digging the last morsels out of the bottom of the MRE entrée pouches and Mountain House meals. Another good item to have is a travel-sized roll of duct tape. Everyone knows duct tape is one of the greatest products for universal jimmy-rigging. Don't get crazy here and bring an entire roll, which is fairly heavy. Most hardware stores actually sell the smaller travel-sized rolls.

Even though you will likely be carrying a sleeping bag of some sort, it is always important to have an emergency blanket for…well, emergencies. Emergency blankets are the shiny silver, thin blankets that help reflect your body heat back towards your body. It could potentially save your life if the nighttime temperature suddenly dipped far below the seasonal average and what you had prepared for with your current sleeping bag configuration. This is especially true in the northern climates where a rare winter storm or "cold snap" could unseasonably push the temperatures below freezing or subzero conditions. It is important not to skimp here. The ones you can buy for one dollar aren't that effective: they tear easily and they aren't quilted. For a few more dollars, get the NDuR brand emergency blanket ($7); it is slightly quilted and has an Olive Drab exterior. You want the silver side to reflect the heat back to your body and not reflect the sun to the rest of the world, showing them where you are hiding.

The big drawback to emergency blankets is that most aren't breathable. If you use a cheap emergency blanket in conjunction with your sleeping bag for extra warmth on an unseasonably cold night, you will likely wake up wet with perspiration. If you have the extra money, I would highly recommend the Survive Outdoors Longer Escape Bivvy ($55) which is a BREATHABLE emergency blanket. Except in the coldest of subzero nights, if you use this in conjunction with your three season sleeping bag, you should stay plenty warm. This is the system I use and weighing in at only 9 ounces, it shaves about three pounds off my pack over carrying the much heavier winter weight sleeping bag. I also carry this in my assault pack in case of getting stranded overnight away from my retreat. If you do go the route of the SOL Escape Bivvy, just be aware that it is a bit bulkier than the NDuR brand blanket and will no longer fit in your accessory pouch.

The last Item in my accessory pouch would be my set of bump keys/picklock set. There is probably going to come a time when you need to get into a locked door for whatever reason. You can either carry around a battering ram and a large set of bolt cutters, or you can go the lock-picking route. Lock-picking is a skill that takes practice to get good at, so I recommend that you practice beforehand! Personally, I prefer to carry a set of bump keys and padlock shims which are a lot lighter and take less skill to master than a lock pick set. A good set of bump keys will unlock almost 95% percent of the home door handle locks and dead bolts on the market within a few seconds if you've done a little practice. It is also a lot quieter than kicking down a door in the dead of night. In a post-SHTF world, QUIET is our friend.

One important caveat to lock picking equipment is to make sure you check your local laws before purchasing these items. Due to criminals currently using these items to break into houses, both bump keys and padlock shims are typically frowned upon by most local law enforcement officers. Even though they may be legal in your area, I would still only carry these in my main BOB and lone wolf pack and only AFTER the SHTF. Even though you are a law-abiding citizen, I wouldn't lug these items around with you in the trunk of your car or in a get home bag; you're just asking for trouble. The best place I have found to purchase these items is a website called *Scamstuff.com*.

In nearly every bag you carry, except for the assault bag, I would carry an extra pair of socks. Taking care of your feet when you need to get somewhere is vitally important. If you can't walk, then you can't travel. Sweaty socks will hold moisture against your skin causing the outer layers of skin to soften and flake off. This may be okay on day 1, but over the course of a couple days you could end up with red, inflamed feet and possibly trench foot in the extreme. A good pair of breathable boots or shoes goes a long way here, too. In a BOB, I would also include an extra moisture-wicking T-shirt. In a lone wolf pack, I would include an entire extra change of clothes and underwear.

The next item is a little more controversial and there are numerous opinions as to the best way to procure firewood when needed. When I was a SERE instructor, we carried a 3.5 pound axe to chop down, bolt up, and split firewood. During the winter months, I am not exaggerating when I say we spent multiple hours a day gathering firewood to maintain a fire throughout the day. I am not bragging when I say I became an expert on cutting and splitting trees with precision strokes. Becoming proficient with an axe is a time-consuming process similar to learning how to hit a curveball in baseball. If you don't have the time to learn this skill, then I highly recommend that you leave your axe at home when bugging out. Axes are dangerous. To an unskilled, exhausted traveler you are just as likely to stick that sharp axe in your shin as you are to stick it into the piece of wood you are trying to split.

There are much more efficient ways to cut trees without burning nearly as many calories. Some people choose to carry a small camp hatchet, which I never understood, except for the fact that maybe they are thinking about weight and size of the item. Hatchets are nearly worthless at almost every task you put them to short of splitting small, very dry logs with very straight grain into kindling. If you use this for bolting up firewood or chopping down trees, you are doing it wrong and using WAY more energy than you need to. The other drawback to hatchets and axes is that they also produce a lot more noise in the quiet forest as opposed to the different types of hand saws. There are better options for procuring firewood that weigh considerably less than an axe or camp hatchet.

On the cheap side, I would recommend a pocket chainsaw, which is a section of chainsaw blade with two sturdy handles on each side. Do not buy the "survival" wire saws as they are worthless in cutting down anything more than a sapling the size of your thumb. A couple things to remember when buying a pocket saw is not to buy the cheapest one out there even if you're on a budget. This is an instrument that gets harsh use and a broken piece of webbing on one of the hand straps will make it useless (speaking from experience). Expect to pay around $25 to $30 for a good quality pocket chainsaw.

One major drawback to these saws is your initial cut when felling a tree. Once you get about two-thirds of the way through your cut and the tree starts to lean, it may pinch the blade and make the process of finishing your cut nearly impossible. Two ways around this would be to carry a small wedge or to cut up trees that have already fallen (just make sure the tree is off the ground a bit and not waterlogged). You also want to stick with smaller trees that are less than 5 inches in diameter as you will expend less energy and you will be using your bolt knife to split them. The last thing to remember is to always wear gloves when using a pocket chainsaw. Even if you have well-calloused hands from your day job, you will develop blisters very quickly on the sides of your hands next to your pinky fingers if you don't.

Even though I continued to carry a 3.5 pound axe for years when backpacking, I recently discovered a much better tool for the job that weighs a fraction of the weight. A good folding handsaw is the way to go. You use far less energy than an axe or a pocket chainsaw. The only drawback is that you are still limited to smaller trees, around 5 inches in diameter, especially if you intend to split them with your bolt knife. When I said a quality hand saw, what I actually meant is that you should buy a Silky brand handsaw. I have tried other brands with varying success but the patented tooth design that Silky uses far surpasses all others. In fact, they advertise that some of their larger saws can actually compete with a small chainsaw. Silky makes pruning and hand saws of varying size and they even sell a model almost two feet long, which is very popular with back country snowmobilers for cutting large trees out of their paths. For a BOB, I highly recommend the 9.5 inch Silky Ultra Accel which can be purchased for around $60. Yes, you can find similar looking handsaws at Home Depot for much less, but you are also getting much less performance and quality, which means more energy expended.

It is absolutely vital that you include paper maps of the areas between your home and bug out location in your BOB. You can't rely on GPS devices functioning, although I wouldn't discourage you from including one in addition to your paper maps. You have no way of knowing in advance if your pre-planned bug-out route is going to be impassable due to a serious accident or gridlocked traffic jam blocking your way. It's important that you're able to reference a map and find a way around any obstacle. Maybe you planned on taking the highway all the way to your bug-out location, only to find the highway completely overcrowded on day three (much sooner than you or I anticipated). In that case, you'll have to move off the major highway and take secondary roads.

An item that goes hand-in-hand with your maps is a quality compass. The most important feature that you want to look for when choosing a compass is to be sure it's a "lensatic" or "sighting" compass. Don't buy the flat camping or button style compasses which aren't efficient when performing point-to-point navigation. You'll want a folding compass with the sighting wire which will enable you to hold it to your cheek and pick out a target on your heading. Point-to-point navigation with the proper compass can be very precise if you learn how to use it properly and practice with it. The gold standard for compasses is the Cammenga brand Official US Military Tritium Lensatic Compass, which can be purchased for around $75. On a budget, you can find knock-off compasses without Tritium for a lot less. But don't go too cheap. Be sure the compass is made by a major manufacturer; don't buy the cheap plastic ones found on eBay. Expect to pay $20 to $25 for a metal, military-style lensatic compass.

The last essential item in your BOB would be a quality sleeping bag. It's hard to discuss sleeping bags without also bringing your tent into the same equation as your choice in one depends on the other. For families with just a husband, wife, and a single small child, I recommend using your Military Surplus Ponchos as your shelter. If you go this route, you have to realize that it's not a completely stormproof shelter. If you're on a budget, buying a military surplus Extreme Cold Weather System (ECWS) sleeping bag system for each adult or teenager in your family is the way to go. They can be purchased in like-new condition on eBay and Amazon for around $100. You won't get more bang for your buck anywhere. This sleep system includes a waterproof stuff sack, Patrol (summer weight) bag, Intermediate (cold weather) bag, and a Gore-Tex bivy sack. If you use both bags and the bivy sack, it is comfort rated to -10 degrees Fahrenheit. The only drawback to this system is its weight which comes in at a whopping ten pounds (when using all three bags together in the winter). You can definitely drop about five pounds if you're willing to spend the extra hundreds of dollars on an ultralight sleeping bag.

The most important part of this system is the Gore-Tex Bivy bag. If you already have a sleeping bag you like, or want to purchase a lighter, more expensive down sleeping bag, I would still highly recommend that you purchase the Gore-Tex bivy bag on eBay for around $40 to go over top of it. The bivy bag is waterproof yet still breathable and almost acts as its own shelter. This system prevents you from having to carry a tent with its bulky and hard-to-pack poles.

Like I mentioned earlier, using a Gore-Tex bivy bag over your sleeping bag allows you to crawl under the bows of a pine tree or under a fallen log, cover yourself with your poncho, and stay hidden in a dangerous environment. You can't do that with a normal tent which requires a large level spot to erect it, and a tent stands out in the woods like a sore thumb. If you do go the route of the ECWS sleeping bag system, just be sure you aren't buying a knock-off system which typically sell for the same price on websites like *SportsmansGuide.com*. Be sure it is true military surplus in excellent, used condition.

If you have a larger family or a bigger group you are bugging out with, you can simply carry a larger piece of waterproof tarp. I recommend a SilNylon tarp which is a very lightweight yet ripstop, silicone impregnated nylon. A 10'x 10' SilNylon tarp will typically run you less than $100 online yet only weighs 18 ounces. Compare that to carrying a family tent, which could easily weigh over five pounds and needs bulky, awkward poles. On a budget, check out the Noah's Tarps made by Kelty. You can purchase a 12'x 12' Noah's tarp on Amazon for about $70.

If you are traveling with a small toddler or baby, you won't have the option of putting them in their own sleeping bag, especially in winter. In this case, I recommend buying an oversized two person sleeping bag so the small child can sleep between you and your mate for warmth. I have also found a couple companies that sell two-person waterproof bivy sacks: PIEPS, Oware, and *BackpackingLight.com*. This style of sleeping bag/tent system is what I would recommend as it's lightweight and easy to set up in a hidden location, yet still offers protection. Other options include carrying a tent and poles or even a compact hammock-style tent. You have many options; consider the weather environment where you will be travelling, as well as the topography, and make the best decision for your family.

* Check the back of the book for multiple BOB checklists…

Chapter 13
Additional BOB Items to Consider

In the previous two chapters, I discussed what I consider to be the most important and vital pieces of gear that you will need for a bug-out bag. I also mentioned that there are many additional items you should consider, depending on the geographical area you will be travelling and the time of year you are bugging out. There are also other considerations for those of you that live or travel far away from your retreat location. These same additional items should be included in your lone wolf packs that you have ready to go at a moment's notice by the back door of your retreat. When looking at other people's BOB lists, I typically see a lot of the items in this chapter. However, most of them are items you won't need for a three to five day bugout and just add dead weight; only incorporate them if they apply to these special scenarios or a bug-out trip expected to last longer than 5 days.

But before we get into those, I want to mention an absolutely essential item for your BOB if you don't have a specific location or retreat to bug-out to. If you haven't had the time or the finances to fully prepare for a SHTF scenario before it happens, then you need to include a large quantity of survival seeds in your BOB. They will be vital if you are forced to look for a rural farmer, stay at a vacant rural cabin, or show up at a rural distant relative's place to ride out the storm. Having a hundred thousand survival seeds in a Mylar pouch is a huge bargaining chip to trade for room and board and can be used to barter with the locals for supplies you may need (along with having proper weapons to provide security for the rural and elderly farmer's property). Besides, survival seed is extremely cheap compared to most other things you'll need to purchase for your long-term survival and it weighs very little in your BOB. On a side note, leave your gold bullion at home or stashed at your retreat. No one is going to trade food for your stockpiled silver and gold bullion (not to mention the significant amount of weight in your BOB) until a long time after the SHTF.

Two unnecessary items that I see a lot of people putting in their 3-day BOBs are fishing kits and snaring kits. The purpose of bugging out is to get out of town early and get to a safer location as quickly as possible before things start to fall apart. Taking time out of your day to fish or run a snare line is just silly. Those are items you will need if you were forced to live off the land, but they should be kept at your retreat or bug-out location packed inside your lone wolf pack, not adding needless weight to your BOB. For your lone wolf pack, I would suggest taking a very compact survival fishing kit with you, similar to the ones you see packed into a sardine can. Also, unless you are sure there is a fully stocked pond at your retreat, I wouldn't spend much time fishing post-SHTF. Most rivers and streams will be "fished out" similar to most big game being killed off in the forests; there are a lot more productive things to do with your time. Fishing would be a good activity for early teens in your camp when they're not doing chores, but be aware they'll also wipe out the fish population in your neighboring stream or pond fairly quickly. One fishing item I would highly recommend is a mechanical Yo-Yo fishing reel. Yo-Yos are a spring-loaded fishing reel you hang from a branch over the edge of a creek or pond. This allows you to fish without actually being there. You set them and then check them once a day, similar to a snare line.

It's hard to make a specific recommendation on the type and size snares you'll need because it largely depends on the local game available in your geographical area. For a lone wolf pack, I recommend buying a small spool of Vietnam-era military trip wire which can be found on eBay. That will allow you to make snares for most small- to medium-sized game. For larger game, you'll need to do some research on what local trappers are using in your area.

It's important that you have a good survival manual with you when are forced to abandon your retreat location and lone wolf your survival for a time. While I may be somewhat partial because it was the book I was trained from in SERE, I believe the best survival manual available is the Air Force Survival Manual 64-4 which can be purchased on Amazon ($15). Unfortunately, it is over 600 pages long and weighs 3.5 pounds. If you are new to surviving in the wilderness, I would still pack it in a lone wolf pack as it will probably save your life at some point. I would wrap it in a good waterproof bag and then stash it at my campsite. If you already have a lot of wilderness skills, I would still consider a condensed survival manual like the SAS Survival Handbook, or better yet a used copy of AF Pamphlet 64-5 (just be sure to get the spiral-bound water resistant version). Other books I would recommend for a lone wolf pack would be an "edible plants" book for your specific geographical area and a compact bible to keep your spirits up. If you are traveling in a group, you can also consider a deck of playing cards for recreation.

For an extended bug out, you will need some personal hygiene items that you wouldn't bother to pack in a 3-day BOB. First on the list would be a compact toothbrush and travel toothpaste. One of the worst things that you could encounter in a SHTF scenario is a tooth infection, especially with no dentists around. It is vital that you stay on top of your dental care pre-SHTF and maintain your dental hygiene afterwards. I would also carry some soap for washing and bathing. A lot of preppers push the "scentless" soaps, but I wouldn't worry about that. Your clothes are likely going to stink regardless, and if a threat gets close enough to smell your cucumber-vanilla body wash, your OPSEC needs serious work. Look for an all-in-one shampoo and body wash as there is no reason to carry multiple bottles of various soaps. Two items I would consider mandatory are ChapStick and a good quality hand lotion, especially in the winter months when dry skin and cracked lips can become a serious issue. Along with these hygiene items you would pack for a longer bug-out, it's important that you include a variety of medicines like Sudafed, cough medicine, anti-diarrheal, and a big supply of pain medicine like Tylenol.

A vital piece of gear needed for an extended outing is going to be a good quality knife sharpener. It's important that you do a little research on knife "bevel angles" before you purchase a sharpener. For instance, most pocket knives will come with a 20-22-degree bevel angle from the factory. If you buy a compact hand sharpener made for standard kitchen knives or filet knives, they will typically come set at a bevel in the 18-degree range. Why does this matter? If you try to sharpen your knife with a shallower angled sharpener, you are going to literally spend hours grinding away at the sides of your 22-degree bevel until you've got it shaved down to an 18-degree bevel. Until you go through this work, the sharpener isn't even making contact or having any effect on the knife's cutting edge. You can do that; however, the shallower 18-degree bevel will not be as sturdy for the type of hard use a survival pocket knife gets and you'll need to sharpen it more often.

Now that is an extreme example of different bevels, but even if the sharpener for your knife is only 1 degree off, it could mean hours of work to match your knife edge to the shape of the sharpening stones set in your sharpener. The time to figure this out is not when you are in the back country with a dull knife; it is when you first purchase the sharpener. Most quality knife manufacturers will tell you what bevel angle your specific knife has from the factory. I would use that information when purchasing a knife sharpener.

There are many expensive options for the best knife sharpeners (like Lansky), but most would not be easy to pack in a lone wolf pack. On a budget, I would recommend the Smith's 50264 manual knife sharpener which offers adjustments to set your bevel anywhere between 14 and 24 degrees.

Don't forget that your bolt knife and pocket knife will likely have slightly different bevels. I would recommend setting both bevels to be sharpened from the same small travel sharpener or get the adjustable one like I mentioned above. You could also go the route of using a sharpening rod, a flat diamond stone sharpener, or a double-sided circular whetstone (my personal preference) to sharpen your knives in the field. However, sharpening a knife with one of these tools is an acquired skill requiring practice of holding your knife blade at the precise angle while you pass the blade along the stone or rod. Again, being on an extended outing is not the time to fumble through teaching yourself how to sharpen your knife with one of these methods.

An item that I pack in both my BOB and my lone wolf pack would be a section of mosquito netting. Mosquitos are my arch nemesis when I'm backpacking. My personal recommendation is to buy a full-sized mosquito net like the ones designed to go over your whole sleeping bag and cut a 3'x 3' section out of it. I wear this over my boonie cap with the bottom of it tucked into the neck of my t-shirt during the day (when needed). At night I hang it from the ridge line of my poncho shelter with a piece of 550 cord so it hangs down over the head hole of my sleeping bag. I don't see the necessity of purchasing a separate head net and a full sized mosquito net that needlessly covers the bottom half of my sleeping bag. If you have mosquitos in your area that can bite you through your sleeping bag, you need to find a new bug-out location....

Something to consider for an extended outing would be to have a writing utensil of some sort and a small notebook or tablet. Standard pens and pencils may not last long or allow you to write in damp conditions. My personal recommendation is to purchase what are known as "space pens." A space pen will write at any angle, in extreme hot or cold weather conditions, and even in the rain. My personal favorite is the Fisher 400B Bullet Pen ($16). It's all good to have a pen that will write in the rain, but only if you pair it with a tablet of paper that won't disintegrate in wet conditions. I highly recommend the Rite in the Rain brand of notebooks that come in multiple shapes and sizes. I've used them for years and they have held up really well, even in pouring down rain.

There are a couple small items you should consider also. The first is camo face paint, especially if you are travelling a long distance where evasion will come into play. There are a plethora of face paint compacts that you can choose from and feel free to pick your favorite. Personally, I only carry a small tube of black liquid-style face paint. It's much easier to apply in a hurry when needed and it comes off easily with a single baby wipe. The drawback is that the liquid-style camo face paint also comes off more easily in hard rain or if you are sweating profusely. Second, you should consider a signal mirror like the Cohglans 9900 series. While also useful as a personal hygiene tool, a signal mirror is great for communicating at a distance if needed; for instance, signaling your retreat's watch tower upon approach or signaling between security team members while setting up an ambush or trying to by-pass one. You should also pack a couple black contractor bags, which is almost as universal an item as duct tape. There is an article by Survival Life online titled "30 Uses for Trash Bags in Your Bug-out Bag" that you should definitely read to learn more about their universal use.

A small item that you should include in a lone wolf pack would be a survival sewing kit. You never know when the stitching on your pack's shoulder strap is going to tear free or a button on your pants is going to fall off. In fact, be sure to pay attention to the buttons on your clothes; if you find a loose one, fix it immediately before it falls off and is lost for good. You can easily find a compact sewing kit on eBay for under $10. Just be sure it includes a couple larger needles for heavier duty sewing as you can always sew little items with a big needle, but you can't sew beefier material with a small needle. Last, be sure that your sewing kit includes a small assortment of buttons as well.

Depending on how long you plan to be away from your retreat, you will likely need a way to recharge your flashlight and radio batteries at some point. There are many companies that make small solar chargers for multiple devices, but this is another area where you shouldn't skimp. Be sure you are buying from a reputable company as most of the off-brand solar chargers are made in China with very inferior panels and battery systems. For recharging AA and AAA batteries, I recommend the GoalZero Guide 10 Plus Solar Kit which also offers a port for recharging USB devices like phones and cameras. Coming in at only 19 ounces, it would fall in the middle-sized range of solar battery chargers and can be found on Amazon for around $80. There are a lot of other companies that may offer a similar product at a much higher cost; feel free to consider them if your budget allows. But for the price point, durability, and functionality, I don't think you'll find a better alternative for backpacking solar power than the GoalZero Guide 10 plus Solar Kit.

A similar item that I see a lot of people packing into their BOBs are hand-crank emergency radios. For a 3- to 5-day bug out, I don't see the necessity of carrying the extra weight and bulk with you on your journey. Besides, I don't know that I would trust the information being broadcast over emergency radio stations from the government. Their main objective after a societal collapse scenario is going to be preventing panic. Also, if you have packed an effective BOB, you shouldn't need to hear NOAA (National Oceanic and Atmospheric Administration) weather broadcasts, either. You should have the appropriate gear to deal with whatever adverse weather conditions may arise while on your trip. Keep in mind that in the event of a grid-down scenario, the NOAA and most other radio stations probably won't be broadcasting anyway.

With that being said, in the event of a financial collapse or less severe SHTF scenario like a pandemic, a hand-crank radio could be useful. Even so, I still wouldn't pack one in my regular BOB, but I may consider packing into my lone wolf pack at my retreat. If that's the case, then I would recommend the Eton FRX5 radio ($80). It has multiple charging methods including a solar panel on the back which charges an internal lithium battery, a hand crank, and it accepts AA batteries. It can also charge external devices using a USB cable. Unfortunately, it does most of these charging jobs poorly when comparing it to the Goal Zero Guide 10 Solar Kit. You would literally have to spend hours cranking away before the internal battery was fully charged enough to "dump" even a partial charge via USB cable to an electronic device. Neither the solar panel nor the internal lithium battery in the FRX5 is very large or efficient. Maybe someday they will create a hand-crank radio that does multiple tasks well, but as yet, I haven't discovered one.

It would be better to have the Goal Zero Guide 10 plus Solar kit paired with a portable handheld Ham radio transceiver or other communication device that receives emergency and NOAA weather channels. However, unless you are meeting up with other people in your retreat group at a rally point, I don't see the necessity of carrying radios while bugging out. They are an essential item for your retreat or bug-out location, but I personally don't carry a radio in my BOB. Don't forget, in a grid-down scenario, the ham radio repeating towers likely won't be operational and your handheld ham radio won't function much better than traditional FRS walkie talkies (especially in hilly and heavily treed areas).

The subject of survival radio applications is way too convoluted to provide even basic advice in this limited space; it's a whole topic in and of itself. There are many different frequencies like FRS, GMRS, MURS and Ham radio frequencies and pros and cons to each. The one point I want to make is that it will be vitally important to have some sort of radio communication after the SHTF. There are a lot of factors to consider when choosing a survival radio like frequencies, transmit distance, battery type and life, as well as being able to transmit on secure frequencies. It is not illegal to own the more powerful radios that transmit further distances, but it IS illegal to use them pre-SHTF without the proper licensing. Unfortunately, these complicated radios aren't an item that you can just buy, store in a faraday cage, and bust out after the SHTF and expect to be able to figure out their operation. A lot of them require an operational computer and special software to program them. Like most of your survival knowledge, radio frequencies and ham radio operation is something you should get experience and practice with pre-SHTF.

I would actually recommend taking a ham radio operators class and getting licensed. Even if you don't use the radios often before things go south, the knowledge you will gain from such a class will help you decide which type of survival communications will work best for your group, depending on its size and the geographical area in which you will be using the radios. If you have the financial resources, I would ultimately recommend having a large 100w ham radio base station at your retreat with the proper antenna tower to transmit and receive broadcasts from long distances away. Emergency radio transmissions from the government won't be reliable and you'd be better off getting your information from the numerous survival ham radio groups that you could join online. You'll also need some sort of smaller handheld radios that you can use while walking patrols on your property. Again, I can't recommend specific radios because it depends on how large your property is and how hilly the terrain is.

The last item I would recommend in the communications department would be military surplus field phones. Having an actual "landline" set up between your watchtower, cabin, and LP/OPs would offer a lot more security than transmitting on standard frequencies that a looting force might be capable of intercepting. Don't forget to purchase enough of the appropriate cable (wire) for your field phones to reach from your retreat to your LP/OP or other security watch location.

The big thing to remember with any additional accessories you pack into your lone wolf Pack is that you have to CARRY it all.

Bringing everything and the kitchen sink will quickly take your pack upwards of 100 pounds and prevent you from being very mobile. Whatever you DO decide to pack, make sure you aren't sacrificing food for equipment. You can't eat your hand crank radio when you're starving.

* Check the back of the book for multiple BOB checklists...

Chapter 14
Guns, Guns, Guns

I fully expect this chapter to be the most controversial and the chapter I get the most review comments based on. Which weapon to purchase is nearly a religious experience for a lot of people and they are very passionate about their particular weapon for specific reasons. Regardless of what I write below, I am going to have people wringing their hands and cursing me a fool because of reason X, Y, and Z. So please, to all my keyboard commandos out there, when I recommend Weapon X or gear item Z, I am not insinuating that your pick in battle rifle is crap. So calm down, take a breath, and don't take my recommendations personally. The weapon you chose for whatever reason may be the perfect gun for your specific situation or purpose. Unlike 95% percent of gun magazine article recommendations and internet keyboard commandos, my weapon and gear recommendations revolve SOLELY around a long-term SHTF scenario. So it's important that you understand where I am coming from. My recommendations are exclusively based on a weapon's long-term reliability and the ability to score spare parts and ammo for the weapon after a societal collapse scenario. The following chapter is my opinion based on years of research and training with VERY qualified individuals with Special Operations training and many hours of discussions with various professional tactical instructors.

In a lot of cases, my advice is going to be different from the front page article you read in the latest gun magazine and their weapon's new wiz-bang technological improvements. For example, I realize that your 6.8 AR has better ballistics than my 5.56 AR and might be an overall better man stopper, but if you run out of ammunition you have virtually zero chance of finding, procuring, or bartering for more 6.8 ammo. "Well, I have 10,000 rounds of 6.8 in my cabin," you say. What happens when you have to bug out at the last second because a large looting force is rolling down your street or your cabin burns down because you didn't learn how to properly clean your chimney? For that reason alone I would not recommend your rifle even though it costs three times more than mine and 9 out of 10 gun magazine articles recommend yours over mine.

Many people also make the mistake of buying a weapon based on the "expert" advice from their local gun store owner or their friend who is a police officer or competitive shooter. In most of these cases, a policeman's weapon experience revolves around what weapon they are issued in their department and a couple range sessions a year. If you look at FBI police shooting statistics, you'll see that when police officers fire their weapons in the line of duty, they have about a 22% hit rate. I am not bad-mouthing police officers and there are a lot of them that could run circles around me at the range! What I am saying is that IN MOST DEPARTMENTS, the amount of annual weapons training the average police officer receives is woefully insufficient to stay frosty. Typically, the only police officers that get up to date training, the latest gear, and plenty of range time are SWAT officers.

In the case of gun shop owners, their advice usually revolves around manufacturer's product advertisement pamphlets (which can be grossly misleading and inaccurate), online articles they have read, and in some cases they recommend weapons that have been sitting in their inventory too long. I recently had a half hour conversation with a local gun store OWNER who literally tried to convince me that there is no difference between a cheap commercial AR and a mil-spec AR. He insisted that DPMS makes the highest quality ARs you can buy today. He went through all the technical aspects of their facility and it sounded like he was regurgitating a pamphlet ad sent to their gun shop by DPMS. Some gun shop employees are just that: minimum wage employees with no real life experience. They have never spent years on the battlefield and trusted their life to the weapon they are recommending that you purchase. You need to know where the advice you are receiving is coming from and their qualifications for giving you said advice! Gunfighting technology and techniques are constantly changing and improving and the individual you are receiving advice from may have received their "professional training" 30 years ago with far outdated information and training techniques.

There are so many online weapon myths in existence that you could literally write an entire book on the subject. My favorite is when a gun store employee tells me that the best weapon "to fit" my wife's small hands is a little, pink, pocket-sized .380 or some other similar tiny handgun. The entire "pocket guns for chicks" advice is terrible and potentially deadly, yet you'll get the same advice from nearly every gun shop you visit. Anyone with even the smallest amount of range experience knows that a tiny .380 is going to recoil in your hands sharper than a sub-compact 9mm. The slides on those tiny guns are usually much harder to pull back than a larger handgun with more slide mass and weight. The sights are so close together on the tiny barrel that a person with limited training would be lucky to hit the broad side of a barn at 25 yards. They only hold five or six rounds of a woefully underpowered cartridge and without a perfect shot to the eye socket, the rapist will probably have plenty of time to disarm and kill your wife before they have a chance to bleed out. Add into the equation that you may have multiple attackers and then you're really screwed. So three "bad guys" start shooting up the store you're in and you quickly react, pushing your kids into the corner of the store under a display rack. You turn around and they are coming your direction and blocking your exit or retreat. Are you seriously going to take on 3 guys with only six rounds of .380 out of a 3" barrel? Okay, so you are Chris Kyle incarnate. What about your wife?

Why the hell are so many of these terribly underpowered handguns sold to women for self-protection?! Answer…because there is some expert in some popular gun magazine that says it's the best thing since sliced bread after he was "given" one by the manufacturer to test. Instead of selling a woman a false sense of security, gun store owners need to explain why those little pocket guns are not the best choice for self-protection and explain that a larger caliber handgun is much better for self-defense. They need to tell the customer that she is going to have to learn to dress around the larger handgun or deal with a little extra weight in her purse. I am not saying that there is never a time where packing a smaller .380 for personal defense is warranted. But if you pull that thing out, you better have spent some SERIOUS range time with it or you are going to empty your magazine and be wondering why the man in front of you isn't dead. In most cases, a gun store is the WORST place to make a decision on which gun to purchase. It's kind of like grocery shopping when you're really hungry.

A perfect example of the keyboard commandos wreaking havoc on the review forums was after I wrote my first book and mentioned that the main character carried a Kel-Tec SU-16C. I really got hammered over that even though I explained straight out that the Kel-Tec was not a proven battle rifle and that the character only bought it because that was all he could afford and he wanted to stay group standard with the rest of his squad (the SU-16 is chambered in 5.56 and uses standard AR mags). When I was writing that section back in 2010, most mil-spec ARs where running well over $1,300 and the Kel-Tec SU-16C could be purchased for just over $500. That is no longer the case today (2016), with Mil-spec ARs like the Colt LE6920 selling for as little as $900 new and the Kel-Tec SU-16C selling for over $700 (when you can even find them). Just before print, I really pondered changing the main character's rifle at the last minute to an AR just to avoid "the controversy." It wouldn't have mattered though, because then I would have had the AK crowd getting mad at me. What I was trying to show in my first book was that not everyone can afford a LaRue AR and you may have to use what you have on hand.

So what is my personal pick for a SHTF battle rifle? I prefer a true Mil-Spec AR/M4 from a reputable company. Some would bring up the common myth that the AR platform is unreliable which is completely false. Some of that comes from the original roll out of the weapon in Vietnam when the military issued it to soldiers in a wet environment without lubricating oil or cleaning kits and proper training on how to handle possible malfunctions. The fact of the matter is the AR/M4 platform is the battle rifle with the longest running use in our military's history. It has been around for 50 years and there have been hundreds of manufacturers over the years that have sent their new, state of the art battle rifles to the Department of Defense to compete against the AR. After literally a billion dollars of research and torture tests by the DOD, the AR/M4 is still the primary battle rifle of the US military and has proven to be most reliable weapon every single time. That is an undisputable fact.

Even in sandy environments it functions well, which is another misconception of the AR platform. Some say that it won't function "dirty," which is just not true. The secret to keeping your AR functioning is lubrication, lubrication, lubrication! The AR needs to be "wet" to function reliably. In the most recent AR class I took, the instructor was informing the class about the "dirty" AR myth and I didn't believe him because I'd read the opposite in most AR forums from keyboard commandos. Everyone insists that you have to clean your AR constantly for it to perform flawlessly. The instructor broke down his LaRue AR and showed us the dirtiest bolt and chamber I have ever seen! The chrome bolt was caked so thick with carbon that I couldn't believe the rifle would even function. He insisted he had fired over 5000 rounds since his last cleaning while only "snaking" the barrel a handful of times and regularly adding lube. He added some lube before class and his rifle functioned flawlessly both days. I also recently read an article by another reputable instructor who had fired 20,000 rounds through his AR while only adding lube and occasionally snaking his barrel (there were pictures of his bolt and chamber for proof). Please note: neither were advocating that you don't keep you're your AR clean, they were just proving that if you have a quality Mil-Spec AR and keep it well lubricated, it will continue to function and keep you in the fight.

So the question at the end of the day is would I still buy an SU-16 over an AR-15? Yes and No. If you are on a budget and can't afford a quality mil-spec AR-15, I would highly recommend you save up until you can afford one. If you are operating on a very tight budget, and you can still find the SU-16c for around $500, then I would still recommend the SU-16 over most super cheap non Mil-Spec ARs in the same price range. Also, the AK-47 is a reliable, proven battle rifle if you can still find them cheap (quality AKs have gone up a lot the last couple years). Again, I still think it would be better to save up for a mil-spec AR, but either way, I would recommend a rifle chambered in 5.56 because the overwhelming availability of ammo in a SHTF scenario. The AR-15 is hands down the most popular battle rifle in the continental US. It at least gives you a shot in the dark at scoring a spare part or ammo after the SHTF. With a more exotic battle rifle like an HK 93, you may end up with a really expensive club if you lose a spring or a part breaks.

Once again, I am not saying that the AR is the ONLY battle rifle you can buy if you want to survive the upcoming zombie apocalypse. There are plenty of variables about your specific circumstances and where you live in which a different battle rifle might be better suited. For instance, if you live in South Dakota with flat, wide open spaces, a battle rifle in 7.62 (.308) may be better suited for your retreat. The important thing is to stay group standard with your squad and to get everyone on the same page. So I'm sure you will end up having some lively debates on this subject.

If money is no object, my go-to rifle would be a Larue Tactical PredatOBR AR. Larue makes the highest quality, mil-spec AR platform rifles on the market today. After that, I would go with either a Daniel Defense, Bravo Company, or a distant last Colt (Specifically the LE6920 model as they also offer non-Mil-spec ARs as well), in that order. Although great for plinking, I would not trust my life through a long-term SHTF scenario with a low-end, non-mil-spec AR-15 as you are just asking for problems. Regardless of which company you go with, if you are going to choose the AR platform as your go-to rifle, you need to make sure you always carry LUBRICATION, and an extra bolt on you at all times while keeping a spare parts/spring kit at your retreat.

As far as optics, I am a firm believer in being proficient with iron sights before moving to an optic. At that point, I highly recommend a red dot over a scope on a battle rifle for Close Quarter Battles (CQB). My favorite red dots are Aimpoints and the Meprolight M21 or MOR. The Meprolight M21 ($450) is Israeli Special Forces issue and have been proven reliable after years on the battle field. The red dot operates with fiber optic during the day and tritium at night and it never needs batteries. Therefore, it is constantly on and if you are ambushed, you don't have to worry about fumbling for a button or knob (which is also great about the Aimpoints and their unbelievably long battery life). Since there are no electronics, the M21 is supposed to be EMP-proof as well. The only drawback to the M21 is that the red dot can be kind of faint when firing from a dark room into open sunlight. To combat this, Meprolight has a new model called the MOR which also adds battery operation on top of the tritium and fiber optic. The MOR contains a pressure pad operated red laser and possible IR laser (depending on if you can find this model for sale in the US), all built into the same lightweight unit. Unfortunately, the MOR also costs over $1,000 when you can even find them for sale.

Aimpoint red dots is also a top choice for me. The Aimpoint PRO (Patrol Rifle Optic) can be purchased for under $400 on Amazon and the batteries last for 3 years constantly on, which I am a big fan of. That is my biggest issue with EoTech red dots which has an almost cult-like following. While EoTech batteries also last a long time, every model of EoTech has an automatic shutoff feature to their reticle after 8 hours of non-use. That feature cannot be turned off and it's insane to me that you might be on a night patrol longer than eight hours and run into an ambush. You shoulder your weapon to return fire and...no red dot! Now you are taking precious seconds in the middle of a firefight frantically fumbling for the "on" switch to your red dot. No, thank you! If I turn my red dot on, I want it to stay on the entire time I may need it. That is the main reason I solidly advise against EoTechs. I'm not sure if it's true or not, but I've also read that EoTech has some reliability issues with their red dots and to me their reticles seem washed out and blurry anyway (just my personal opinion).

Having a 3 or 5 times multiplier on a flip-to-side mount is also a good option if you need to reach out and touch someone. The only time I would consider a scope for a battle rifle was if I was absolutely certain that I wasn't going to get into a firefight within twenty-five yards. However, I can see where a scope would make sense in certain open plain areas out west. If I did go the scope route, I would want one on the low power side like a 2-7 power or, better yet, the newer 1-6 power optics, just in case of CQB (Close Quarters Battle). From personal experience while deer hunting, there was a time years ago where I had to pass on a shot because a large buck was too close and moving too fast in a thicket for me to keep the crosshairs on him with my 4-16 power scope. It was very frustrating and I moved to a 2-12 power hunting scope after that with greater success in the brush.

There are two things that I would steer clear of when purchasing or building an AR-15 platform rifle. The first is adding a "piston" system. I know that adding one is quite the rage lately and prevents your rifle from getting dirty as quickly as a normal gas impingement AR, but you are asking for problems down the line. The AR platform was never designed for the added stress that a piston puts on the rifle's bolt carrier group and buffer spring tube. At some point, you are going to experience what is known as "carrier tilt." Depending on the quality of your rifle, you can start experiencing malfunctions in the 5,000-10,000 round range, with some people having issues starting with as few as 1,000 rounds fired. It is not a matter of *if* but a matter of *when* you will experience carrier tilt. Carrier tilt will seriously diminish your rifle's reliability and in some cases can cause a complete failure to your rifle. I would steer clear of aftermarket "piston" kits for your AR. Don't take me the wrong way and think I am against piston rifles in general; I am just against adding them onto the AR platform. The AK-47, ACR, and SCAR rifles where specifically designed to prevent carrier tilt while utilizing a gas piston in their rifles.

The second thing I would avoid (not as big a deal in bolt action rifles) is steel cased ammo. I am not saying to "never" use it; for instance, if you were running low at your retreat and found or bartered for more ammo and that's all you could get, then use it. However, I wouldn't purchase it or use it on a regular basis in semi-automatic weapons as the steel case produces a lot more wear on your gun than brass cased ammo. Besides, the companies that sell steel cased ammo are typically using other sub-par components in their ammo, the most common of which is "dirty" powder and poor quality primers. You have a lot higher chance of experiencing a malfunction when using cheap steel ammo than when buying from a quality manufacturer like Lake City or Federal. In a SHTF scenario, you need to be able to trust your life to your ammo functioning flawlessly!

So now that I have given you my personal recommendations, remember that my intention is not to bash anyone's choice of battle rifle. There are a lot of proven battle rifles to pick from. What is much more important than the rifle you choose is making sure you are proficient with it. Professional firearms training is an absolute must! However, taking your black rifle to the nearest range once every couple months, sitting behind a bench with sandbags, and plinking away at paper targets is practically worthless. You can teach a monkey to put a red dot in a circle and pull a trigger. A firefight is pure chaos and confusion. Any scenario you end up in where there is someone shooting at you will most assuredly never happen when you are seated behind a shooting bench with sandbags. Practice shooting prone, on your knees, while running, while lying on your back, while standing on your head (you get the drift). You need to learn how to operate your rifle while moving to cover. And please, if you don't know the difference between cover and concealment, Google it right now; it could save your life. If you can't "move and shoot" at your local gun range, then you need to join a new one or make a range at a friend's farm.

No matter how high speed you think you are from watching Instructor Zero on YouTube (FYI, that's a joke, not a recommendation...), it is vital to go through a first-rate carbine operator course with a professional instructor. That does not include your local NRA course or going to the range with your buddy who "shoots a lot" and served in Vietnam. If you are a beginner, then a couple of range sessions with someone like that may be beneficial to show you the safe operation of your weapon and some basics, but you may also be picking up bad habits or outdated operational standards. You need to ask around and find an actual operators course with a vetted professional tactical instructor. The best rifle in the world won't help you if you don't know how to make it sing properly.

In the meantime, I highly recommend Kyle Lamb's training DVDs, which you can purchase through Viking Tactics for practicing at home and at your local range. Practicing in your living room on a regular basis is actually more valuable than range time. Place a pillow on the floor and practice mag changes from your battle belt until they become second nature. Practice clearing jams and double feeds (hypothetically! Do not practice with live rounds indoors…obviously). Practice ready-up drills. Focus at a point on the wall and practice raising your rifle quickly to your shoulder (and drawing your pistol) until it becomes second nature and your sites automatically line up with the point you were previously focusing on. Repeat, repeat, repeat. Those three simple drills will make you ten times more proficient in a real life situation than someone putting thousands of rounds downrange sitting behind a bench, and it won't cost you a dime.

If you are part of a retreat group (and you should be), you also need to train together in small squad tactics. You need to work together until you can read each other's minds and then train some more. This brings me to probably one of my more debatable philosophies. Most preppers are learning and teaching themselves the wrong squad tactics! I love the SAS Survival Manual and the Army's field manuals. That is great stuff, but some of it is not designed for a SHTF scenario. Most military training is designed for pitched battles and winning wars by advancing the fight. Those tactics are great if you are ordered to take a hillside during a war. In combat, your job is to kill the enemy with the realization that the friendly forces may take some casualties as well in order to gain the objective. As a soldier, if you get shot in the melee, there is likely a medic nearby who will call in a rescue helicopter to transport you to the nearest Forward Operating Base and a professional medical team with the latest and greatest medical technology for treating battlefield wounds. There are no hospitals in a SHTF scenario and you'll probably never make it to the nearest doctor. Getting shot (even a minor wound) is life-threatening, especially if it gets infected. You need to avoid shootouts like the plague! Forget all the Rambo crap. You are NOT Travis Haley just because you watched the Magpul Tactical Carbine DVDs and bought all the same tacticool gear he has.

Your tactics should be based on guerrilla warfare. If bullets start to fly, forget winning. Your squad's ONLY objective should be to retreat by bounding under heavy cover fire. Every engagement should be immediately handled by disengaging as quickly as possible and retreating! At that point, you can rally up and decide whether or not to set your own ambush for your pursuers. Make them come to you! That doesn't make you a coward; it makes you smart and will keep you alive. If you absolutely MUST engage an enemy, then make sure it is on your own terms. Night vision optics and suppressors are absolute game changers in this department and I would highly recommend outfitting your squad and training with both. Again, if you must engage, use guerrilla tactics and hit the enemy quickly from a distance and retreat just as quickly. Never try to win a pitched battle. It isn't worth it if valuable members of your team or loved ones are killed over no real practical objective other than killing the guy(s) that took a pot shot at you.

Another topic of conversation I'd like to discuss where battle rifles are concerned is the area of accessories. Everyone has been to their local range and seen Tacticool Bobby all decked out in MultiCam and wearing a Shemagh scarf. His AR looks like a Christmas tree with every available accessory, including but not limited to, a tactical light, a red laser, an IR laser, a front grip, and a bipod all mounted to his quad rail with a 3x flip-to-side multiplier mounted behind his Eotech. Bobby takes about ten shots before he has to lower his arms to the low ready and give his aching shoulders a break. I am not saying that every one of those items doesn't have a specific place in your arsenal. What I am saying is that you don't need all that crap on your bug-out rifle doubling the weight of your weapon, which you are going to be carrying around for the next three to five days. Keep all that stuff at your retreat or bug-out location. The one exception would be a good quality tactical light. I'd recommend having a fast attach on your flashlight and carrying it in an accessory pouch on your battle belt, and only mounting it on your quad rail once it gets dark.

On the subject of tactical flashlights, I have an opinion that is quite contrary to most of the "experts" out there which I touched on while discussing flashlights for your BOB. Flashlights have come an incredibly long way in the last decade with extremely high-lumen CREE LED flashlights available that Maglite probably never dreamed were possible twenty years ago. Unlike the lower lumen flashlight you carry in your BOB, your weapon-mounted tactical light should be at least 500 lumens. Even when working on a budget, you can still find decent quality 500-900 lumen flashlights in the $50 range. I already went off on a rant the last time I discussed flashlights and I'm going to try and contain myself this time. Here is the deal: you do NOT want a strobe feature on your 600 lumen tactical light...PERIOD! I realize that 95% of the "experts" out there will tell you differently, but their expertise is outdated and just plain wrong.

If you do a Google or YouTube search on the effectiveness of the strobe feature on a tactical light, they will almost all sing its praises. What you have to realize is that a lot of their advice is based on the 100 lumen flashlight era of five years ago. If you only have a 100 lumen tactical light then yes, there is a smidgeon of viability that a strobe feature will help disorient an attacker a tiny bit more than 100 straight lumens in their eyes. The drawback to the strobe feature is that it also has a disorienting effect on you, as well as any of your compadres that may be standing to your left and right. If your attacker is standing in front of a reflective surface or brightly painted wall, that strobe is also going to reflect right back at you.

Most experts recommend the strobe because it is harder to see movement under strobe and one of the other members of your squad can slowly move alongside the attacker without him seeing your partner approach. Make special note of this next point: The strobe has the same disorienting effect on you and your partner, making it harder for you to see your attacker's movements, as well. Is he reaching into his back pocket for a gun? Maybe he is pulling out his wallet to flash his badge because he's an off-duty police officer. It will be a lot harder for you to determine exactly what he is pulling out from his back pocket compared to a steady stream of light. This forces you to make a less informed, split-second decision on whether or not to squeeze your trigger. If you make the wrong decision, you are likely to have your life ruined by spending all your money on defense lawyers while being villainized by the anti-gun media.

The biggest area where I see them push the strobe nonsense is for the "frail college girl" on campus to flash into the suspected rapist's eyes, allowing her enough time to run away and escape. Sorry, guys. This isn't pepper spray. The second she turns to run, the flashlight will no longer be shining in his eyes and he's probably going to catch up to her (unless she's an Olympic track star) and be more pissed than he was a moment earlier. The theory that flashing a strobe light into an attacker's eyes will buy you time to escape is laughable at best. If you actually dig into the research and studies these "experts" are quoting, you will find a 100-200 lumen flashlight used in EVERY SINGLE TIME.

So is there a time and place for a strobe feature on your weapon light? Maybe five years ago, but not with today's 500+ lumen tactical lights. Unfortunately, because there is such a misconception about strobes and because they are in such high demand from customers, it's not as common to find a tactical light without a strobe these days. If you shine a 500-900 lumen flashlight into someone's face at night they are going to be disoriented and be forced to divert or cover their eyes…every time with no exceptions (unless they have superhuman pupils). Strobing them does not add to the effect at all because their eyes are already diverted. The only person it affects at that point IS YOU! If you are indoors (especially with light colored paint on the walls), the only person you are disorienting is yourself and those with you. I am not just pulling this out of my posterior. I have actually experienced it.

The last advanced pistol training class I attended included a night shoot portion. The negative effect of a strobe light was the instructor's main point and he drove it home during that training with real world demonstrations. He demonstrated different scenarios with different lumen flashlights and the strobe features turned on and off, indoors and out. It was very thorough, and I could say without a doubt that he was absolutely correct. At the end of the day, if you buy a 100 lumen light, than by all means get the disco ball feature on your flashlight, even though I still believe the negatives of strobes far outweigh the positives. If you are going to get up to speed with the times and get a 500+ lumen weapon light, then make sure you don't get the strobe feature. Unfortunately, like I mentioned, they are much harder to find so you'll need to get a light where the strobe can be programmed out.

The most important feature to a weapon-mounted light is the tailcap switch should ONLY turn the flashlight on and off and NOT cycle through various settings. When you toggle that switch on in an emergency, you don't want to cycle through 5 different modes to get to high. I don't care if it remembers the last setting when you turned it off, stick with a strictly on/off tail switch. I am also not a big fan of pressure pads for your weapon mounted flashlight, either. The wires leading from the flashlight to the pressure pad have a tendency to catch on objects and rip the pad off your gun or rip the cord out of the back of the flashlight. If you don't carry the other tailcap switch in your bug-out bag or assault pack, then you end up with a paper weight on the end of your rifle. One other thing that you need to realize is that you won't get over 300 lumens with standard batteries in most cases. So you need to stock up at your retreat with rechargeable CR123 batteries or whatever battery your high lumen flashlight takes.

My best recommendation for those of you with the means is the 600 lumen Surefire P2X Fury (single mode option) flashlight ($149). Surefire is a proven name on the battlefield and their quality is top tier. If you are on a budget, then for just about any other flashlight, I recommend the Nitecore brand. Their company, I'll admit, is newer and they haven't been around long enough to be proven in the "sandbox," but their build quality is excellent for the price point. For a battle rifle, check out the 920 lumen Nitecore MT10A ($55 on Amazon). The MT10A has a standard tail switch on/off activation with the ability to purchase a pressure pad if you so choose.

Switching between the different modes is on the side of the flashlight in the form of two rubber buttons for easy step up or step down in power. Be sure to mount these buttons toward your quad rail so they aren't bumped accidently. The MT10A remembers the last mode you were on, so when you hit the tail cap you will always get the turbo mode (or whatever mode you have it set at). It does contain a strobe feature but you need to do some serious gymnastics with your fingers between multiple buttons to activate it, reducing the risk of accidently switching it on in a gunfight. Another great feature is that it has a mini low-lumen red LED built into the lens for when you want to retain your night vision. Now the kicker: the Nitecore MT10A flashlight uses rechargeable 14500 batteries (which are required to get the 920 lumens); however, it will ALSO uses standard AA batteries (obviously at lower lumens)! This means that if you run out of the 14500s or lose the charger after the SHTF, you don't just have an expensive paperweight. The only drawback to the MT10A is that it has a short run time. If you are looking for a longer run time, check out the Nitecore MT26 ($59) which runs about the same price but uses 18650/CR123 batteries as opposed to 14500/AA batteries. Another great budget flashlight company I would consider would be the Foursevens brand.

For a pistol-mounted light I'd highly recommend the Surefire X300 Ultra ($195). A pistol light is an item that gets a good amount of abuse and has to handle constant recoil. Don't skimp here; I wouldn't recommend any other brand of cheap pistol lights. Don't forget to buy the proper gun holster for your battle belt that will hold your specific pistol mounted light. After going through a night shoot with a professional instructor, I discovered that regardless of what method I used to hold my flashlight in my off hand, my accuracy suffered dramatically when I couldn't use both hands to grip my pistol. I know that it's important to train one handed (and I do), but it would probably take decades of doing so to achieve anywhere near the accuracy you'll get while using a proper two-hand grip. After the night shoot I attended, I am convinced there is no way I EVER want to get into a firefight at night without a light mounted on my pistol. Since that day, I now conceal carry my Glock 19 everywhere I go with a light attached. The light does add a little weight to the front of your barrel but it also helps mitigate recoil to a degree and I found my rapid fire groups closing up faster than when not having the weapon light mounted.

The next area of weapons I want to cover is handguns. This is the easiest section of the chapter for me to write. The best brand of handgun for a SHTF situation is Glock, end of story. I have owned many handguns over the years and to tell the truth, they have all given me pretty good service and most were reliable. However, Glock is the best SHTF handgun you can own. It may not be pretty, and it may not "fit" your hand perfect, but when you pull the trigger, it goes bang every…single…time. I have at least 10,000 rounds through my Glocks with not a single issue and they have eaten every kind of ammo I have fed them. I don't know if there is another handgun in the world that has been more rigorously tested and abused yet has still continued to function.

But reliability is not my only requirement for a SHTF handgun; simplicity is also very important. Again, a gunfight is an enormously chaotic event, even for the best trained police officers and soldiers. Nothing goes according to plan and the only hope you have is if you have trained extensively and your tactical training takes over as second nature. I have read that when confronted with opposing fire, even some of the best trained soldiers get "club hands" and fumble and bumble through their mag changes and operating their rifle or handgun. It is also not uncommon to hear stories of well-trained police officers racking the slide on their weapon after they draw, sending an unused round flying, all because that was their normal routine on their range days.

If I am transitioning to my handgun, it is because my rifle has failed, or I have run out of spare magazines for it. In either case, your handgun is your last ditch effort to get out of a bad situation. I don't want to have to think about whether I have the safety on or not while I'm drawing. I know there are going to be people who disagree with me and insist their weapon have an external safety. But, for the average Joe with minimal training in a firefight, that is one extra step to fumble through before your weapon is operational, and fractions of a second can mean the difference between life and death. A handgun without a safety in a proper holster is EVERY BIT as safe as a handgun with an external safety! True weapon safety is more about keeping your barrel pointed in a safe direction at all times and proper trigger finger control than whether or not you have a physical safety on your weapon.

When choosing a Glock, I would stick with models chambered in 9mm or 40 caliber for ease of acquiring ammo in a SHTF scenario. You could go with a Glock chambered in 45 ACP as well, but you are limited to fewer rounds per magazine. In a firefight, I want as many rounds packed into the magazine as possible. With the Glock models 17 and 19, you have 17 and 15 rounds per magazine available respectively. In each of my backup mags for my everyday carry Glock 19, I have also Glock factory +2 baseplates installed, allowing me to carry 19 rounds in my Glock 17 spare mags (FYI, the larger Glock 17 mags fit the Glock 19). Another great thing about Glock is that a lot of their parts are interchangeable even between models of different calibers. Lastly, similar to the AR platform for rifles, Glocks are probably the most popular handgun in the country with many police departments having them standard issue, so finding a replacement part after the SHTF is still a possibility.

Glock is NOT the only handgun suitable for a SHTF scenario, but it is far and away the best, in my opinion. The Smith and Wesson M&P line would be a distant second choice for me, especially for people with smaller hands. There are the HK, 1911, and revolver faithful out there that will swear by their handgun and curse me for not recommending their weapon....fine. If you properly train with your handgun and you are comfortable with it, then good for you. A good example of this is a retired police officer that was issued handgun X and has used it exclusively for 20 years. While I would still recommend cross-training to the Glock, if you aren't serious about spending the needed range time becoming proficient with a new weapon platform, stick with what you are proficient with. My recommendations are for the weekend warriors, those purchasing their first handgun, and those who don't have the time to train four times per month. Remember, your handgun may be your last ditch effort to save your life. I want a handgun that is simple to operate, reliable, and has a high capacity magazine.

The next weapon I'd like to cover is the bolt action rifle. This is an area where I am a lot more flexible. Most bolt action rifles from the big manufacturers are reliable, which is my number one requirement for any SHTF weapon. I realize that there are plenty of fantastic long-range calibers available for a bolt gun, but I would recommend sticking with .308 (7.62) or a far distant second 30-06. These are arguably the most common hunting cartridges in the US today and your best chance at re-supply if needed. The other options I would consider would be a detachable box magazine (to carry spare magazines for faster reloading) and a threaded barrel for adding a suppressor.

My personal rifle recommendations would be a Remington 700 or a Tikka CTR, both chambered in .308. The Remmy 700 is a very common weapon with a lot of aftermarket options. The only problem with the 700 is if you buy a base model, you are probably going to want to upgrade both the stock trigger and stock to make it high speed. My personal favorite rifle is the Tikka CTR (Combat Tactical Rifle). Tikka arguably makes the most accurate out-of-the-box rifles for under $1,000. Tikka triggers are fantastic straight from the box and the buttery soft smoothness of their bolt actions are unparalleled for the price. The CTR comes standard with a Teflon coated bolt, a 20" threaded semi-heavy barrel, and a 10-round steel box mag. The only drawback on the Tikka is that it would be hard to find a spare part for it if something broke. Fortunately for bolt guns, this is rarely the case. Once again, I am not belittling your personal pick in bolt rifle as I am really flexible on this weapon platform. As with most rifles, be sure to get plenty of practice with it.

I would also highly recommend buying a good quality laser rangefinder to use with your bolt rifle and memorizing the ballistic charts for your particular brand of rifle cartridge. I hand wrote and laminated a small ballistic chart with common ranges for both my standard rounds and my subsonic rounds and taped it inside the rear flip up scope cover on my rifle. With a quick glance up, I can find the bullet drop at multiple distances for both rounds. Professional training with a rifle is important, but definitely lower on the priority list than attending multiple pistol and carbine training courses. After some of the AR training courses I have attended recently, I no longer recommend the Magpul Carbine DVDs. However, Magpul's Long Range Rifle DVDs are stellar and I highly recommend them to learn the basics of accurate long-range shooting skills.

As far as optics go for your bolt gun, it's hard for me to make recommendations because everyone's geographical locations are different. In the foothills of West Virginia, a low power 2-7 power scope is sufficient because the likelihood of finding a shot farther than 300 yards is rare. If you live in the open planes of Montana, a 4-16 power or higher scope would make more sense. A good rule of thumb is that you should spend around the same amount of money on your optic as you do your rifle. I realize that those of you on a budget can't afford this. However, if you pay less than $100 for a cheap scope, you are REALLY doing your weapon a disservice and you are hamstringing your ability to shoot accurately at longer distances, which is the whole point of a bolt gun! If you are on a budget, look at scopes from Nikon, Burris, and Vortex in the $150-200 range.

My personal favorite scope on a budget, and the one I currently have on my Tikka, is the Vortex Diamondback 2-7x35 ($189 on Amazon) with the bullet drop reticle. Their glass is superb for the price and easily competes with Leupold's entry level scopes. The best part of the Vortex Diamondback scope is the excellent FOV (Field of View) at 100 yards that is comparable to much more expensive scopes. At 100 yards, the Vortex's FOV on 7 power is 19.3 feet! Compare that to Nikon's 2-7x35 scope which has decent glass but the FOV is only 12.7 feet on the same 7 power. That is almost 50% more FOV from the Vortex than the comparable scopes in the same price range! What a larger FOV means is that you'll have a lot less "Tunnel Vision" effect out of the Vortex than other scopes and you'll be able to see a 50% larger area where you are looking. Make note and be sure you get the Diamondback model of scope and not Vortex's lower-priced Crossfire series. The Crossfire scopes use a far inferior quality of glass. If you are not on a budget, you have thousands of quality options like Leupold, Zeiss, Schmidt & Bender, etc.... One of my clients has a Leupold VX6 2-12x42 scope with the illuminated FireDot reticle, and I absolutely love it. At 2 power, with both eyes open, you can almost run it like you would a red dot on a battle rifle and follow moving targets really efficiently. At the end of the day, you need to do your own research on scopes that are suitable for your particular area of the country.

I will be perfectly honest: I am not a big fan of shotguns for a SHTF weapon. They definitely have their place for certain scenarios and I know that there are a lot of prepper "experts" out there that tout shotguns as the best all-around SHTF gun you can have, but I strongly disagree. I personally think a shotgun is a great idea to have for cabin self-defense as it's a devastating man-killer at close range and won't penetrate walls indoors like a rifle or pistol round will. Shotguns are also great for bird hunting. At the same time though, shotguns recoil quite a bit, their ammo is expensive and bulky, and they can't be easily suppressed (I realize there are new suppressors for shotguns, but they are thousands of dollars). Shotguns are absolutely NOT a substitute for a battle rifle or long range hunting rifle! Just like your knives, please don't try to multi-purpose your guns. I realize that some of you are on an extremely tight budget, but if you end up in a gunfight with a shotgun against a looter brandishing a battle rifle, you are at an extreme disadvantage regardless of your skill with your shotgun. I would only purchase a shotgun after you have purchased a handgun, battle rifle, and bolt gun (in that order).

For self-defense shotguns, I would go with a Mossberg 590 or a Remington 870. They are both great weapons that have been around for a long time, there are plenty in circulation, and there are lots of aftermarket accessories you can purchase for them. If you are on a real tight budget, you can also get a standard break open 12 gauge from a reputable manufacturer for under $200.

Once you have purchased a handgun, a battle rifle, and a bolt gun, (and a year's worth of long term food storage!), there are other SHTF guns you might want to consider. The first would be a reliable semi-automatic .22 rifle. Once again, this is a weapon that I regularly hear some other prepper "experts" recommending as their go-to SHTF weapon. They are dead wrong. I admit a well-placed shot with a .22 can kill a man...over time. However, you could also shoot them 20 times and still have to wait ten minutes for them to bleed out as they return fire. A .22 caliber gun IS NOT a substitute for a battle rifle...period! There is no debate here and anyone debating it is wrong! A .22 is really great in a couple other aspects though. For one, their ammo is extremely cheap and easy to buy in bulk compared to other calibers. You can easily suppress a .22 and use it for hunting small game around your retreat, and with its limited recoil it also makes a great first gun for a young teen or your spouse to learn on if they are new to shooting.

My personal recommendation for a semi-automatic .22 is the Ruger 10-22 Tactical model with the threaded barrel. The 10-22 has been around for decades, there's a ton of them in circulation, and the aftermarket accessories available are endless. They are also, arguably, the most reliable semi-automatic .22 you can buy. A lot of other companies' semi-automatic .22 rifles can be very picky about what brand of ammo you run through them. Reliability in SHTF weapons is paramount! The one exception to the Ruger 10-22 I would consider is the Smith and Wesson M&P 15-22. This is an AR clone with a functioning charging handle and magazines that resemble standard AR mags. Most of the models also come with threaded barrels. This would be a great gun to get some serious AR range time on a budget without buying the much more expensive 5.56 ammo. I don't personally own one, but most reviews I've read say they function pretty well and will eat various brands of .22 ammo.

A newer caliber on the market that would make a great secondary battle rifle is the .300 Blackout cartridge, which was actually designed around being fired through a suppressor from a 9" barrel. The .300 Blackout is essentially a 5.56 cartridge trimmed back to fit a larger and heavier .30 caliber bullet. Instead of carrying a bolt gun in a scabbard while you bug out, you should highly consider buying a 16" .300 Blackout upper with a fixed scope for your AR and carrying three spare AR mags with subsonic .300 Blackout ammo. With a quick swap out of your battle rifle's upper, you could have a silenced semi-automatic rifle effective out to 150 yards. Now this may not work out West, as 150 yards isn't that far, but in that situation you could use .300 Blackout supersonic ammo and still have a pretty quiet and hard hitting rifle out to 700 yards. This platform would make a fantastic weapon to set an ambush against an attacking force.

A great thing about this round is that you can buy a .300 Blackout upper for your 5.56 AR lower and everything else on your rifle functions the same way, including using the same bolt carrier group and the same 30 round 5.56 AR mags. When utilizing supersonic ammo, the .300 Blackout's ballistics are similar to the hard hitting 7.62x39 AK round. When utilizing subsonic ammo, you are essentially shooting a .45 caliber weight bullet (208 grains at 975 feet per second) with better ballistics out to 150 yards. The other great thing about the .300 Blackout round is it's designed to fire reliably out of a short 9" AR pistol barrel. (Important Note: putting a 9" pistol length barrel on your AR lower with a stock makes it a Short Barreled Rifle [SBR] by ATF standards, so be sure you don't do this without the proper ATF paperwork or buy an AR pistol lower to mount it on!) This makes a great, compact, and silent CQB weapon. I would however, only purchase this as a backup weapon for a specific purpose and NOT buy this as your primary battle rifle. Since it's a newer caliber on the market, there are not a lot of these weapons around yet and the ammo is quite expensive, making it hard to come by post-SHTF. On the flipside, if you have your own reloading equipment, you can make your own .300 Blackout brass from spent 5.56 casings, giving you an unlimited supply of .300 Blackout ammo as long as you have the proper components and equipment to size down the 5.56 brass and reload them.

I would also consider picking up a .45 caliber handgun with a threaded barrel and a .45 caliber suppressor. For quiet "wet work," this gun is fantastic. If you had to quietly enter a house where a retreat member was being held, this would be a great handgun to do that with. With a quality "wet" silencer, the .45 is truly whisper quiet. On top of that, you don't need to buy expensive subsonic ammo as most .45 caliber rounds in circulation are already subsonic. If you have some extra money to spend, pick up a semi-auto HK UMP carbine converted from a USC (make sure it was legally converted or buy a USC and do the conversion yourself). A friend of mine has one of these, and with a suppressor attached and 25 round UMP mags, it truly is a whisper-quiet death machine and a total blast to shoot. However, they are also extremely expensive and will probably run you well over $2,000 to get a used one.

If you can afford to drop $2,500 on an HK UMP, then you will probably be a good candidate to pick up my next recommendation: a Barrett model 82A1. Having a semi-automatic .50 caliber rifle to keep in your retreat's watchtower could be a game changer if your retreat is assaulted by a large looting group driving armored vehicles. I am NOT making the case that your little band of merry men go toe-to-toe with a professional military force (foreign or domestic). But there is always a chance that in the societal fallout after the SHTF, some of the larger gangs of looters may get their hands on military trucks and hardware after the rural reserve bases have been abandoned. A Barret chambered in 50BMG will easily cut through the engine block of most light-armored vehicles and disable them in their tracks. With its large, specifically engineered muzzle brake and a heavy recoil spring, the 82A1 is surprisingly very comfortable to shoot. The recoil is more of a slow push on your shoulder and less of a sharp snap like you would get from a larger caliber hunting rifles. In fact, the 82A1 is more comfortable to shoot than my little .308 Tikka T3 Lite deer rifle. However, expect to pay over $10,000 to pick one up with a scope and extra magazines. Obviously, this weapon is not a bug-out weapon as it weighs over 30 pounds before you even add a magazine, scope, and ammo. However it is a force multiplier and huge asset for a "fixed" firing position at your retreat.

On the same subject of weapons and personal protection, I would like to add a couple other recommendations for your retreat. I've already discussed the advantages of having night vision optics for your weapons, but an additional item for security you should consider is a FLIR (Forward Looking Infrared) optic which produces an image based on an object's heat signature. With night vision, an enemy combatant can still be unnoticed at distance if they are in a static position and stay still. However, it is almost impossible to hide from a FLIR optic. If you have a watchtower at your retreat, you should really consider a FLIR optic for scanning your perimeter at night. Unfortunately, to buy a quality FLIR unit you are looking between $4,000 and $10,000.

For daytime perimeter security, I recommend buying a good quality spotting scope. There may come a time when your bolt rifle's scope and its standard magnification won't be powerful enough to verify a potential threat at distance. Before you start throwing rounds down range at a "potential' threat, having a 20-60 power spotting scope on standby could help you verify if you are shooting at an armed looter or the neighbor's kid who accidently wandered onto your property. Last, I would highly recommend buying some full-size silhouette (18" x30") or equivalent-sized AR500 steel targets. Besides being able to use them on a homemade range pre-SHTF to increase your shooting proficiency, you can also use them post-SHTF for ballistic protection in multiple locations around your compound. Some could be placed below the windows of your watchtower, in a sniper hole, or at other security positions like your LP/OP (Listening Post/Observation Post). You could also use them to protect a vehicle if you were forced to make a supply run or leave your retreat in an emergency. With improvised brackets, you could weld them to the outside of your driver and passenger doors or place them upright in the bed of a pickup to protect your squad while travelling.

There are a plethora of other weapons that I haven't covered and you could literally write an entire book on the subject. Again, if I didn't mention your personal choice in rifle or handgun, I'm not saying that you are wrong or your weapon is crap. This chapter is just my opinion based on years of research and experience on which weapons are most reliable and best to consider SPECIFICALLY for a long-term SHTF scenario. Whatever weapon you end up choosing, make sure it is reliable and chambered in a common cartridge, get plenty of professional training on its use, and practice, practice, practice!

Chapter 15
Tactical Gear and Clothing

Tactical Gear is one area that has changed dramatically in the last decade. With the advent of new types of holsters, mag pouches, slings, optics, etc., the tactics and techniques of "gun fighting" have changed significantly in recent years. A lot of this new gear has been used with great success during the recent wars in the Middle East and helped soldiers and SWAT team members become faster and more accurate at their profession. Just ten years ago, you had a handful of companies making holsters and your options for carrying your handgun were fairly simple: you could get a leather holster or a nylon one and that was about it. Today, if you have a common handgun model, your options are endless and can be quite confusing. So where do we start?

I would say that the most important thing to look for when purchasing ANY type of survival or tactical gear is quality. When I first started preparing for hard times, I was on a tight budget and spent a lot of time trying to research and buy a cheaper version of the gear I needed that would "get me by." Please don't do this when at all possible. I literally have a huge box of unused gear I've purchased that either didn't last or was insufficient for the task at hand and I ended up having to buy another piece of gear to replace it. If I had just saved up the money and bought a quality piece of gear in the first place, I would have spent less money in the long run.

There are a few things I look for when purchasing a handgun holster, but you first need to take into consideration how you are intending to carry. When carrying concealed, a lot of people choose tiny "pocket" guns for ease of concealment. I strongly discourage you from doing this. If you are getting robbed at your local mini mart and end up in a gunfight, you will wish you had a larger handgun with more rounds in the magazine...guaranteed. If you are going to make the conscious decision to carry concealed in your everyday life, then you need to make the conscious decision to dress around a practical gun-fighting-worthy handgun.

Pocket guns are fine to be carried in an ankle holster as a backup or when your dress won't allow otherwise. For instance, I worked for a few years in a professional environment where khaki slacks and tucked in dress shirts were required. This prevented me from carrying my normal, everyday-carry Glock 19 and I was forced to keep it in my pack that I carried to work each day. But in all other circumstances I dressed "around my gun" to make sure I wasn't obviously printing. If your normal style of dress is the new fad of tight "skinny" jeans and tight t-shirts, then you need to switch it up when you carry. Your pants should allow you room to carry in the waistband (IWB) style holster.

When I first got my concealed carry permit many years ago, I was regulated to carrying my Glock 19 in a shoulder holster, which limited me to carrying only when I could wear an unbuttoned shirt over the holster or a coat in the fall and winter. There weren't a lot of good holster options for concealed carry (that I knew about) back then and it resulted in me not carrying very often during the hotter summer months. Then I owned my own business for seven years and it was important for me to carry on a daily basis. I sold the bulkier Glock 19 and purchased a Kahr P9 which I carried for years in a nylon IWB pouch. I was never really happy with the decision as the single stack magazine limited me to 6 rounds and I was never able to get nearly as proficient with it as I had been with my Glock. Around 2007, a friend of mine bought a Crossbreed Supertuck IWB holster for his Glock 19 and boldly touted it as a revolutionary new way to carry concealed. He let me borrow it for a few days and I quickly determined that I could carry his Glock 19 way more comfortably than the much smaller Kahr P9 in the nylon IWB holster. It was a literal game changer for concealed carry and I quickly sold my Kahr with its limited magazine capacity and bought another Glock 19 with a Crossbreed holster. Since 2007, I have never looked back.

Today there are literally hundreds of companies online and on eBay making similar Kydex IWB holsters that you can choose from including the bigger companies like Galco, which makes the King Tut holster ($60). Basically, this holster style utilizes a large piece of thick, flat leather that goes on the inside of the holster against your body and prevents the various curves and edges of your weapon from digging into your skin (which is why it's more comfortable than any other style of IWB holster). It is wider than the actual gun holster section and it attaches to your belt with two metal clips on both sides of the holster. Using two clips instead of one (like the older nylon pouches) makes the holster stay in place very firmly when drawing, and your weapon doesn't cant or tilt forward and back like the older holsters with a single point of attachment to your belt.

The holster itself is made from Kydex, which is a type of plastic that becomes flexible when heated, and it is molded for your specific model of handgun and any accessories you may have on it. This allows great retention for your weapon with a slightly audible snap when holstering. In fact, I can do a literal handstand and on occasion have gotten into a friendly grappling match with a close friend without my weapon coming loose. At the same time, a swift tug from the holster brings your weapon to bear without the added step of releasing a retention strap. A big benefit of a Kydex holster is that it retains its shape after you draw, unlike the old leather and nylon pancake holsters which flatten out after you draw your weapon. This allows you to easily re-holster your weapon with one hand, which is beneficial if you have your support hand occupied (i.e., keeping your attacker's arm pinned behind his back while he is on the ground).

One thing to consider when purchasing this style of holster is to get the "combat cut" option if offered (some companies already do this or you can use a sharp razor to do it yourself). Essentially, you want to be sure the upper part of the leather near your handgun's beaver tail is cut away in the same shape as your beaver tail, allowing you to reach full grip without the leather digging into the webbing between your thumb and finger. I highly recommend the Crossbreed Supertuck and Minituck models, which can be bought for around $70. I have had mixed luck buying knock-off brands from the various companies on eBay which sell them for around $40. You can roll the dice and try to save a few bucks, but you may end up buying a second one and you would have been better off just buying the Crossbreed from the get go.

The next style of holster is a regular on-the-hip style or Outside the Waistband (OWB) holster. Once again, this used to be dominated by your older leather and nylon pancake style holsters. Today, different type of polymers and plastics (especially Kydex) have taken over the market, allowing a more rigid and sturdy holster while eliminating the need for a retention strap. This is probably going to be the most comfortable way for you to carry your weapon after the SHTF if you are on a budget. The company that introduced this style of holster was Raven Concealment and they are still considered the gold standard when purchasing Kydex OWB holsters. Just like with Crossbreed's IWB holsters, there are dozens of companies online and on eBay that have copied the Raven Concealment's OWB holster. You will typically pay around $100 for a Raven holster, yet you can find companies on EBay that sell similar holsters for around $45. Purchase them at your own risk or if you are on a tight budget, but you may end up with a dud (on the bright side, if you purchase a holster from one of the companies that sell on eBay, they will usually work hard to replace it or fix the problem as they dread getting a bad review).

The most important thing to consider when carrying any holster OWB, is to make sure you are using an actual pistol belt. Your run of the mill Walmart belt will not hold the weight of a pistol and it will inevitably result in your holster leaning out away from your body due to the weight of the fully loaded magazine. There are multiple options for pistol belts, yet most are quite expensive. A good quality brand-named leather or reinforced nylon webbing pistol belt will typically run you well over $60. If you are on a budget, check out Lutzs Leather (*lutzsleather.com*) where they sell good quality leather pistol belts starting around $30, depending on the options you select. I received one of their belts as a Christmas present from my dad and after wearing it regularly for three years now, it's still rigid and in great shape.

The subject of holsters leads me into what I believe to be the most important piece of tactical gear you can buy for a SHTF scenario: a high quality battle belt. After society falls apart, it is going to be vital to your safety that you carry a weapon on you at ALL TIMES with no exceptions! This does not mean leaning your rifle against a tree twenty yards away while you garden. You may not have time to reach it if a starving, desperate person appears from the edge of the woods suddenly. I would even take this a step further and recommend every late teenage and adult member of your group be armed at all times as well. The minute you get lazy in this area will likely be the time that a bad situation arises where you need to protect yourself.

Can you get by with a simple OWB holster and spare mag pouch or two on your support hand side? Sure, but it will not be the most comfortable way to stay armed…every day…all day. A good quality "Battle Belt" will support the load much better and allow you to carry more gear in relative comfort. On my battle belt, I carry two spare pistol mags and two spare rifle mags on my support side. On my strong hand side, I carry my Glock 19 as well as my trauma kit and sometimes a dump pouch on the rear of my battle belt. That's it. I've seen battle belts that are loaded to the hilt with gear for assaulting a compound. That is not the purpose here. You are trying to carry the bare minimum as this will become a part of your everyday wardrobe for the foreseeable future.

As far as the actual battle belt goes, this is another area I would not skimp on. This piece of gear will get all-day, everyday use and you want something that will hold up over the long haul without the webbing and fabric tearing or coming apart. The two belts that I would recommend the most are the HSGI Sure Grip battle belt and the VTAC Brokos battle belt. If I had to pick my favorite between the two, it would be the HSGI because it is lined with Sure-Grip, a soft Neoprene-type material to "grip" your hips, allowing for a snug fit while staying comfortable. However, I tend to sweat, and in the hot summer months the idea of having a wide Neoprene battle belt snug around my hips while gardening or patrolling doesn't appeal to me. For you, that may not be an issue. It is for that reason only that I personally went with the VTAC Brokos belt; it is still very sturdy yet offers a lot more breathability. Both of these belts come in various tactical colors and versions of camo for around $80. One thing to remember is that nearly every battle belt I have seen runs really small (short). I would highly recommend ordering the next larger size than you think you'll need.

Remember when buying a battle belt that they don't include an "inner belt." This is one area where you can skimp a little bit, but I still don't recommend doing so for long term use. The inner belt that I personally use is the Viking Tactics (VTAC) Cobra Belt which costs around $60. On a budget, there are a lot of "tactical" belts you can find on eBay for around $20 which will get the job done. One of the most important features to consider when purchasing an inner belt for your battle belt is having some type of "buckle" fastening on the front. Don't get your typical nylon tactical belt that weaves through the buckle to fasten. For one, they almost always loosen over time and this will be compounded once you add a little weight to your battle belt. Second, you want something that you can quickly throw on and take off without adjusting each time you put it on. The one thing I would avoid, if possible, are the typical plastic buckles that come on most cheaper tactical belts; this is an item you will be using frequently and the plastic buckle is likely to break over time. If you are on a budget and that's all you can afford, then I would recommend buying an extra buckle in case (or for when) the first one breaks. I would highly recommend that you purchase a tactical belt with a "Cobra" brand buckle, but you are unlikely to do so on a smaller budget.

When buying mag pouches for the molle webbing on your battle belt, there are a few important things you'll want to remember. First, don't buy the classic nylon or canvas mag pouches with the velcro flap on them. In fact, I would steer clear of these types of Vietnam-era mag pouches in nearly every situation except maybe for spare mag pouches on the outside of your bug-out bag. In any instance where you are in a gunfight and you need to reach for your next magazine quickly, you NEVER want to fumble with a velcro strap to get to the magazine. That is wasted time when fractions of a second count. The only reason those mag pouches were ever used were for retention purposes before today's newer technology. The other drawback to those types of mag pouches is the difficulty in replacing a magazine in the pouch one-handed while performing a tactical reload. Similar to the old leather pancake pistol holsters "flattening out" after you draw, those flimsy fabric mag pouches make it nearly impossible to rotate your magazines from your vest to your battle belt one-handed when you get a break in the action.

My personal recommendation for mag pouches is HSGI Taco Pouches which have quickly become the gold standard. They have adjustable magazine retention built in without using a strap over top, stay open after you pull your mag, and come in most camo choices. As an alternative to Taco pouches, both G-Code and Wilder Tactical are now making similar style mag pouches you can consider for around the same price. Another alternative would be BladeTech mag pouches which are made from a rigid plastic and are popular with competition shooters. Last, you could also consider Kydex mag pouches from Raven Concealment or other sellers on eBay if you are on a budget.

One of the biggest things to remember is to get "single-stack" mag pouches and not "double-stack." Double-stack mag pouches are too bulky and will get in the way if you need to lay prone (especially when you put them on your vest or plate carrier). They are also much more likely to snag on things as they stick out from your body too far. You want to be as lean as possible. Most importantly, you will experience slower mag changes as it's much harder to grip a magazine when it's pressed tight against another magazine. When attaching the mag pouches to my battle belt, I prefer to have two pistol mag pouches and two rifle mag pouches (some people prefer to only carry one spare rifle mag on their belt). I position my pistol mag pouches with one at the 11 o'clock and one at the 10 o'clock position. My rifle mag pouches go at the 9 o'clock and 8 o'clock positions. Never put your rifle mags in front of your pistol mags as it makes the pistol mags much harder to get to in a hurry.

On the weapon side of my battle belt, I position my holster at the 2 o'clock position and my trauma kit at the 4 o'clock position. I've seen some people wear their trauma kit in front of their pistol, but I find it digs into my stomach when I sit down. The most important thing is to make sure that your trauma kit does not interfere in any way when you draw your pistol.

On that note, I also chose to buy a specific holster for my battle belt; it has quickly become my favorite holster, hands down. Drawing a sidearm from an OWB belt mounted holster never really felt comfortable or natural for me. I felt as if I needed to contort my body to the left when drawing to make it easier for my weapon to clear the top of the holster. This was compounded the faster I got and the more I practiced. I had always wanted a kydex holster that would be securely fastened to my battle belt but somehow mounted about four inches lower than a standard OWB holster. Don't get me wrong, there are plenty of "duty" type holsters out there that hang from a pistol belt (typically for police officers), but most of them use a thick piece of nylon webbing. This always makes the holster flop around when running and the only way to secure it is to use a leg strap on the bottom, which isn't comfortable if you snug it tight enough to be effective.

Enter the Viper Holsters, Rockwell Tactical Series 1 holster (*ViperHolsters.com*). This holster was designed with direct input from the Rockwell Tactical Group, comprised of Green Berets and ex-military Special Forces and instructors at the Special Forces Advanced Urban Combat School (SFAUC). I was going to describe their holster in my own words, but this direct quote from their website sums it up best:

"Viper was asked to evaluate the battle belt platform and identified certain instabilities in the battle/war belt platform. Viper crafted the Tac 1 specifically to overcome these weaknesses and provide rock solid sidearm transport. The Viper chassis drops and offsets the sidearm, provides clearance and cant for quick deployment and allows lower presentation ability when necessary. The separate chassis component allows us to tune the position of the sidearm specifically to the style of the operator. All this is accomplished while stabilizing a leveraged accessory and dropping it comfortably below the tactical harness/vest or body armor carrier. Although the chassis appears to be one piece, it is actually two layers of Kydex in different thicknesses in order to provide much greater rigidity and strength than a one piece unit. The RTG Tac 1 eliminates the shortcomings of the popular thigh rigs that have seen much service with elite groups."

Within a week of practicing with this holster, I achieved a noticeable increase in my presentation speed with less unnatural contorting of my body while drawing. It IS expensive ($140+), but you get what you pay for and I personally believe this to be the best holster on the market today for a battle belt platform.

The next piece of gear I want to discuss is tactical vests. You can find multiple companies that make universal tactical vests, but I have yet to find one that is functional. When you combine a universal holster, universal mag pouches with Velcro retention straps, and one-size-fits-all approach to sizing, you end up with a very subpar product. In my opinion, a battle belt is a far superior way to carry your gear than a vest, but I also acknowledge that there may be instances where a battle belt won't work for very specific reasons. If you do plan to carry your gear in a vest, do yourself a favor and build one from scratch with a holster and mag pouches specifically designed for your weapon.

Another piece of gear that is very important is a plate carrier and ballistic plates. I recommend keeping your plate carrier at your retreat location or storage unit and not at your home in town. In my opinion, if you bug out on day one or day two after the SHTF, you shouldn't need a plate carrier on your way to your retreat. Things should be relatively calm the first few days and it'll be a week or two before looters start to get organized into groups and start setting ambushes along the roadways. If you are travelling with a battle rifle and dressed as if you mean business, most travelers you encounter on the road should steer well clear of you. Besides, you are going to be carrying plenty of weight on your person already with your pack and battle rifle. There's no need to add an extra 10-18 pounds to that equation. However, if you were ever forced to leave your retreat or it came under attack, having a plate carrier and quality plates readily accessible at your bug-out location would be a very wise idea to protect your vitals during a gunfight.

There are a plethora of options when shopping for bullet-proof vests and plate carriers, and you're going to have to do some research into what's best for you and your retreat members. Some will look towards the Kevlar type vests that the police wear, but in my opinion that is subpar protection for the threats you may face after the SHTF. The vests that police wear are considered soft body armor (typically level IIA protection) and designed for comfort since they need to wear them on a daily basis. Accordingly, they are designed to be lightweight and typically only offer protection from your average handgun rounds. After the SHTF, you are very likely to be squaring off at distance with people carrying their deer rifle or a battle rifle, which most police-style soft body armor won't protect against. I would recommend purchasing stand alone "hard" plates as opposed to soft body armor. At a minimum you should purchase level III plates, which should stop up to six hits from a higher caliber rifle like .308 rounds.

Unfortunately, hard plates are not very comfortable to wear as they are bulky and heavy (just how heavy depends on what type you purchase). In the last five years, there have been a lot of breakthroughs in ballistic plates with newer technology making them much thinner and lighter. You can break down ballistic plates into three categories: AR500 steel plates, ceramic plates, and composite plates. If you are on a budget, the only type of plate you are likely to afford is steel.

There are a couple of factors that you MUST take into consideration before purchasing steel plates, however. First, the steel plate must be made from the proper AR500 steel from a reputable manufacturer with a FULL anti-spalling coating. Anti-spalling coating is a thick layer of Linex-type coating which captures the bullet fragments when it smashes into the steel plate and shatters apart. If you purchase a raw AR500 steel plate and get shot, the bullet will shatter against the plate and send tiny bullet fragments in all directions. They will typically imbed themselves in your neck and upper arm area if your arms are out in front of you (holding a rifle for instance). Those fragments act as miniature bullets themselves and could easily puncture an artery or become infected and life-threatening. A full thickness anti-spalling coating is not optional when buying steel plates!

The second thing to be aware of is that steel plates are by far the heaviest type of plate you can purchase. You're looking at approxiamently 16 pounds of weight when wearing both front and rear steel plates. On the flipside, steel plates are very durable and will last you a lifetime. The other types of hard ballistic plates have shelf lives and the composite ones are sometimes known for the layers coming apart over time with hard use. Most ceramic plates are so fragile that if you dropped one on a hard surface like concrete, you could literally crack it, significantly compromising the bullet-stopping effectiveness of the plate. After doing lots of research, I purchased a set of Spartan brand steel plates ($180) from *Thetargetman.com*. In my opinion, that company is constantly innovating and testing to offer you the best product they can. You may choose to purchase from a different company, just be sure you watch test videos on their anti-spalling coating and make sure it is effective at capturing most bullet fragments.

If money is no option, then I would seriously consider getting one of the newer composite or ceramic plates. Although they are more fragile than steel plates, they literally weigh less than half of what steel plates do (typically around 8 pounds per set). The other drawback is that they will only handle a limited amount of hits (typically 6) before you run the risk of getting penetration from a round. At the same time, I wouldn't let this stop me from getting composite or ceramic plates because if you are taking more than six hits to your chest, you've surely got bigger problems and have likely been shot somewhere else. There are tons of companies that make ceramic and composite plates; you'll have to do your own research as these companies are constantly changing and improving the technology behind their products. The biggest issue with these types of plates is their cost. A good quality set of composite or ceramic plates will typically set you back between $600 and $1,000.

Once you have decided on the type of plate you are going to purchase, you need to make a decision on the type of plate carrier to use. There are multiple companies that make plate carriers, just be sure you don't go with any of the cheaper companies like Condor because they probably won't stand the test of time. Especially if you are carrying 16 pounds of steel plates, whatever plate carrier you choose must be made of quality material and have proper stitching to prevent it from falling apart through hard use. One of the most common types of plate carriers are the ones you typically see SWAT officers wearing with the full cummerbund that wraps around your mid-section and attaches with Velcro at the front of the carrier. I personally don't prefer this type of carrier as they are restrictive, bulky, and can take close to a minute to put on and adjust properly. They also are going to be hot to wear during the summer and, in my opinion, the cummerbund section can sometimes get in the way of your pistol draw from your battle belt. This is compounded if you have mag pouches or gear mounted in that area.

Personally, I prefer a "minimalist" style carrier which is just big enough to hold the plates and that's all. My plate carrier has a piece of webbing and buckles on both sides of the plate carrier to keep it snug to my body. I can literally throw this over my head in a pinch and with one snap of a buckle, I'm ready to go. I also prefer the minimalist type carriers as they don't interfere with my battle belt nearly as much as a full plate carrier with a cummerbund. Again, that is just my personal preference and you may decide to go a different route. Either way, your plate carrier should be kept in a very accessible place at your retreat, because if you ever truly need it, it's probably going to be a "right now" situation!

Some people will purchase plate carriers for their spouse. If your spouse is fully trained and part of your "tactical response team" at your retreat, then you should definitely get her plates as well. If she is not a part of your core team of fighters, than I probably wouldn't go through the expense if you are working on a budget. Same philosophy goes with older teenagers. For younger children, I recommend buying a single composite plate and placing it in their backpack. If a gunfight erupts, you can teach them to lay prone behind their pack for protection. It probably wouldn't be a bad idea to have the same system when you send them to school pre-SHTF (with the rise in mass casualty school shootings today).

For full plate carriers, I recommend the Mayflower and Paraclete brands from SKD Tactical which run around $200 -$300. For a minimalist plate carrier, there aren't as many options. I personally use a Flyye Fast Attack plate carrier ($100 on eBay). To be honest with you, I purchased that plate carrier many years ago when I was on a budget and Flyye is not considered a high-quality brand. I have used that plate carrier on many training exercises and to date it has held up flawlessly with the stitching and material holding up perfectly. I am not saying that this is the best option for you and I will probably look to replace it in the future with a higher quality plate carrier as the Flyye starts to show wear.

I would steer away from overloading your plate carrier with gear and magazines. Once again, you want to stay as low profile as possible. There is no need for double magazine pouches and loading yourself down with a dozen spare mags. Double mag pouches on the front of your vest seriously interfere with your ability to comfortably lay prone will firing. Most special operational soldiers only carry 6 magazines on their person for an assault (unless they are going to be out for a long period of time without resupply), and someone in the squad always has extra magazines available in a pack. For the front of my plate carrier, I have three spare mag pouches. When combined with the two spare mag pouches on my battle belt and the one in my rifle, that makes a total of six magazines and 180 rounds readily available during a fire fight. If I am carrying my assault pack with me, I will also have three spare mags attached to the outside of the pack for quick re-supply. Again, remember, you are not taking the fight "to" the enemy. You should always retreat under cover fire, and 6-9 full magazines should allow you to do so.

I could sit here and make recommendations for gear all day long, but for the sake of "bugging-out" there is one more piece of gear I would highly recommend for your battle rifles: the Vickers Combat Application Sling by Blue Force Gear. Having a regular rifle sling that just goes over your shoulder doesn't allow you to bring your rifle to bear quickly enough when you're ambushed. Most two and three point slings that allow you to carry your rifle in front of you don't secure it very well when you are forced to transition to your side arm or use your hands to ride a bike, climb a ladder, etc. This results in your weapon flopping around in front of you and banging against your knees when you run or snagging on foreign objects around you. The Vickers Sling has a large piece of webbing that you can grab and cinch the rifle close to your body when you need to use both hands for a task. The same piece of webbing allows you to quickly release the tension and bring the weapon to your shoulder. I realize that there are other manufacturers that make similar slings, but most use a knotted loop of para cord to tighten and loosen the sling. Especially when wearing gloves, that loop of para cord can be tough to grasp.

The next thing I'd like to discuss is clothing options. This is an area that gets a lot of discussion on the preparedness forums and the recommendations are all over the board. One myth I want to dispel up front, is the idea of the "grey man" concept. This is typically discussed for people who plan to stay in the big cities after the collapse and scavenge for their supplies. The premise is to blend in with your environment by wearing "normal" clothing for that area or by wearing a black contractor garbage sack to look like a bum. Am I saying that this is never a good strategy? No, but in most cases, you are utilizing this strategy because you have made the absolutely huge mistake of staying in an urban area and you are scavenging for supplies when you should have bugged out in the first place. Wearing a garbage bag over your body would prevent you from carrying a battle rifle with you as the bag would significantly restrict its use. If you wear the rifle slung over the top of the garbage bag, it immediately dispels the myth that you are a "grey man" and you would also have limited access to your mag pouches for quick magazine changes. If you wear your belt or vest over top of the garbage bag, than you might as well stop pretending to be a measly bum on the streets and go the opposite direction by projecting an aura of strength.

When bugging out during the first few days in a grid-down scenario, most people are going to be pretty low key and there won't be any starving and super desperate people yet. Somebody that is experiencing some level of desperation, for whatever reason, during the first week is likely to confront soft targets of opportunity and steer clear of someone dressed like a soldier, mercenary, or operator. Once you hit the 2 weeks to 1 month mark, desperate and starving people are likely to attack you regardless of how you are dressed if they think you have food or something else of value. This is why I recommend that once you reach your retreat or bug-out location, you stay there for the first six months and only leave your property under the most dire and desperate of circumstances.

If you are wandering around and scavenging a month in after the SHTF, nearly every person you encounter is going to present a potentially life-threatening situation. Between months six and twelve, most of the US population will be dead or dying from disease, starvation, and looters pillaging, murdering, and raping. If you are forced to leave the safety of your retreat after the first six months, you are less likely to come across as many travelers or persons wandering around looking for food. On the flip side, if you encounter people away from your retreat after month six, they are going to be one of two groups: other preppers who were prepared ahead of time and will likely be quite suspicious of you, or the best and most savage of looters who were able to live through the SHTF likely by committing terrible acts of violence against their fellow man. Either way, both of those encounters are dangerous, with the second one being an especially deadly interaction.

So what should you wear? First of all, it is imperative that you dress for your environment. It is more important that you are comfortable and protected from the elements than any kind of image you may want to portray. In cold weather be sure to dress in layers so you can layer down as the day and night temperatures fluctuate and you perspire on your hike out of town. Sweating profusely during the winter is almost as bad as being under-dressed. Wet or sweaty clothing can cause you to be chilled even though you are wearing enough clothing. When bugging out, I highly recommend you portray an image of strength and try to dress like a mercenary or operator. However, I would steer clear of military-type fatigues as you don't want to be confused with a soldier. First, there may be people who are angry that the military didn't respond to help them or they may assume you are a deserter (which could go badly for you). Second, you may also experience people flocking to you for help, assistance, or discussions about "what's happening out there?" All of these situations you want to discourage.

For bugging out, I would recommend a pair of Khaki or Olive Drab cargo or "tactical" pants and similar style shirts and jackets. My favorite pair of pants are TRU SPEC Xtreme pants. They are very well built and have a special coating over the knee area that is extremely durable. The other brand of pants I really like are BlackHawk Warrior Wear lightweight tactical pants which are also very well made with more hidden pockets than you can count and a flexible waistband for comfort. Once you reach your retreat or bug-out location, I would make sure you have quality clothing (not Walmart) that will stand the test of time as you farm and live an outdoors type of life far from your previous cubicle job. Consider brands like Carhartt for durability. Make sure you also take into account young children who grow up quickly and be sure you have the next available size of shoes and clothing for them as you can't just run down to the mall for fall school shopping anymore.

Something else to consider would be a universal "uniform" for your retreat members when walking patrols or coordinating an assault. Typically, I see retreat groups buying "tacticool" military camo fatigues. I am not a big fan of this as, once again, you don't want to look like soldiers. Also, there are very few environments in the continental US where standard military camo patterns are even effective. The two exceptions would be Multi-cam and A-Tacs type of camo which blend in to some environments nicely, but you still look para-military. In my opinion, for your retreat, you should buy the best civilian camouflage clothing for your specific area of the country. In the Northeast where I live, Mossy Oak and Realtree are going to blend into the woods significantly better than any of the military camo choices including Multi-cam. You could even go so far as developing an arm band or head band in a universal color to differentiate yourselves from the locals who may be sporting similar camouflage while out hunting.

I realize that not everyone can afford to own all the latest and greatest pieces of tactical gear. But as I mentioned, it's essential that you attend a professional operators course for your handgun and battle rifle. What you will quickly see is that having the proper gear will make you a much better and faster gunfighter than using older and cheaper gear. I'm not saying that you should put off purchasing long-term food and rush out and splurge on all the tactical gear I've mentioned, but you definitely need to make it a priority and a portion of your monthly allowance for long-term preparations. Having the proper weapons, gear, and training could mean the difference between life and death if you ever end up in a gunfight in a lawless post-collapse scenario.

Chapter 16
Long-Term Food

For thousands of years, people around the world have been growing and storing their own food to last them through the non-growing season in their geographical area. Only in the last fifty years has mankind, in developed countries, gotten away from this practice. With on-demand food at our grocery stores, the knowledge of how to grow and store your own food has almost completely disappeared from society. Even most of those "country folk" who grow gardens in the summer, only do so to have fresh vegetables in the summer and fall. Very few of them grow and store enough vegetables to completely live off of them throughout the winter months.

The biggest obstacle that 99% of survivors will face after the loss of the electric grid is the lack of food. Dying from starvation is a very slow and painful process for the unprepared and something you definitely don't want to experience. Even a lot of people who consider themselves prepared are drastically under-estimating the food they will need. You are going to be burning a considerable amount of calories after the SHTF...more than you think. On top of that, most preppers have significantly less food (necessary daily calories) than they think they do.

I hear a lot of rural people tell me, "I'll be alright; I know how to garden and can vegetables." The first thing I always ask them is how many canning jars do they have left over when they get done canning the vegetables in their garden each fall. Almost every single person answers "none" or "very few." That is a life-threatening problem if they are planning to live off canned food and stored vegetables! Most people grow a garden to eliminate their need to buy vegetables at the store and not to actually sustain their family's full diet through an entire winter. Of all the people I have asked that question, not one has had ANYWHERE NEAR the amount of canning jars they would actually need to feed their family from their canned goods. Canning is great, but unless you can afford to have an enormous amount of canning jars, you are going to need to learn how to store your vegetables in a root cellar or "cold cellar" that you may need to dig by hand if you wait till after the SHTF.

If you think you have enough canning jars to survive a winter, than I implore you to do a little exercise. Count how many jars you currently have. Next, figure out your average harvest dates for your garden. I realize that different vegetables have different dates when you plant and harvest them, but for illustration purposes let's say your harvest season is from early June through late October. That means you have around six months during which there are no mature vegetables in the garden (again, this varies dramatically depending on where you live). Assuming you have a family of four, you will probably need AT LEAST two to three quarts worth of food per day just to survive (not thrive). That means your family should have the equivalent of four to five HUNDRED quart jars in storage and three times as many lids. I realize that there a ton of variables here from the length of your growing season to whether you have a root cellar, how many people you are feeding, and whether or not you have other long-term food preparations. My main point is that you can't just look at the stack of jars in your basement and think, "That should be enough." You need to seriously tabulate and calculate on paper exactly what you think you'll need based on your family's needs than add in some extra supplies "just in case." If you do this, you'll probably notice that you need a lot more canning jars, lids, and supplies than you thought, and you'll probably need to grow a much larger garden to fill all those jars. Two things you will also need to seriously consider during this process is purchasing a greenhouse to extend your growing season and digging a large root cellar to store vegetables and limit the amount of jars you will need to purchase.

I am not saying that it's impossible to strictly live off your vegetable garden year-round, but having a year's worth of long-term food storage is definitely advisable. There are many different ways you can store up a year's worth of food with the most popular being the prepared freeze-dried food companies. There are a lot of companies that advertise "1 Year Food Plans," but beware of them! I am not going to call them out by name, but I'm sure you have seen their advertisements on numerous preparedness websites. Even a lot of the big name, conservative talk show hosts advertise for them. In almost every case, these companies' claims are verging on outright lies and their one year's worth of food won't last you six months in most cases. If you actually do the math on the calories provided in those plans, you're going to find that most of them are providing you with far less than half the calories you are going to need each day! At the end of the year (if you make it that long), you will probably look like a holocaust survivor. If the SHTF, they are going to be directly responsible for a lot of people dying who thought they were prepared and I don't make that claim lightly. If you get nothing more out of this chapter, remember this: most long-term food companies' serving sizes have no basis in reality! Completely ignore them when purchasing your long-term food! The only correct way to purchase long-term food is by buying it based on calorie count.

I highly recommend that you have at least a 1-year supply of food for each member of your family. A six-month food supply will not get you through an entire winter, spring and summer until your garden crops have reached time for harvest. I can also almost guarantee your first year's harvest won't go nearly as well as you plan and you'll likely have less food than you think on year two, so having some long-term food left over from year one post-SHTF would be a bonus to help get you through the second winter. Unfortunately, there is no one-size-fits-all "1 year" food insurance plan, period! I have seen 1 year food plans from major companies, ones that you'd surely recognize, that come with as little as 700 calories per day. Another trick they attempt is packing their plans with high sugar calorie-count juice drinks and other side items like chocolate pudding to pad their numbers. The majority of your calories should be coming from actual food items and not sugar-packed side items. If you choose to buy a pre-packaged 1 year plan, pay attention to this tactic.

Also, be wary of following the Recommended Dietary Allowance (RDA) charts to determine your caloric needs as they are designed for the "average" person who is in good physical health and performing minimal exertion throughout the day. These numbers can also fluctuate greatly depending on age, physical health, and your level of activity. Your best bet would be to use a Basal Metabolic Rate (BMR) calculator like the one at www.bmi-calculator.net/bmr-calculator/ to figure out how many calories are needed for each individual member of your family based on their age, sex, height, and weight. This will give you a baseline to start from and the MINIMUM daily calories needed for each member of your family. Please realize that these calories are based on the absolute bare minimum needed for your body if you literally sat still all day. After figuring out the baseline for each member of your family, you then need to multiply the baseline by the Harris Benedict Equation. He offers formulas for each type of lifestyle, but I recommend multiplying your baseline times a "moderate lifestyle" (1.55) or an "active lifestyle" (1.725). Obviously, you're not going to be living a "sedentary" (1.2) or "lightly active" (1.375) lifestyle if you plan to survive. I also wouldn't pick the "extra active" (1.9) lifestyle either because you will certainly have some days with lighter work as well as winter months with less outdoor activity involved.

Take for instance the average American adult male at 35 years old, weighing in at 195 pounds, and standing 5' 9" inches tall. His baseline BMR is 1,663 calories a day. Applying the Harris Benedict Equation for even just a "moderately active" lifestyle, he'd need to multiply his baseline (1,663) by 1.55. That means he will actually need 2,577 calories each day. It is very vital that you do this for each member of your family. Once you add up your family's caloric needs for the year, you will have a better foundation for where to start. If you have already purchased long-term food, contact the company you purchased your food from and get the calorie count for the food they provided you and do the math based on your family's daily caloric needs. If they don't have that information at their fingertips or they refuse to give it to you, it is a safe bet that you have been misled and you have far less food than you think. When they do provide you with the calorie count in the food they sold you, I would be willing to wager you significantly less food than you thought you did.

Once you determine your family's or survival retreat's caloric needs, then you can start deciding what type of food to buy. Although there are benefits to having all freeze-dried meals that are ready to eat, I would not rely on that as your sole source of food for multiple reasons. Something you need to take into consideration is expense. What can you afford? For an average family of four (6,000 calories a day), you would likely be spending over $20,000 for a 1-year supply of strictly Mountain House meals (when figuring 6,000 calories a day and not just their serving sizes or advertised prepackaged 1 year kits). That same amount of calories could be purchased for around $4,000 in a year's worth of raw staples for your whole family. The major drawback to this approach is that your meals become A LOT MORE labor intensive to cook, especially if you are feeding 20 people at a retreat! Most people don't take into consideration that "someone" is going to have to prepare all these meals and clean up afterwards without the help of a dishwasher. Imagine having to cook a Thanksgiving Dinner three times a day, every single day, and then clean up afterward! Everything you do after the SHTF will be harder than before. You are going to have to weigh the pros and cons of each type of meal and what your budget looks like. My best advice would be to combine all the above and have a mixture of canned goods, prepared meals and staples, while also raising your own fresh meat and growing your own vegetables. You can adjust the ratio between them to fit within your budget.

The first area of food storage I would focus on, especially if you are on a budget, is buying extra food that you already eat. This technique could actually save you money...if you do it correctly. However, this technique should only be used if you already live rurally and plan to survive in place. Having a lot of food stored at your house in the city could go really badly if you aren't able to bug out by vehicle for whatever reason and take it with you. If you do go this route, I can't stress enough that having food at your house in town and not being able to take it with you is NOT a legitimate reason to NOT bug out by day two after the grid goes down! Again, staying in town because you're psychologically comfortable there and you have plenty of food there will only get you killed in the long term as more and more desperate people try to take your food. I would be hard pressed to tell you to leave it behind though, so if you did find yourself in this situation, I would go to extraordinary lengths to find someone with a running vehicle or find a route out of town that isn't deadlocked. In fact, if you are on an extreme budget and this is the only way for you to store long-term food, then I would try and locate someone within walking distance (don't wait till the last minute, do this before the SHTF!) that has an old classic car or truck that you can barter for. Worst case scenario, offer to take them with you and share your food; it's not ideal but it sure beats leaving your food behind or staying in town.

The "buy extra food you already eat" technique is actually quite simple. You are essentially storing up the same types of food you already eat on a regular basis. Most canned and boxed goods have a storage life of two to three years. In truth, especially where canned foods are concerned, their storage life is considerably longer when stored properly. The manufacturer has to print the shortest time the food will be good for. For most food (NOT ALL), it doesn't become poisonous the day after it expires, it just starts to lose its nutritional value. As long as you aren't "too" long past the expiration date and the can doesn't stink or smell funny, it's probably safe to eat (again, this is a general rule and one that should only be applied if you are desperate and starving).

The best way to make your food last longer is to store it in as dark and cool of an environment as possible. A good place to consider would be in a dark corner of your basement, as long as it's not damp, which will spoil your boxed goods. If it is damp, you'll need to invest in a dehumidifier. Some people store their food in their garage, but I would refrain from doing so if it isn't temperature controlled and kept between 32 and 70 degrees Fahrenheit (freezing isn't bad, but freezing and thawing multiple times each season is bad). The worst thing you can do for any long-term food is store it where it is going to get hot. If these options don't work for you, consider storing the extra food in an unused closet or under a guest room bed.

The first thing you want to do is sit down with your family and discuss all the items you eat on a regular basis. Make a spreadsheet with the shelf life and calories from each can or box of food. Focus primarily on canned soups, canned vegetables, canned fruit, boxes of pasta, instant potatoes, spices, and anything that has a minimum of one year "eat by" date. If you go through your entire pantry, you'll be surprised how many items you would be able to buy in bulk. Next, you need to estimate how many times a year you eat that food item. For instance, Little Bobby loves SpaghettiOs. Let's say he eats between 1 and 2 cans of SpaghettiOs each week. That would mean that you go through about 75 cans per year. If SpaghettiOs have a two-year shelf life, then you should eventually have 150 cans of SpaghettiOs in storage at any given time.

To get started, pay attention to your local grocery store's weekly flyer and whenever one of the items on your list goes on sale, buy as many as you can afford that week. Having access to a Sam's Club or Costco membership would also help you buy these items in bulk and save some money. The absolute best place to buy in bulk is at a restaurant supply store. Most large cities have them and you would be really surprised at how much cheaper you can buy bulk food compared to your local grocery store or even the Costco type stores. The only drawback is that your SpaghettiOs will probably come in a large #10 can.

Once you stock up and have a one- to two-year supply of your everyday food items stored up, then you are just buying your normal amount of groceries each week and rotating through your stored goods. The best way to keep track of this would be to have a shelving system that you can access from the front and rear. You always pull cans from the front and replenish your shelves from the rear, that way you are always using the oldest cans first. Having a laminated spreadsheet of your food supply hanging from one of the shelves will help you stay organized. I would recommend buying a grocery-store type price labeler like you used to see grocers use in the 80's, and put a sticker with the date on top of each item you place on your shelves. Those labelers are super cheap online (less than $10 on Amazon) and will really help you to keep track of the expiration dates as you go through your food.

Storing up food this way does make your weekly trip to the grocery store a little more labor intensive (because you need to check your supply shelves and find out what you need to replenish), but it is well worth the time and effort. Since you are only buying your food in bulk or when it's on sale, you will also save money in the long run even though it may cost you a little extra in the near term. By using this technique, you should easily be able stockpile a full 2-3 months (possibly 5 or 6 months depending on how much canned and boxed food your family eats) of food for a SHTF scenario. This will minimize the amount of long-term food staples and freeze-dried meals you will need to purchase. On a side note, unless you intend to eat your food past the expiration dates, don't let the food go bad on the shelves and throw it out. A week before expiration, donate those canned goods to your locale soup kitchen and make sure they know the expiration dates are coming up. They'll be sure to use them in time, and be appreciative to you for your donation.

This same technique can be used for those of you that garden and can your own vegetables. Figure out how many jars of vegetables you go through in a year. Instead of growing and canning just enough to get you by till the next harvest, grow and can two to three years of vegetables and rotate through them on a shelf just like you do with your canned goods. Be sure to label and date them. You will only have to do this for one season and then you can go back to growing a smaller garden each year to replenish the vegetables you used the previous year. The other great reason for doing this is that it forces you to buy extra canning jars and lids which is an area where most people who can are severely lacking. It also pushes you into growing a very large garden (instead of your normal sized garden) and forces you to "dry-run" the type of gardening you will be doing after the SHTF. If you combine this technique with buying your everyday food in bulk, you should easily be able to store five to six months of SHTF food for your family at very little to no additional cost.

This is as good as any time to discuss canning foods. This is a skill that you absolutely must learn and master to survive a long-term SHTF scenario. Just like gardening skills, it is not good enough to just buy the supplies and have them ready at your retreat; this is something you need to practice and get proficient in beforehand. Canning is, hands down, the easiest and most efficient way to store the food you grow or kill post-SHTF for a long time. However, it is literally a science that takes into account minute details like the elevation where you live. If you make a mistake and don't pressure-cook your meat at the right pressure or for the right length of time, you could get botulism and literally die from eating it! You need to practice and actually can different types of food and meat, adding them to your weekly diet pre-SHTF. I would recommend having a large water bathing pot as well as a good quality pressure cooker and all the relevant cooking utensils to go along with both. You need to buy multiple books on the subject, especially the "Ball Complete Book of Home Preserving" which is the gold standard for canning books. If you are a hunter, you should also consider getting an extra deer or two and maintaining a three year supply of canned venison. Same goes with those of you who raise your own livestock.

So let's say you ARE on a strict budget and need to buy raw staples and cook each meal individually, where do you start? At the end of this chapter, I included a spreadsheet with an example of the supplies you will need to purchase for a family of four. Remember that this is just a guide and a starting point for you as you will need to adjust the overall calories needed based on your particular family's caloric needs. You may also decide to change the ratios or types of food to support your family's diet. You can purchase a similar interactive spreadsheet from my website which allows you to adjust the individual quantity of each item to fit your family or retreat's needs. The other reference item I would highly recommend purchasing (or downloading for free from their website) is the LDS Preparedness Manual. While I don't agree with some of their philosophical ideas about how society will break down, their food storage and supply guide is very informative.

The cheapest company (yet still reputable) that I have found for purchasing staples is the Rainy Day brand of long-term food, offered at a discount at *FoodAssets.com* (I am not affiliated with them in any way). The Food Assets website provides a lot of good general information about storing food long-term and they carry many brands of long-term food, including Mountain House, Augason Farms and Rainy Day,at very reasonable prices. The biggest reason I recommend Rainy Day over Augason Farms and some of the other companies is strictly because they offer more of their food items in 6 gallon re-sealable buckets (most with a Mylar bag inserts). The price per serving is around 30% LESS when buying Rainy Day's 6-gallon buckets over buying individual cans or cases of #10 cans. The only drawback to this method is if you are buying food strictly for yourself (lone wolf) and you don't think you'll eat the entire bucket of food before it goes bad. At that point, #10 cans would make more sense. The other great resource for buying staples (surprisingly) is the Church of Latter Day Saints. If you go to their website *store.lds.org* and go to their "self-reliance" section, you'll find numerous items available by the case of #10 cans. While their selection is limited, the staples that they do carry are about as cheap as you'll find anywhere else.

Technically, the cheapest way to buy bulk staples is to buy them in a 6 gallon bucket. A lot of preparedness forums and "experts" will encourage you to buy raw staples and prepare them for long-term storage on your own. I highly do NOT recommend this! For instance, a popular technique is to buy a 25-pound bag of rice (which only runs around $13) and put it in a large Mylar bag (which you have to buy) with oxygen absorber packets or dry ice (which you have to buy) and then seal the bag with a sealer (which you have to buy) and then place that item in a sealed bucket (which you also have to buy). Once you figure in your time and effort and buying all the necessary packaging supplies (which the big companies buy in enormous volume at cheaper prices), you are saving very little money, if any, by doing it yourself. There are lots of instructional books and YouTube videos on how to do this, but I personally advise against it for the newcomer. On the same subject are people buying very expensive food dehydrators and freeze driers for storing up long-term food supplies. The same principle applies. You are going to be spending as much as a thousand dollars just to get all the necessary equipment and supplies before you even get started. It would have been much cheaper to just buy the same food already processed by a reputable company.

Freeze-drying, dehydrating, and properly packaging food for long-term storage is a precise science and even a tiny bit of moisture left in a small percentage of your batch (i.e. it was in the bottom corner of the dehydrator and didn't get as much air flow as the rest of the food) can spoil the entire bucket of food. Even though some of these techniques are fairly simple, you are not going to know if you've done it correctly until you open that bucket ten years from now and your family's lives depend on that food. That would be a bad time to discover that you overlooked some minute detail during processing or packaging and your food (your lifeblood) is now spoiled. I am not saying you can't do this stuff yourself, but you better know EXACTLY what you are doing and there is no room for any error. YES, you can save a few bucks by doing it yourself, but my advice is to leave it to the professionals and the companies with many years of experience and proven commercial-grade systems for preparing food for long-term storage. Companies like Wise, Mountain House, Augason Farms, and Rainy Day specialize in packaging staples for long-term storage and know what they are doing. This will also put your mind at ease, because you know that your food will be good whenever you need it. On a side note, if you are buying a food dehydrator for processing and storing food AFTER the SHTF, then I am good with that, as long as your 1-year emergency supply came from a reputable company.

So which staples should you buy? It depends a lot on your budget and what types of food you like to eat. Once again, beware of the "serving sizes" even when buying bulk staples. This is why I recommend going off calorie counts and NEVER on serving sizes. For instance, most companies show a serving of rice to be a quarter cup... really? My three-year-old could scarf down a quarter cup of rice and still be hungry. If you aren't going to count the actual calories of each meal, a safe bet would be to literally double every serving size for the average adult.

If you're on a budget, I would recommend you start by storing plenty of white rice because it is probably one of the cheapest types of bulk food you can buy. Nearly half the world eats rice as a main staple in their diet. While I will acknowledge that eating strictly white rice on a daily basis is not going to provide the nutrients you need in your diet, it can make a great base for a lot of your meals and stews.

To go with your bulk rice, buy bulk freeze-dried or dehydrated vegetables and different types of seasonings from chicken and beef bouillon to teriyaki sauce, which will keep you from eating the same bland white rice regularly. You can also add fresh or canned meat to the meal. I'm not going to give you any specific recipes as everyone's taste buds are different, just use your ingenuity and plan ahead. Another great base would be buying pasta noodles in bulk. If you are using the "every day" food technique, you should have lots of jars of spaghetti sauce saved up already. That won't last you forever though, so I recommend buying bulk spaghetti seasonings (Rainy Day makes them) and making your own sauce each year from your garden's tomato plants. You could also buy stroganoff gravy seasonings to switch up your "spaghetti" intake preventing you from getting tired of pasta noodles.

I would recommend having at least a six-month supply of various freeze-dried or dehydrated vegetables like sweet corn, carrots, peas, beans, broccoli, and the like to get you through until you can start growing and preserving your own vegetables from your garden. Beans are a good alternative source of protein if you are a vegetarian or you can't afford to buy and preserve meat beforehand. There are a lot of various types of beans out there for you to pick from, but beware that they don't last near as long as a lot of your other staples and they will get "harder" the older they get. This requires you to soak them longer to soften them up. I would also recommend a large supply of instant potatoes as a side item to your other meals. Once your garden potatoes are ready to dig up, you can replace the instant potatoes with fresh ones. Some people want to store up large amounts of various grains, and you can do so if you like, but be aware that almost any foods (like fresh bread) you are preparing with grain requires A LOT of preparation, extra stored staples like yeast (which don't store well long-term), a quality grain grinder, and longer cooking times. This makes your "chef's" job a nightmare, especially when they are responsible for feeding a large group of survivors.

A survival staple you must have is plenty of salt. I recommend having around ten pounds of salt per adult person and half that per child. Salt is not only used for seasoning food but it is vital to a lot of the different preservation and canning techniques for meat and vegetables. Personally I would recommend storing sea salt as it is much better for you, but it is also twice the cost of regular iodized table salt. You may also want to consider replacing a portion of your salt storage with "canning" salt. Adding sea salt when canning can cause mineral buildup on your canning jars and may turn the food a slight color. While this doesn't really affect the quality or storage life, it can be a nuisance.

For breakfast meals on a budget, consider buying rolled oats or grits in bulk. You can buy some dehydrated brown sugar, raisins, and dried fruits like blueberries, bananas, and strawberries to switch up the flavor of your oatmeal since you will be eating it often. I also recommend buying hash browns in bulk as a great side item to go with scrambled eggs from your chickens. If you choose not to have chickens (which I highly suggest that you do), then you can store up powdered (real, crystalized) eggs. Just be aware that powdered eggs don't have an extremely long shelf life (roughly 10 years).

Other staples you need to consider are sugar, flour, baking powder and soda, powdered milk, butter powder, honey, soup mixes, gravy mix, pepper and other seasonings, as well as various comfort foods like cocoa mix, coffee, and sweets for special occasions. The last thing I would mention is you'll need a good supply of cooking oil. In most pre-SHTF diets I realize that you'd want to avoid cooking oils as often as possible, but in a SHTF scenario you'll need those extra calories and it's an easy way to add calories to what you're already cooking. Regular vegetable oil only has a shelf life of a year, whereas olive oil and shortening will typically last two years. Those shelf lives are not nearly long enough and you'll be forced to replace those items too often at considerable expense. I recommend Augason Farms who carry a shortening powder with a shelf life of 10 years. No other company I've found offer cooking oils or shortening powders that last nearly as long.

Some people are going to say, "Holy cow! White rice, pasta, shortening, and oatmeal doesn't sound like a healthy diet!" I agree with you. If you had a choice in the matter, it would be heathier for you to continue shopping on a daily basis for your fresh foods at your local Whole Foods grocery store. Since that isn't going to be an option after the SHTF, the closest you are going to get to that kind of natural and healthy diet is to grow your own vegetables and raise your own meat. If you don't live rurally already and can't afford a retreat to go to, then you don't really have any choice in the matter and it may be six months or longer till your garden is ready for harvest. It is not an optimal diet and it is not the healthiest choice in food, but again, we are talking about survival here and any extra unhealthy calories you may be consuming will mostly be burned off and offset to some degree by the extra physical labor you will be doing on a daily basis. But even the extra physical labor is not going to counteract the deficiency in nutrients you are going to experience.

To combat this, the most vital part to surviving long term is going to have a solid 1- to 2- year supply of quality multi-vitamins for every member of your family. You are still going to need a lot of calories each day for energy, but multi-vitamins will help keep your immune system functioning properly on a poor diet and help prevent you from getting sick as easily. Not all multi-vitamins are created equal, however. Be sure to avoid "gel caps" when purchasing vitamins because they have a tendency to go rancid unlike dry pills. Be sure to do some research on the subject and find out what is best for your age group, gender, and health level. From my research, I recommend the "Alive!" brand of multi-vitamins which you can find at Costco for a reasonable price. I would also stock up on vitamin C tablets which boost your immune system and can really help fend off a cold if you catch it early by loading up on vitamin C. At worst, it will help make your symptoms less severe in most cases. Unlike food, which can make you sick if eaten way past its expiration date, most vitamins don't necessarily "go bad," they just start to lose their potency the older they get, meaning you may have to take a higher dose. Most multi-vitamins have a shelf life of only a few years and this item is a costly item you don't want to replace every few years. My recommendation is to buy a large "chest style" deep freezer to keep in your basement or garage. You can now store your vitamins and other medications almost indefinitely till the SHTF. I wouldn't worry about keeping the freezer running after the SHTF, as you will then have two years that your vitamins will still have their full potency. A freezer is also vital to store some cooking oil and many other staples you will need but don't have a long shelf life.

If you can afford to purchase prepackaged freeze-dried meals, I would highly suggest you do. Again, I would not recommend trying to live solely off these meals long-term, but they make great tasting occasional meals to break up the monotony of your bland meals from staples and they can be made really quickly when you don't have time to prepare and cook a full meal. In almost all cases, these meals are very high in sodium and nutrient deficient. The healthier freeze-dried alternatives that some companies offer usually don't taste very good. Prepackaged and complete freeze-dried foods like Mountain House should not make up more than half of your diet, at most. Also, don't buy a ton of food without actually trying samples of it first.

While I realize that it is overall survival we're talking about, you don't want to hate the food you are stuck with for the next year. That will make your life a lot more depressing than it has to be. Sitting down to the table in the evening for a hot meal should be an enjoyable time of day, not something you dread. In my opinion, I have found that a lot of the "cheaper" freeze-dried company's meals don't taste very good. I prefer Mountain House which, I believe, makes some of the best tasting meals around. However, those freeze-dried complete meals are very expensive compared to purchasing the raw staples.

They may not seem so expensive at face value, but this is another area where you need to literally double the amount of serving sizes they advertise for the average adult. Costco is currently offering a 1-year supply of Mountain House meals, claiming 1,986 calories per day for around $4,500. What you need to realize is that Costco adds 40 pounds of high calorie peanut butter and 34 pounds of crackers to the kit. Who eats 40 pounds of peanut butter a year? Better yet, how could you eat 40 pounds of peanut butter in a year? You have to watch out for gimmicks like this when buying a long-term food "kit." If you subtract the calories from the peanut butter and crackers, you're now down to 1,529 calories per day. As we've already discussed, that's only 3/5 of what the average man would need in daily calories (2,577). Don't get me wrong, I actually think that is a really good price for Mountain House food. In fact, it's actually about 40% cheaper than buying it by the individual case of #10 cans. Just know what you are buying before you swipe your credit card. The other problem to buying these kits is that most people aren't going to be able to save up enough to drop almost five grand in one transaction, let alone buy multiple kits for their entire family. It is usually easier to make your long-term food purchases a little each month.

When you do buy Mountain House type meals, be sure you buy them by the case of #10 cans. Buying them by the individual 2-serving bags will cost you significantly more than buying them by the case of #10 cans. Be sure to check Costco. They have a limited supply of menu choices for cases of Mountain House #10 cans, but the cases they do carry are somehow 40% cheaper than I have found anywhere else including Amazon and Walmart online.

With any of the above methods of storing long-term food, don't forget to have the proper cookware to cook the items, especially if you are going to be feeding more than 8-10 people on a daily basis. You are going to need very large pots, skillets, and pans. In the case of rice, you may want to purchase a large steamer insert for your largest pot. If you can afford it, you may also want to consider getting a quality set of cast iron pots and pans, which will last indefinitely. While they will lose their anti-stick coating over time, you can re-season (re-apply a non-stick coating) your cast iron cookware as opposed to Teflon and other cheaper non-stick cookware where once you chip off the thin non-stick coating, it is gone for good. The only thing to remember is there are specific ways to care for cast iron, so be sure you have the necessary supplies and knowledge on how to "season" your cookware.

In a nutshell, if you have the funds and wish to have the lowest maintenance meals possible, then buy primarily pre-made freeze-dried meals and supplement that with some staples and fresh livestock for meat and eggs. This, however, is the most expensive way to go. The cheapest way to achieve a full year's worth of food would be to combine all the methods. Start with a full two years of "foods you already eat" and foods you have canned like meat, stews, and veggies. Don't forget that these methods work best if you live at your retreat already and they won't cost much as you'll eat them throughout the year in your normal diet. After the SHTF you could probably feed your entire family for up to six months with just those two methods. At that point, you'd only need to buy six months of long-term food storage which the average family unit should be able to do for under $2,000 if buying strictly staples. I bet a lot of you are spending more than that each year on just your car insurance. What are your family's lives worth?

This is a condensed example of my **Long-Term Food Storage Plan** that I offer through GridDownConsulting.com. It is fully customizable and comes with a version for both a family and a larger survival retreat.

LONG-TERM FOOD STORAGE PLAN - FAMILY OF FOUR

Grid Down Consulting
McConnellsburg, PA 17233

GridDownConsulting.com

Daily Caloric Needs for a Typical Family of 4

Be sure to find your own family's caloric needs using a basal metobolic calculator first, then apply the Harris Benedict Equation

4 person family EXAMPLE figured with 1male (2.400 cal. day). 1female (1600 cal. day), and 2 children (1000 cal. day X 2)

2.400 + 1600 + (2 X 1000) = 6,000 calories of food per day X 365 days = 2.190,000 calories per year needed for your entire family

Long Term Staples

It #	Product	Quantity	Total Serv.	Total Cal.	Shelf Life	Price Ea.	Total
1	Rainy Day White Rice - 6 gal	6	1,332	426,240	25	$ 35.37	$ 212.22
2	Rainy Day 16 Bean Mix - 6 gal	3	621	203,067	25	$ 68.80	$ 206.40
3	Rainy Day Beef Bouillon - #10 can	1	1,446		25	$ 33.77	$ 33.77
4	Rainy Day Chicken Bouillon - #10 can	1	1,446		25	$ 22.51	$ 22.51
5	Rainy Day Shredded Cheddar - #10 case(6)	1	450	39,150	20	$ 208.24	$ 208.24
6	Rainy Day Garlic Granules -#2.5 can	1	255		20	$ 12.30	$ 12.30
7	Rainy Day Montreal Steak Seasoning - #10 can	2	908		20	$ 10.70	$ 21.40
8	Rainy Day Iodized FAlt - 6 gal	2	7,560		20	$ 25.68	$ 51.36
9	Rainy Day Black Pepper - #2.5 can	2	454		20	$ 12.46	$ 24.92
10	Rainy Day Spaghetti Seasoning - #2.5 can	2	136		25	$ 9.37	$ 18.74
11	Rainy Day Spaghetti Noodles - 6 gal	3	852	179,772	20	$ 58.63	$ 175.89
12	Rainy Day Butter Mashed Potatoes - 6 gal	1	709	53,884	20	$ 64.64	$ 64.64
13	Rainy Day Potatoe Hashbrowns - 6 gal	4	640	100,480	20	$ 49.15	$ 196.60
14	Rainy Day Honey - 45 lb Bucket	1	64	62,208	35	$ 110.50	$ 110.50
15	Rainy Day White Sugar - 6 gal	1	15	76,545	25	$ 59.35	$ 59.35
16	Rainy Day AP Flour - 6 gal	1	302	67,950	12	$ 28.10	$ 28.10
17	Rainy Day Margarine - #10 case(6)	1	1,068	56,604	4	$ 76.38	$ 76.38
18	Rainy Day Beef Gravy - #10 can	2	486	14,580	15	$ 18.22	$ 36.44
19	Rainy Day Quick Rolled Oats - 6 gal	3	1,149	119,496	30	$ 26.27	$ 78.81
20	Rainy Day Brown Sugar - #10 can	2	1,330	13,300	15	$ 9.85	$ 19.70
21	Rainy Day Cinnamon - #2.5 can	1	257		7	$ 8.56	$ 8.56
22	MH FD Apple Slices - #10 case(6)	3	216	10,800	25	$ 79.99	$ 239.97
23	Rainy Day Instant Milk - 6 gal	2	1,184	94,720	25	$ 97.32	$ 194.64
24	Rainy Day Baking Soda - #10 can	2	1,316		4	$ 9.21	$ 18.42
25	Rainy Day Baking Powder - #10 can	3	6,804		4	$ 15.03	$ 45.09
26	Rainy Day Dehydrated Sweet Corn - 6 gal	3	960	236,160	20	$ 112.24	$ 336.72
27	Rainy Day Dehydrated Sweet Peas - 6 gal	2	1,620	74,520	20	$ 128.79	$ 257.58
28	Rainy Day Dehydrated Broccoli - 6 gal	2	648	33,696	25	$ 88.83	$ 177.66
29	Rainy Day Dehydrated Carrot Dices - 6 gal	2	864	62,208	25	$ 79.40	$ 158.80
30	Rainy Day Dehydrated Raisins - #10 can	4	192	18,624	20	$ 24.12	$ 96.48
31	Rainy Day Dehydrated Banana Slices - 6 gal	5	1,120	164,640	25	$ 33.18	$ 165.90
32	Rainy Day Orange Drink Mix - #10 case(6)	1	552	60,720	20	$ 105.32	$ 105.32
33	Rainy Day Cocoa Drink Mix - #10 can	2	196	27,440	12	$ 20.50	$ 41.00
34	Augason Farms Shortening Powder - #10 can	6	1,068	53,400	10	$ 9.22	$ 55.32
35	Adult Daily Multi-Vitamin - 200 count	4	-	-	FR	$ 19.99	$ 79.96
36	Childrens Daily Multi-Vitamin - 200 count	4	-	-	FR	$ 11.99	$ 47.96
37			-	-			$ -
38			-	-			$ -
	Totals			2,250,204			$ 3,687.65

Mountain House Entrees

It #	Product	Quantity	Total Serv.	Total Cal.	Shelf Life	Price Ea.	Total
1	MH FD Vegetable Stew w/ Beef - #10 case(6)	18	918	192,780	25	$ 179.94	$ 3,238.92
2	MH FD Beef Stew - #10 case(6)	18	1,080	226,800	25	$ 227.94	$ 4,102.92
3	MH FD Chicken ala King - #10 case(6)	18	1,188	344,520	25	$ 217.92	$ 3,922.56
4	MH FD Chili Mac w/ Beef - #10 case(6)	20	1,200	288,000	25	$ 173.94	$ 3,478.80
5	MH FD Pasta Primavera - #10 case(6)	16	864	198,720	25	$ 185.94	$ 2,975.04
6	MH FD Chicken Stew - #10 case(6)	24	1,440	331,200	25	$ 139.99	$ 3,359.76
7	MH FD Beef Stroganoff - #10 case(6)	24	1,440	374,400	25	$ 119.99	$ 2,879.76
8	MH FD Granola, Milk, Blueberries - #10 case(6	8	960	240,000	25	$ 169.99	$ 1,359.92
9			-	-			$ -
	Totals		9,090	2,196,420			$ 25,317.68

Chapter 17
"Chickens, Rabbits, and Goats, Oh My!"

I have already explained how to store up a year's worth of food on multiple budgets. You will notice the one thing lacking on the sample long-term food spreadsheet I included is meat. Yes, you can buy freeze-dried meat, but it is very expensive at $3 to $4 per "realistic" serving size, unless you buy imitation meat like TVP (textured vegetable protein) which defeats the purpose and to be honest, freaks me out a little. My recommendation is to raise and process your own meat for long term survival. "But I live in the city and it's not feasible or legal for me to raise a cow in my backyard...," you say. That's okay. I'll explain how to get around this. But first, let's discuss the absolute, hands down, no debate, BEST animal for prepping...rabbits! "Rabbits, you say?" Yes....rabbits!

Rabbits

Rabbits are an extraordinary animal and the perfect solution for long term sustenance. Everyone has heard the term "breed like rabbits," and there is a reason why the term is so well known. The gestation period for a rabbit is only 31 days! When breeding them on a schedule, the average female rabbit will have around 64 kits (babies) every year equaling 320 pounds of meat! A single female rabbit for each member of your family or retreat community will provide you with all the meat you will need for the entire year. This reduces the amount of time you will need to spend hunting, which will become a seemingly dauntless task a month after the SHTF when most wild animals have been killed off to the edge of extinction. This will also keep you safer as there will be considerable risk involved every time you leave your retreat to hunt.

The other great thing about rabbits is that you don't need to keep and feed twenty rabbits before the SHTF for your 20-person retreat. Because their gestation period is so short, you can just keep four does (female) and a buck (male), and let them breed the day after the SHTF and within a month you'll probably have around 16 baby does (and 16 bucks for immediate butchering), which brings your doe breeding stock up to 20 (including the original four does). Just be sure to breed your four does at least once or twice prior to the SHTF to make sure they are fertile and good mothers. You also want to prevent letting the does get too overweight as this can hinder their ability to produce healthy litters.

Rabbit meat is one of the healthiest meats you can eat. It is an excellent source of protein, it has less cholesterol and fat than chicken, beef, lamb or pork, and it has an almost ideal fatty acid ratio of 4:1 omega-6 to beneficial omega-3 fatty acids. A single pound of rabbit meat has 617 calories, 91 grams of protein, and only 25 grams of fat. A single female rabbit producing 64 kits and 340 pounds of meat each year will add 788,400 yearly calories for each member of your retreat. That could be between 30-60% of daily calories needed depending on the size of individual! Rabbits are also relatively easy to care for and require only a fraction of the feed as raising cows. A pound of rabbit meat can be produced from a pound and a half of feed compared to beef which requires six pounds of feed per pound of meat produced. Rabbits are also perfectly compatible with your retreat's OPSEC (Operational Security). Compared to most other farm animals, rabbits are a very quiet animal, helping you keep a low profile and preventing unwanted guests wandering in from the sound of normal livestock.

While I highly recommend you already have a large supply of canned meats ready for the SHTF, rabbits eliminate the need for re-using those canning jars for meat in the future, making them available for vegetables. What I mean by this is that once you have your rabbit operation up and running, you will be producing a steady supply of rabbit meat year round and will be butchering and processing the rabbits AS YOU EAT THEM. On the opposite side of the equation are large animals like cows or pigs, where there are long periods between butchering and you will need to can or preserve a large quantity of meat from a single animal to make it last till you get around to eating it all. Raising rabbit meat prevents you from needing tons of extra canning jars or going through the time-consuming process of preserving or cold-smoking your meats from the larger animals. As a bonus, rabbit manure makes some of the best fertilizer and it isn't "hot," meaning you don't need to compost it. You can literally add it directly to your garden vegetables, unlike manure from most other livestock. Compared to other livestock, rabbits can be raised in a much smaller footprint than the acres needed for larger animals. While I don't recommend keeping your rabbits in small cages, it is possible to do so if you are limited in the amount of fencing you have on hand or can afford to store up. If you are forced to keep your rabbits in smaller cages, just be sure you have a good "rabbit run" so you can let them out each day to stretch their legs while you feed and water them.

A minor drawback to raising rabbits is that most breeds don't do very well in extremely hot environments like the southern states. Heat stress can cause bucks (male rabbits) to go sterile for months at a time and at worst it can cause a rabbit to have heat stroke and die. If you are going to raise rabbits in these areas, you must find a way to keep them cool during the day in the summer. On YouTube, one homesteader attached an energy efficient cooling fan from an old computer to each hutch and ran them off a single battery powered by a small solar panel. If you do live in these areas, be sure to research the best breeds for hot weather; a simple Google search will provide many web resources. On the flipside, rabbits do quite well when it's cold outside. As long as you are providing them a dry space out of the wind and plenty of food and straw for their nesting box, they will weather the winter months relatively easily. Although I recommend you buy multiple books on raising rabbits and get hands-on experience from someone locally, the best resource for raising rabbits in a SHTF environment I have found is Nick Klein at *HostileHare.com*. He is amazing to work with and I highly recommend him for general information as well as purchasing cages and small fodder systems for feeding them.

As I mentioned earlier, rabbits eat significantly less feed than other livestock. The most common method of feeding rabbits is with rabbit pellets and hay. The only drawback to this is there won't be any place to buy your rabbit pellets after the SHTF. From my research, most rabbit pellets start to lose their nutritional value and turn color after about six months of storage. While you may be able to store pellets in mylar bags inside 5 gallon buckets, there isn't a lot of information readily available on how to do this online or if it is even effective in keeping your pellets from going bad in long-term storage. The best and easiest way to feed your rabbits is by using a grain fodder system. Fodder is also a more natural way to feed your animals and closer to their natural diet than feeding them straight pellets and grain.

Grain Fodder Systems

A grain fodder system is simple to operate and mostly fool proof. All you are doing is taking a fast germinating grain like barley or wheat and growing it in rotating trays inside of a hydroponic environment until it is three to four inches tall. Hydroponic growing is 50% faster than traditional farming and removes the need for soil, eliminating soil-borne diseases and pests, weeds, and the use of herbicides and pesticides. Mineral and vitamin levels in hydroponically-sprouted grain are also a lot higher than those in dry grain and they are absorbed more efficiently in the animal due to the lack of enzyme inhibitors in sprouted grain. Grain sprouts provide a good supply of vitamins A, E, C and B complex. The vitamin content of some seeds can increase by as much as 20 times their original value within several days of sprouting. Barley, which is one of the easiest grains to grow hydroponically, has a protein percentage of 12.7 percent and a crude fiber percentage of 5.4 percent over a dry seed. Amazingly, these percentages jump to a crude protein percentage of 15.5 percent and a crude fiber percentage of 14.1 percent after an average of seven days of sprouting. By sprouting, the digestibility of the grain also increases from 40 percent to 80 percent so livestock will not need to consume as much fodder compared to commercial feed because they are obtaining more nutrition from a smaller volume of feed.

Since fodder systems are a relatively new way to feed livestock, most of the big named companies building fodder systems today are producing very large and very expensive systems meant to feed entire herds of livestock. For smaller in-home systems, check out *HostileHare.com* and *Half-PintHomestead.com*. One of the best features of a fodder system is they aren't very time consuming and only require about ten minutes of work each morning. The only down-side is that you'll need to keep a constant temperature between 60 and 70 degrees for maximum growth and minimal mold issues. While keeping the fodder system in these temperature ranges isn't hard pre-SHTF in most air-conditioned homes, after the SHTF you may need to keep them in a cooler basement (make sure it has a window, even a small one) in the summer and keep it upstairs closer to your heat source in the winter. Luckily, sprouting seeds takes very little light and a single small window in a laundry room or basement will do the trick.

Unlike store bought rabbit food, unprocessed grain like wheat and barley stores very well. You can buy and store a year or two of grain very easily for your fodder system in airtight 55 gallon drums.

Besides fodder, rabbits are also going to need some roughage (hay) to eat as well. However, when feeding them fodder as their main course, you don't need to buy high quality hay as it is mainly for their digestive health at that point. I would highly recommend that you grow a small field of Timothy or Orchard Grass at your retreat location and maintain it. It doesn't have to be very big, but be sure it's enough to feed your rabbits year round if you run out of grain for your fodder system or your grain storage spoils. This is another benefit of rabbits: unlike other livestock that require enormous amounts of fresh hay and specialty commercial grain feed, rabbits don't eat nearly as much, allowing you to literally use a scythe to harvest your orchard grass fields for the winter as opposed to using noisy tractors that require precious fuel to operate and will likely attract looters from a long distance away.

What if you don't currently live rurally on a homestead or at your bug-out retreat location? This brings me to our original question at the beginning of the chapter, "But I live in the city and it's not feasible or legal for me to raise livestock in my backyard...." That's most likely not true today. Over the last decade, a lot of people have jumped on the "live green" movement and even big city hipsters are getting into raising some of their own food in their tiny backyards. Because of this, most cities have incorporated bylaws to allow a certain amount of small livestock like chickens and rabbits. Even if your town doesn't, I would personally consider a little civil disobedience in this situation (that's just me; I would never officially advocate that you actually break the law). Rabbits are a very quiet animal to raise and your neighbors and local government would probably never even know you had them. When the SHTF and you need to bug out, you can throw all your does into one portable cage to make the journey (remember to put your buck in a separate cage to keep him from fighting or breeding with the does). If I was forced to bug out by foot with a shopping cart, I would definitely make sure that I had my rabbits even at the expense of leaving some of my pantry food behind. Extra canned food won't feed you as long as your rabbits, which are your most important long-term protein provider.

There are a lot of companies online that you can purchase rabbit cages or hutches from, or you can make them yourself if you are on a budget. Rabbits can be kept in pretty small spaces, but it's not very humane if you can afford to give them some extra space to move about. I recommend each cage be a minimum 30" wide by 24" deep and 18" high. This gives you just enough space to have a nest box and allow your kits (babies) to stay with momma the first few weeks while they are nursing. You can go wider with the cages, but I wouldn't recommend going deeper as it will make it harder for you to reach your rabbit in the back of the cage. For limited space, you should consider buying stackable cages, typically three high from websites like *KWCages.com, Klubertanz.com*, and *Bassequipment.com*. You can definitely build the cages yourself and save a few bucks, but there will be a considerable amount of time and effort involved.

A couple things are imperative to consider when shopping for or building your own rabbit cages. Be sure they have removable trays under each cage for ease of cleaning and to prevent urine and feces from falling onto the rabbits below (when stacking cages). Also, be sure they have "urine guards" on every cage to prevent urine overspray from getting on the rabbits below and to keep small baby rabbits from falling through the wire on the side walls. Pay a couple extra bucks and be sure your cage floor is made from ½"x ½" galvanized wire as opposed to ½"x1" wire as it will be a lot better for your rabbits' long-term paw health. Be sure that the rabbits don't have any access to wood framing as they will chew through it over time, and make sure you have extra water bottles in storage as they tend to leak over time. I would also recommend that you buy permanent nesting boxes for each cage or you can build your own out of 1x lumber.

There are a lot of other things to consider and many different ways to house your rabbits depending on your climate. Even if you are on a tight budget, I would still recommend you find a way to make rabbits work for you. If that means buying the extra cage material and storing it at your bug-out location with the rest of your food, then make it a priority. You could probably do so for a couple hundred dollars. Just be sure that you know how to build the cages when the time comes and you aren't short any material or building tools. This is the worst-case scenario and I strongly recommend you have at least the same amount of rabbit cages as you have people pre-built at your bug-out location, with some extra cage materials ready to go if you need to build more.

When you do build your cages, be sure to build them within sight of your watch tower or your main security post (that should be manned 24-7). This goes with your chicken coop as well and any other livestock you may consider raising. Predators, including the two-legged variety, can quickly wipe out your entire flock of hens or rabbits. Building the proper fencing structures to keep out all the different types of predators from the high-jumping, deep-digging, and flying varieties of predators can be very expensive, especially if you plan to free-range your livestock and let them forage over a large area. It is vital that you take the basic security procedures for your coop and pens and then make sure they are in full view and within earshot of your watch location so any attacks on your animals can be quickly thwarted.

Chickens

If your city allows it, I would do the same thing with chickens as you do rabbits and keep a handful in your backyard. An average chicken lays around 225 eggs a year, depending on the breed of chicken. At 70 calories per egg, you are adding around 16,000 calories to your family's diet per hen. Unfortunately, chickens (especially roosters) are more likely to cause some problems with your close neighbors who may not want to rise at daybreak every day. While keeping rabbits at your home location is imperative, in my opinion, you may want to consider getting your chickens from a farmer close to your bug-out location if you can't keep them in town.

If you go this route, drive around the back roads near your retreat location to find a nearby farmer or homesteader that has chickens and make it a priority to barter for some as soon as you arrive at your retreat post-SHTF. The longer you wait to approach the farmer after the SHTF, the less likely he is going to be to part with any of his birds. In fact, consider introducing yourself pre-SHTF and tell him you live in the area and are looking to possibly raise chickens in the future and ask for any advice. Most country folk are good natured and would be happy to show you around their operation and share with you some pointers. During this conversation, it's important to find out if he keeps chickens year round or if he just buys some chicks each spring and sends them to butcher each fall. You wouldn't want to show up in the winter to find the person with a reduced flock as he'll probably be less likely to part with any of them. Also, find out if he keeps broody hens (we'll discuss this later) or if he culls them and only keeps the most proficient egg layers. You are going to want at least a couple broody hens (which are looked down upon by most farmers who strictly want eggs). You won't be able to get chicks mailed to you each spring after the SHTF and running a heat lamp to keep the chicks warm in your off-grid cabin could be a problem.

Chickens are an incredible resource for a homestead and retreat; being able to have fresh eggs each morning is something you need to seriously consider. Over the last eighty years, the way chickens are raised has dramatically changed. Before electricity, chickens were mostly free roamers on the average farm and fended for themselves. Today, farmers want as many eggs as possible out of their birds and therefore most chickens are raised on specific diets of various grains. While this may work great for an egg farmer, you are going to want your chickens to be as self-sufficient as possible. There are numerous breeds out there and some forage better than others, but some may not handle your particular cold/hot climate as well as another breed. You need to find local homesteaders in your area and find out which chickens do best in your area.

There are also different things to consider when raising chickens for a SHTF scenario as opposed to normal times when you are able to supply and feed your chickens solely from the local feed store. You should strive to have as free range of birds as possible while still enticing them back to your coop each night. If you don't provide your birds ANY food, they are likely to start roosting out in the trees and laying their eggs in the bushes. If they are completely free range, what do they need you for? Over time, you'll start to lose more and more hens to predators and your dreams of picking eggs out of nest boxes each morning will be gone. At the same time, keeping your birds cooped up (no pun intended) all the time requires you to be their sole source of food each day and you may not be able to afford storing a year's worth of chicken feed when you're trying to put away a years' worth of food for yourself and your family members.

There are as many ways to raise chickens as there are ways to raise your own kids. Here is my advice: For the average family, keep at least ten birds ready to go for when the SHTF, including at least one rooster. Research which chicken breeds are good egg layers that will also forage well in your geographical area and make them the majority of your flock. Always keep at least two birds that are broody at all times even if they are a different breed than your other hens. The broody hens will usually be more than happy to raise another breed of chicks as their own. It is important that you allow a broody hen to raise the baby chicks as opposed to raising them indoors in a box. Chicks that are raised indoors on chick feed won't be nearly as proficient at foraging as chicks raised by a broody hen that will help teach them to forage as they grow. I would also recommend having an enclosed chicken run off your coop for periods of harsh weather. The chicken run is vital to keep your chickens protected when you have a predator move into the area as it may take you a day or two to dispatch of it. Each morning let your chickens out of the coop to free range around your property (you will likely need to build a fence around your garden) so they get the majority of their sustenance on their own. In the evening, just before dusk, it is imperative that you entice your birds back to the coop, and that is typically done with a tasty treat. This can be done with daily table scraps and garden leftovers if you run out of chicken scratch. If you do this every night, your birds will get in the habit of coming back to the chicken run each evening and roosting where they belong, back in the protection of the coop.

As far as feed goes, you should strive for your birds to be as self-sufficient as possible. In the evenings a small amount of scratch and some grain fodder can help give them some extra nutrients to lay more eggs. In the winter months, during the days when there is snow on the ground, you will need to significantly increase the amount of feed and fodder you give them. Once again, having a fodder system for your rabbits and chickens is an extremely effective way to feed them off grid. You do, however, need to be sure your chickens are getting the proper amount of protein and calcium to maintain their ability to produce eggs regularly.

Other Animals

There are other farm animals that homesteaders and preppers like to raise. Goats and pigs are very common, as are certain breeds of cattle. I am not against any animal you wish to raise, just be aware that larger animals require a lot more food to maintain and if you can't run to the local feed store or realistically store a year's worth of grains for them, you may want to consider something smaller and more self-sufficient. Goats are a very hardy and self-sufficient animal that can forage for most of their diet if given enough room to roam. They are also a fun animal to have around the farm, and don't be surprised to find hoof prints on the hood of your truck. Goats are also the best source of milk for your retreat. While goats produce far less milk per day than a cow, the milk is far easier for your body to digest and as close to a human's breast milk as you are going to get. Even most people that are lactose intolerant or have milk allergies can handle goat's milk.

In the end, while there are endless options for raising animals at your survival retreat, rabbits and chickens are by far the most productive on the least amount of and most easily produced feed. Rabbits, especially, are hands down the best option for people that have a retreat far from home and can't maintain livestock at their actual retreat. If you get nothing else out of this book, I seriously implore you to consider raising a handful of rabbits for a possible SHTF scenario.

Chapter 18
Survival Retreat Recommendations

I realize that in the preparedness community there is a lot of discussion about "off-grid retreats," and like any other subject on prepping, the advice you get can be all over the map. When I travel around the country and help clients set up off-grid retreats, there are hundreds of prerequisites that I am looking for in an effective retreat location. I could literally write an entire book on that one subject (and I may at some point). But in the meantime, I am going to cover some of the basics, some fresh ideas that I consider important, and some items you may not have considered before. This is NOT a complete list of retreat considerations, though, and do not base a major property purchase on just the information in this chapter.

I realize that it may sound self-serving, but if you are a wealthy individual who is considering the purchase of a remote survival retreat or a dual-purpose weekend getaway, it is ABSOLUTELY imperative that you hire an expert like myself to help find a proper and effective retreat property location. I can't count the number of times that I have emailed, had phone consultations with, and visited clients with retreats that may have been far from a big city but still had serious, life-threatening OPSEC (operational security) issues. Some of them were nearly, if not completely, impossible to solve without selling the property and starting over. I literally hate telling a client that their recently built retreat is in a bad location. It makes me feel horrible, but I feel it is more important to tell a client the truth than to give them a false sense of security.

First of all, it is important to remember to put into practice things like gardening, canning, and raising rabbits BEFORE the SHTF whether you have a retreat or not. Some people plan to buy a retreat and wait till society falls apart before they implement any of their survival skills they learned in a book or watched on YouTube videos. It is vitally important that you don't do this; the learning curve on a lot of these skills is extreme and there is no margin for error when your family's lives depend on said skills. That is where my first recommendation comes in. Even though a lot of prepper experts recommend buying property 500 miles from the nearest city, don't do it! The one exception to this rule is if you are able to make a living and provide for your family while living at your retreat location. At that point, yes, get as far away from civilization as you can (or your wife will allow you). Don't forget that if you live 50 miles from the nearest small town, then you (or your wife) will be putting serious miles on your vehicle travelling to and from town just to get basic groceries and supplies each week.

Most people that are preparing for hard times still need to live near a major city for work purposes. This brings me to my point: one of the biggest mistakes you can make when buying a retreat is to buy property so far away from your everyday life that it makes it unfeasible to go there regularly on the weekends and maintain it or actually put into practice your preparedness skills. I've talked to numerous clients that have bought retreats hundreds of miles away from where they live. They went there regularly at first, but after the first year, the novelty wore off and now they only make the tedious, four-hour drive a couple times a year. How are you supposed to install and maintain a garden at your retreat like that? It is very important that your retreat be less than a three-hour drive from home otherwise you'll probably not use it very often. Owning a retreat then becomes a burden instead of a weekend getaway and you'll spend half your weekend "free time" stuck behind the wheel of a car as opposed to relaxing in front of a warm fire.

It's also impossible to build a retreat 500 miles from the nearest city on the east coast without driving into the next big metropolitan area. So how far should you be from a major city? There is no definite answer because each city is different and the topography surrounding each city varies as well. For example, some big cities are very centralized and as soon as you drive out of the city limits you enter massive corn fields or mountains. On the flip side, some cities have large suburbs and small towns that surround the cities for fifty miles or more in every direction. My recommendation would be to have your retreat at least 75 miles away from the outside edge of any major population areas, while 130 miles would be ideal (this makes it around a two-hour drive in most cases).

This is not set in stone, though. If you live in Las Vegas (bad idea from the start) and you drive 75 miles from town, you are still in the middle of the desert. I have also seen a very effective retreat location tucked away nicely while only 40 miles from a major city in Pennsylvania. It was five turns from any major road, at the end of a dead end country lane. The cabin wasn't viewable from the road and was surrounded by a thousand acres of state game lands. It also had a very deep and steep ravine that circled the back half of the property making an approach from any direction outside of the only road in nearly impossible. For an additional 50 reasons I don't have time to get into, I would actually take that location over a lot of the other retreats I've visited that were hundreds of miles from a major city yet had one or more very serious OPSEC concerns. At the same time, it takes a very trained eye to find an effective retreat property less than 100 miles away from a large city.

It's not just the major cities that you need to steer clear of, though. You need to be at least five to ten miles away from any small towns (less than 1,000 people) as well. I realize that some experts may tell you that moving to a tiny country town will help you survive in a SHTF scenario. This information is false! I currently live a two-hour drive from our family retreat inside a tiny town of less than 1,000 people in the mountains of Pennsylvania. This town is surrounded by farm land and farmers with plenty of livestock. If my town had to survive for under a month, it would probably make it through. However, in a long-term SHTF scenario where transportation and food deliveries shut down, you are no safer surrounded by 1,000 starving mouths than you are if you are surrounded by a million. If you have food in your basement and the starving masses surrounding you don't, they will eventually take it from you by force if necessary. There is just no way to feed 1,000 mouths without electricity unless you had a fully functioning, town-sized, off-grid food infrastructure in place BEFORE the collapse (which I have yet to hear about any town having in place).

Conventional wisdom from people who have never crunched the numbers would tell you that a small country town would do just fine following a collapse. Even though there may be a few thousand cows on farms surrounding the town, those will not last very long. A thousand people eat an incredible amount of food on a daily basis. Once the food runs out, the smaller towns may keep law and order in check for a while longer than the big cities, but after a month or two with no food, many people will be dying on a daily basis from starvation. Even though the "country folk" in a small town may generally have a better work ethic and set of morals than the inner city masses, making them more likely to work together for a while, all that goes out the window once true starvation sets in. Once the average dad watches his young child withering away before his eyes, he will do ANYTHING to get food for that child. I don't care if he is blue collar, white collar, redneck, urban hipster, white, black, or purple. Human desperation brought on by starvation affects everyone the same regardless of background or upbringing. The looting, murder, and pillaging in the tiny towns across this nation will be just as severe as in the inner city once people get hungry and desperate enough.

When most people think of a "survival retreat," they instantly picture a concrete home with steel shutters. I am actually of a different mindset; I believe that building a "fortress" is a telltale sign to your neighbors (and anyone who visits your home pre-SHTF or stumbles upon you post-SHTF) that you have valuable supplies, like food, worthy of taking by force if necessary. Outside of the most hardened structures (very expensive), almost every compound can be overcome in time by a handful of well-trained guys, whether it's burning you out, destroying your utilities, or just laying siege to your retreat for weeks. A "fortress looking" retreat is something a looting force will be likely to lose a few men over and spend some serious time and effort to get inside. I realize that a lot of preppers think they are John Wayne incarnate…you are not! Those of you with Special Forces training know what I'm saying is true. You can only hold a location (even a good defensible location) against a much larger force for so long without re-supply and reinforcements. It's very unlikely that you'll do so without taking serious casualties and injuries over time. If the majority of your food and other supplies are properly hidden from the looters on your property, is "defending your castle" worth losing family members over? Hiding in plain site with a normal looking cabin is far better. You can still do a lot of things to increase the defenses of your property without building an obvious fortress.

Staying hidden from prying eyes is the most important part of having a retreat. Being in a location that very few people stumble upon is much better than having a reinforced concrete fortress to fight from out in the open. A lot of preparedness experts will try and teach you how to make your retreat a fortress so you can utilize it like the Alamo. If it comes down to a last stand against a superior force, your fate will likely be the same as those who fought at the Alamo. You are far better off hiding than you are fighting regardless of how well trained you are and your conventional OPSEC plans.

The first basic to staying hidden is to make sure your cabin, garden and livestock are not visible from ANY roads and preferably hidden from any neighbors as well. When designing a retreat from scratch, I prefer to have as long of a driveway off the road as financially feasible to the landowner. Even if you are a billionaire, this is not the time to pave your driveway for convenience sake. The first fifty feet of your driveway leading off the road should look very minimally travelled with maybe a couple strips of gravel for your tire tracks. Just off the road you need to install a secure gate without easy access around it. Not any gate (especially decorative ones) will do, though. Find out what type of gate the oil companies, cell tower companies, or utility companies use in your area and purchase a gate from the same manufacturer or have one made that resembles them. Have a sign company make a replica sign from a picture you supply them from the cell tower (or other) company's gate and place it on your gate. Essentially, you want your driveway to look exactly like an access road and NOT A DRIVEWAY. This will deter most non-local looters right from the get go and severely minimize the amount of random travelers wandering down your lane and begging for food. Make sure you also take down any property number signs or mailboxes immediately after the SHTF that will give away the fact that it is a driveway and not an access road.

At the same time, you don't want someone being able to look back a long driveway. After around thirty yards, it's important that your driveway make an "S" bend back in the trees. After that "S" bend, and as long as it's not visible from the road, feel free to install heavy gravel or asphalt for convenience sake. I would also try and have the last segment of driveway that leads to your cabin (or watchtower) as long and straight as possible. You want to be able to see hungry stragglers approaching from as far away as possible from your watch location. Another thing to consider would be to have a spare sheet of plywood available to make a very forceful no trespassing sign after the SHTF. You don't want a professional made sign as you want it to appear as if an average homeowner made it using a can of spray paint. I would consider the following language or something similar, "No Trespassing – If you proceed past this point, you will be shot on sight with no questions asked! (We don't have any food either…).'' I know it may sound a little corny, but you have to understand the mentality of a starving individual who is looking for easy targets of opportunity. I am not insinuating that you actually kill hungry people on sight, but you want them to fear that you will.

I would install this sign along your driveway at the furthest point visible from your watchtower while not being visible from the main road (this is a backup to your gate utility sign to deter hungry stragglers and neighbors). The reason you want it visible from the watchtower is that you'll want to know if someone was deterred by the sign and left. At that point, you'll know someone was on your property and you can follow them and confront them on your terms down the road and make them leave the area, or follow them from a distance to make sure they actually leave the area and aren't trying to find another way onto your property or looting a neighbor's house.

Another idea that works great with this is to hang a steel target or piece of metal fifty feet past the no trespassing sign that has the words "Turn Around!" spray painted on it. If someone ignores the no trespassing sign and continues down your driveway, then your watch (preferably someone with a suppressed rifle) takes a shot at the metal gong and sends it spinning. If the no trespassing sign doesn't make them leave, then a rifle round pinging off a sign/target right next to them with the words "Turn Around!" most assuredly will. If it doesn't and they continue on, it's time to raise the alarm!

Next, I want to discuss your actual cabin at your retreat. There is a gung-ho segment of the preparedness community that wants to build mini fortresses for their retreat cabin. There is nothing that screams "prepper" and "person with food" louder to your neighbors and local community as building a concrete fortress or installing extravagant steel shutters on your cabin. Besides, regardless of where you build your retreat, there may come a time when a large raiding force attacks your compound. This is not going to be like the movies or an episode of the *Walking Dead*. The looters aren't going to blindly rush your compound across an open expanse like they are storming a medieval castle's walls. In all likelihood, they will post up at rifle range and slowly pick you off one by one as you leave your cabin or retreat to garden or bring in firewood. It is very hard to defend against this or prevent it from happening! You will likely lose at least part of your group defending your "castle."

What if your father gets killed? Or your sister? What if it's your young daughter who takes a random ricochet? Your wet dream of having a shootout with Zombies is not going to be a reality in this situation regardless of how tactically prepared you think you are. If a large looting force approaches your retreat, they have likely been assaulting retreats for a long while and are probably very good at it. Do you think you are the only group that has members that were ex-special forces or ones that could qualify as snipers? How do you plan to make your last stand if every time a member of your group sticks their head up to fire at the assaulting force some random sniper takes them out? What if they raided an Army Reserve base down the road and they're driving MRAPs with ballistic protection? What if they have fifty-caliber machine guns mounted to their vehicles that cut through your concrete walls like Swiss cheese? How sturdy do you think your fortress really is? Is it fire proof? Even a redneck can figure out how to make Molotov cocktails.

My point in this is that it's far better (and cheaper) to fly under the radar and build a normal looking cabin than something that screams Prepper Retreat. You should have a mindset of retreating and living to fight another day rather than dying while protecting your supplies like Custer's Last Stand. The best way to do this would be to have an escape tunnel leading out of your cabin into the surrounding woods or brush. If you hide the entrance to the tunnel out of the basement of your cabin well enough, you could actually use it to hold up in for a day or two and wait till the following night to actually leave under the cover of darkness. You could also use the same tunnel to bypass their scouts, sneak back into your cabin in the middle of the night with suppressed weapons and catch the looters off-guard while they sleep. I realize that in the scheme of things a tunnel like this could be a considerable expense, but it is one that I very highly recommend. If you don't have a way of escaping your retreat when you're surrounded by an overwhelming force, most of your other preps don't matter. I'm not saying that you run at the first sign of danger, but there may come a time when things go south very quickly while defending your retreat and it makes more tactical sense to leave than take numerous casualties.

If you go this route, it would be wise to have some food and ammo supplies stored in the escape tunnels (personally, I would store each person's BOB/lone wolf pack in there as well) in case you are fleeing in a hurry. Most assaulting forces aren't going to move into your retreat and set up a base there. They need to stay on the move to prevent being over-run by a larger force themselves or being attacked guerrilla warfare style from the locals. They'll probably ransack your cabin, take what they need or can find, and be gone within a few hours or the next day.

Having an escape tunnel goes hand in hand with not having all of your food inside the four walls of your retreat. This will make the prospect of retreating through an escape tunnel a much better option without worrying if the looters will find your stash and clean you out. I recommend having a full underground storage location hidden on your property, outside the four walls of your retreat. Some people will cordon off a section of their existing basement, but that is very hard to conceal and anyone looking for a hidden room will notice that the basement is smaller than the upstairs footprint of your cabin. Eventually they will find your hidden door. If building from scratch, it's better to have your storage room under a garage, shed, or barn. Even if it's separated from the cabin, you can always connect the two by a tunnel. If you are on a budget, they make plastic barrels with re-sealable lids made for burying supplies around your property that you can purchase as you can afford them. Just try not to put all your eggs in one basket. It's best if you keep about ten percent of your supplies easily found by the looters (lightly hidden) in your cabin. This will make them think they have found your entire stash and hopefully, they'll stop scouring your property and cabin for more food.

If you do go the route of hidden underground storage (or for any hidden storage facility), then I also recommend a "double blind" storage room using the same ten percent principle. Let' say, for instance, your underground storage facility is located under your 14' x 24' mini barn you had built for your rabbits and other animals. I would have a dividing wall poured at 6 feet allowing two separate rooms. One would be 6 foot x 14 feet while the other is 18 feet x 14 feet. Obviously you'll want a hidden door into the 6 foot storage room where you keep ten percent of your supplies. Have a second hidden door from inside the 6 foot room leading into the larger storage room. If the looters find their way into the initial 6 foot room, they will assume they have found your hidden stash and will likely stop looking for additional hidden doors. Wherever you put your main storage facility, it's vital that you have a quality vault door installed to protect it.

Another thing I would highly recommend is to have a sniper hole or two facing your cabin and garden. This is a small space (roughly 7 foot long x 4 feet wide x 4 feet deep at a minimum) dug underground where a member of your retreat can hide himself for a few days while taking random shots at any enemy patrols or any of the looters that are hanging around your cabin or trying to raid your garden. A couple important things to remember here: first, a suppressed bolt gun (or a scoped and suppressed .300 blackout upper for your AR) would be highly recommended in this situation. Second, the purpose of this is NOT to engage the enemy in a shootout. You should only take a SINGLE shot every few hours. Your purpose is to slowly take the enemy out one by one and/or make their life a living hell while they occupy your cabin. A single suppressed shot will make it very hard for the looters to locate the source of the shot. Shooting multiple times from the same location in short successions (even suppressed) will help the enemy pinpoint your general location and make it easier for them to find where you are hidden.

This is also where two sniper holes in different areas could really keep the enemy guessing where the random rounds are coming from. You should keep a sleeping bag in a waterproof stuff sack, a set of shooting sticks or rifle bipod, army cot, and some food in these locations as the person may need to be there for a few days till the enemy force gets tired of getting shot at. If you don't have suppressed rifles, you need to be at least 300 yards away. If you are using a suppressed rifle and subsonic rounds, you can be as close as 100-150 yards away from your cabin. Third, make sure the entrance is hidden to perfection and your firing hole is as small as possible with the ability to close it off and be unnoticeable from the outside. A good way to do this would be to have a large log lying across where your firing hole is sticking out above the ground level.

Even though you want to avoid having the appearance of a fortress, you can—and should—add security items to the cabin that will not be so obvious. The first item I would consider would be to have very solid and secure exterior doors. Depending on your budget, you can go as light as a solid steel core door or buy custom wood doors that have steel plates sandwiched in the middle. Regardless of which door you choose, the weakest link is your locking mechanism. Standard household locksets are easily defeated and can be opened with a set of bump keys in less than a few seconds. If you can afford to, buy entry doors from Master Security Doors or a similar company that makes nearly impenetrable doors that will still blend in with your cabin. If working on a budget, consider deadbolts from companies like Bilock and Abloy, which typically run between $200 and $400 for each dead bolt. On a tight budget, you can find deadbolts from Kwickset and Master Lock that advertise their $40 deadbolts as bump proof, but that is only for when you are physically in the house. On a side note, if you do plan to escape through your tunnel system and turn over your retreat to a large invading force, don't lock the doors when you bug out. Leave them unlocked. Why have them destroy the door to your cabin when you plan to move back in after they are gone?

Another thing I strongly discourage is the use of "bullet proof" glass windows in your cabin. Bullet-resistant glass that is thick enough to defeat rifle rounds is VERY thick and VERY heavy for a normal window-sized opening. This also prevents you from having functioning windows that open in the summer to get a breeze through your non-air conditioned cabin. Besides, most rifle rounds will easily penetrate multiple walls when they don't hit a stud. There is no reason for bullet-proof windows when shots can go right through the walls surrounding the windows.

Another drawback to bullet-proof glass is they grow "cloudy" over time as they get tiny surface scratches on them. So while I don't recommend bullet proof glass, I do highly recommend Anderson's Stormwatch hurricane-proof windows placed, at minimum, in all your first floor window locations. Anderson sandwiches a clear, very strong polymer sheet between two panes of glass, making it very resistant to intruders. It would probably take five to ten minutes to smash your way through one of these windows with a normal hammer. These windows won't keep someone out indefinitely, but it will definitely slow them down. This is great for a non-occupied cabin as it takes them longer to get into your cabin and if you have a security system at your retreat, it allows more time for the rural police officers to arrive and catch the intruders in the act.

If you go this route, I recommend keeping your window sizes on your cabin as uniform as possible so you can keep an extra window pane or two on hand to replace a broken window. The best part of the Anderson Stormwatch windows is they don't cost much more than a standard high quality window. In fact, they would actually be cheaper than making functional steel shutters like I've read a lot about on prepping forums and various books. In order for security shutters to be even remotely effective, they would have to be made out of some pretty hefty AR500 steel and probably cost five times as much as just installing Anderson's hurricane proof windows. Steel shutters are another thing that screams, "Prepper retreat!" which, again, is something you definitely want to avoid.

Another item that screams "prepper retreat" are large banks of solar panels on your property. While solar panels may work great in some areas of the country like out West, there are a lot of areas in this country that have considerable cloud cover throughout the year, making solar power quite inefficient. In fact, where I live, we'd be lucky to get 30 solid days of sun each year. Even if you do live out West, those large sections of panels can be seen from a long way off and will draw looters like moths to a flame. You also run the risk of installing an incredibly expensive piece of infrastructure that may end up getting fried in the event of an EMP attack or massive solar flare. I have yet to find a solar panel company that can assure me that an EMP or solar flare won't fry their panels. I realize that solar power is all the rage lately, but I recommend attaining your post-SHTF electrical power from a different source.

While there are a lot of ingenious ways to get power, my preferred method of off-grid power is with a propane-powered generator hooked up to a battery bank. With a diesel generator you have a serious issue with the storage life of the diesel in your storage tanks. Even with addition of fuel stabilizer, diesel fuel can only be stored for 6 months to 1 year without significant fuel degradation and only if you keep it perfectly clean, cool and dry. What this means is that if you're not running this system pre-SHTF, it is going to be very costly to consistently replace and maintain a large supply of diesel for a SHTF scenario. Properly stored propane will last indefinitely and doesn't degrade over time, making it a perfect option for a SHTF fuel source.

The major drawback to any generator sourced power is going to be the amount of noise they produce. However, this can be greatly minimized with a reasonable amount of expense. Two ways to accomplish this is to build an underground enclosure for it or a double-walled shed. In both instances, it is very important that you have proper ventilation installed. With the addition of acoustic paneling, you can greatly reduce the amount of sound produced by the actual generator.

The generator exhaust is a different matter, though, and you will need to get creative to minimize the sound from the exhaust. There are plenty of resources online on the subject of silencing generators. You are, however, going to have some level of ambient sound produced, so I recommend that you only run the generator in the middle of the night when most people will be sleeping. You can also add all your electrical equipment, like your battery bank and inverter, into the generator enclosure or shed and EMP proof it by following the advice of Scott Hunt in his DVD available through The Survival Summit titled "Home EMProvements." This DVD is full of invaluable resources on EMP-proofing your retreat and I highly recommend it.

The last thing you'll have to figure out on your own is what size generator to purchase and how large of a battery bank you will need for your cabin. These two points can fluctuate greatly depending on what you plan to power in your cabin after the SHTF. Ideally, your generator should only run for about two hours a day, just long enough to recharge the battery bank. Anything that requires excess electricity like showering, laundry, or running power tools, should be scheduled during the two hours when your generator is actually running. During the day, when you are operating off the battery bank, all uses of power should be kept to a bare minimum. If you are only running your generator an hour or two each day, a 2,000 gallon underground propane tank should provide you power for at least a year or two.

Another security feature I would definitely have inside the cabin is a full Burglar Bomb system. The Burglar Bomb Repulsar IV is a system of motion-activated pepper spray canisters that are ceiling-mounted and look like your typical smoke detector. When activated, and after sensing movement in your cabin, they release a full canister of OC aerosol spray into your cabin, preventing anyone from entering for multiple hours. Once the first canister goes off, the system resets. There are three backup canisters on standby for the next three attempts at entry. If you had a couple of these strategically mounted throughout your cabin, you could literally keep an assaulting force out of your cabin for most of a day, allowing you to get set up in your sniper holes and start creating havoc amongst their ranks. Even if they had NBC masks, they would likely enter your cabin just long enough to raid your pantry and any other low hanging fruit available to them. It's doubtful they would stick around long. This would also be great for a security system to prevent burglars from breaking into your cabin pre-SHTF. If the neighbor kid tries to break in and gets a face full of pepper spray, he's likely to leave just as fast as he entered. The best thing about this system (per their ads) is that it leaves no residue behind to clean up.

I saved my biggest piece of advice for last. One of the absolute best items you can put into your survival retreat cabin is a Masonry Heater, sometimes referred to as a Russian or Finnish Stove. Over the last few years, I have seen the rise in popularity across the prepping community of "rocket wood stoves" whose technology is actually very similar to masonry stoves. In essence, a masonry stove looks like an enclosed fireplace (with a door) but instead of the chimney flu going straight up through your roof and taking most of the heat with it, a masonry stove has channels built with fire brick that weave back and forth above and beside the firebox. These channels absorb all the heat from the fire and store the heat in the stone mass of the fireplace while slowly radiating the heat throughout your house over the following 18 to 24 hours. It is an extremely even radiant heat and you don't suffer the extreme temperature differences in your home that a wood stove produces (hot when the fire is blazing and cold when the fire dies down). Most preppers are putting wood stoves into their cabins for warmth and for cooking, but a masonry heater is far more efficient. In fact, they are so efficient that 90% of new home construction in Finland uses this method of heating. Except in the absolutely coldest climates and subzero conditions, you can easily heat a 2,000 square foot, open-floorplan cabin with a masonry stove while only building a SINGLE large fire each morning or evening! With a wood stove you are constantly adding wood throughout the day and night, fighting to maintain a constant temperature. In addition, wood stoves consume four times (or more) as much wood as a masonry stove/heater.

The biggest issue with standard wood stoves is that they produce smoke from your chimney which can be seen from miles away. This is a huge OPSEC issue that could attract hungry neighbors and looters in your area. A masonry heater burns at nearly 2,000 degrees, as opposed to the average wood stove which burns at only 700 degrees. Because of the high burn temperature, every ounce of your wood is consumed and even the gases produced by the wood are burned. This means that you literally have zero smoke and no creosote buildup in your chimney system. The exhaust that does vent out of your chimney is actually cool to the touch as all the heat has been absorbed by the fire brick and stone mass.

The only drawback to a masonry heater is that you need to find a qualified mason to custom build it, and their services can be fairly expensive. They typically run over $6,000 for a small masonry stove for a smaller cabin, upwards of over $10,000 for a larger or more decorative masonry heater. Regardless, I would make whatever concessions you can to put one in your retreat cabin. Over time they will definitely pay for themselves. They are more efficient, use considerably less wood, produce no smoke, and produce a much more even heat for your cabin. Do your own research on masonry stoves and highly consider installing one at your retreat.

In closing, these recommendations are literally the tip of the iceberg of information needed to set up an effective survival retreat. You will find a lot of good information online that will be useful in building a full retreat. However, for every good piece of information, there are probably twice as many terrible recommendations from "survival experts" and bloggers who have no idea what they are talking about. There are a handful of good Survival Retreat Consultants you can find with a simple Google search, but make sure you thoroughly vet them first to find out where their expertise comes from.

It's also important to find out which threat they recommend their clients prepare for, as that will tell you how they will be tailoring their prepping recommendations. For instance, if a consultant thinks the most likely SHTF event is a financial collapse, then his recommendations likely won't protect you from a grid-down scenario. Especially when dropping hundreds of thousands of dollars building a retreat, it's best to prepare for the worst and hope for the best. If you are prepared for a grid-down scenario, a financial collapse will be no problem. If you prepare for a financial collapse, you'll likely not have enough food storage, an inoperable electrical infrastructure for your cabin, and many other issues that could have been solved by just building it differently in the first place. If you'd like to discuss hiring me to help you set up your family's survival retreat, you can contact me via email through my website, *GridDownConsulting.com.*

𝔄fterward
A Biblical Perspective on Preparedness

In the books that I published in the past, I have made clear my faith and the importance of relying on God through hard times. In this chapter, I would like to discuss the biblical perspective on being prepared. When discussing biblical theology, I realize it can be as contentious an issue as which gun is best suited to a SHTF situation, but I feel it is an important discussion to have. The chapter below is MY OPINION and beliefs on the subject. If you are a believer and have a personal relationship with Jesus, then I want to make one point overwhelmingly clear: this chapter is a general guide. At no point does it take any precedence over what God is specifically calling you to do. Again, please pay heed to that still small voice that resides in each one of us and listen to the leading of the Holy Spirit to help guide your decision-making process through the hard times ahead.

I have had multiple discussions with my pastor on the subject and, as with all aspects of prepping and life, I am always willing to evolve my thinking and stance on the subject as new sound biblical information is put before me. Please feel free to contact me through my website and let me know what you believe on the subject. But before you do, please research and pray about it and don't just take a one-sided stance for contentious purposes.

There are two sides to the biblical argument on prepping. There are the Christians who will cite stories, like those of Joseph, on being prepared for hard times, and there are the Christians who will cite the example of the Israelites fleeing Egypt and how God miraculously supplied their every need during forty years of wandering through the wilderness. So what should we, as Christians, do? Should we make advanced preparations or rely solely on God's miraculous provisions if hard times were to come about? I believe the answer is actually both.

However, before I start discussing scripture on the subject, let me first remind you of the three main reasons people (including Christians) don't prepare for hard times. The first is ignorance, that is to say, not being educated on the subject. The second is the "ostrich head in the sand" syndrome: it's much more comfortable to hope it will never happen. And the third is (especially for Americans) the assumption that the government will come to their aid.

Educating yourself takes time and work, and the topic can be depressing (especially if you don't have faith and a reliance on God to see you through). The mainstream media is NOT a good source and you have to dig for yourself to find any solid information. Remember, in November of 2014, Admiral Rodgers, the Director of Cyber Security for our nation, told Congress that what he fears the most is a cyber attack on our critical infrastructure (the electric grid) that could lead to massive loss of life and industry, that he believes it will happen in the very near future, and that they are completely unable to stop it. That is a huge revelation! Yet the mainstream media completely ignored that story. Be careful about what the media is feeding you and pray for discernment to see through the spin they put on stories to push their agenda. The information you need is out there, but not on the 6:00 Evening News.

Just because the media aren't covering the threat does not mean that it won't affect you and your family once it happens. And just because it is a frightening scenario and you'd rather just not think about it or just pretend it doesn't exist, it does not lessen the severity of the impending societal breakdown. You can't just "blink" and miss it. And banking on the military and FEMA to help not only you, but 300+ million additional starving people all at the same time? It's seriously not even realistic to think that would work, even with full electrical and communication systems working. The threat of EMP and the vulnerability of the electric grid have been widely known in the government since the 1960s. That's over forty years and ten presidential administrations (Republican and Democrat alike) that have done nothing to harden our critical infrastructure or protect the electric grid. It would only cost around $2-$4 billion dollars to harden the grid, which is less than what we give Pakistan in aid each year. The politicians don't care! Voting for this doesn't buy them any votes come election time because very few people are even aware that a threat exists. It's hard for me to fathom as all the information is out there, yet no one is talking about it. I think it's time for Christians to WRESTLE with this, rise up and take the lead.

I feel it is imperative that you educate yourself on the threat. What I mean by this is that if you are putting away tons of food and supplies for no specific reason, then you are a bit crazy. That is why "preppers" have been shown in a bad light by the media. The liberal media think that everything is going wonderfully in our rapidly growing technological society and that there is no threat to our food supply and no one needs a gun to protect himself because the police will protect you (when in truth they will usually show up ten minutes later to clean up the mess and call the coroner's office for your dead body). Since the media have no interest in researching the threat, there obviously isn't one and you're crazy for putting some extra food in your basement.

Information and education on the subject is paramount before making decision. Researching the theology behind "prepping" is completely irrelevant if you don't believe there are hard times ahead for our country. I strongly challenge you to go to my website and spend AT LEAST a full day's worth of time (over time if need be) looking at the evidence I put forth on the likelihood of a grid-down scenario. That does not mean just read through what I wrote. Even though I put a lot of information on my website, it is literally the tip of the iceberg of evidence towards a grid-down scenario. Do your own research! Click on the hundreds of links I supply to government reports, news articles, and videos on the subject. Do your homework and pray about it before deciding if preparing for hard times makes sense for you and your family. I believe that the amount of evidence I put forth is irrefutable and if you don't bury your head in the sand in fear, you will come to the same conclusions that I have about the undeniable threats that face this country in the near future. Once you have done that or if you are already convinced that hard times lay ahead for other reasons, then continue.

I have a close friend that I graduated high school with, whom I respect enormously and I know that he loves the Lord immensely. During a discussion a while back about my profession as an emergency preparedness consultant, he mentioned that his stance is not to worry about the future and he is going to just trust in God when the time comes. He also mentioned the story of the Israelites escaping Egypt in Exodus and how God supplied their every need. That challenged me a bit, and made me second guess myself. It forced me to research that story and pray and deliberate on it. Did I not have enough faith? Was I not trusting God to miraculously supply my family's needs should the worst come to pass?

Here is what I've come to personally believe. First, God took the Israelites out of Egypt and into a "wilderness" to wander for 40 years. This area is essentially a desert. To this day it would be very hard to grow crops or raise livestock in this area of the Middle East, not to mention that there were approximately 3 million Israelites to be fed and watered each day. This is not a situation where the Israelites WERE capable of taking care of themselves. This was a situation where God led them to that place and only a miracle by God (manna) could sustain them and keep them alive, forcing them to wholly put their trust and faith in God. I believe this is a great example of how God can supply our needs miraculously when he chooses to do so.

If I were to go for a week-long backpacking trip in the dry desert of Arizona, I would take supplies for myself to make sure I would have enough food and water. I wouldn't just head out with the shirt on my back and expect God to miraculously save me and feed me. I am not insinuating that he couldn't, I am just saying that it would not be a wise decision on my part to test Him. I think God expects us to be smart and responsible in our decision-making processes. This leads to the preparedness side of the story. The Israelites were slaves and had no way to or even enough time to prepare for their quick departure out of Egypt. They didn't have time to grow large crops and store away food to take with them or raise large quantities of livestock for their journey (not that the Egyptians would have let them do that anyway). This is an instance where God used many miracles to harden Pharaoh's heart and let them escape the oppression of the Egyptians. God miraculously brought them out of the land of Egypt and miraculously provided for their needs. This is a wonderful story about God's ability to do miraculous things to save His people. There is nothing in this story that I could find "against" preparing for hard times.

Another common example I hear against prepping is the story of Elijah in 1 Kings 17 where God directed ravens to come down and miraculously feed him during a famine:

2 Then the word of the Lord came to Elijah: 3 "Leave here, turn eastward and hide in the Kerith Ravine, east of the Jordan. 4 You will drink from the brook, and I have directed the ravens to supply you with food there." 1 Kings 17:2-4 (NIV)

This is not an example where Elijah chose to go there and forgot to take food with him. This is an example where God specifically spoke to Elijah and instructed him to go somewhere while telling him that "He" would supply his needs while there. This is an instance where God specifically told Elijah to go somewhere and "rely on His provision." There is nothing in this story against preparing for hard times, it is a story about how when you are obedient to God's will, He can and will miraculously provide for your needs. It is a story about trusting God. Ask any missionary who has ever sold their home and moved to a third world country, and they will tell you that if you are obedient to God, he will take care of your needs.

Last, there is the following passage which some Christians will use against prepping:

25 "Therefore I tell you, do not worry about your life, what you will eat or drink; or about your body, what you will wear. Is not life more than food, and the body more than clothes? 26 Look at the birds of the air; they do not sow or reap or store away in barns, and yet your heavenly Father feeds them. Are you not much more valuable than they? 27 Can any one of you by worrying add a single hour to your life?

28 "And why do you worry about clothes? See how the flowers of the field grow. They do not labor or spin. 29 Yet I tell you that not even Solomon in all his splendor was dressed like one of these. 30 If that is how God clothes the grass of the field, which is here today and tomorrow is thrown into the fire, will he not much more clothe you—you of little faith? 31 So do not worry, saying, 'What shall we eat?' or 'What shall we drink?' or 'What shall we wear?' 32 For the pagans run after all these things, and your heavenly Father knows that you need them. 33 But seek first his kingdom and his righteousness, and all these things will be given to you as well. 34 Therefore do not worry about tomorrow, for tomorrow will worry about itself. Each day has enough trouble of its own." Matthew 6:25-34

I think some people misinterpret these verses. These verses are specifically about worrying, NOT seeking worldly pleasures, and making sure that you seek God first in hard times. It does not tell you not to buy clothes, or food for tomorrow evening's dinner. It is telling you not to worry about those things; that if you trust in Him, God will provide for you regardless of your financial circumstances.

Do you sit at your table each night waiting for birds to drop food on your plate to eat like Elijah? No, that's silly. You go to the grocery store and buy all the food that your family will need for the upcoming week planning out each evening's meal and making sure that you buy all the ingredients to cook them. You probably even make a list of the food (supplies) you will need. Why? Because if you didn't do this then you would have a hard time feeding your family next week and they would go hungry. Why is this so different than making a list of supplies you may need next year if there were food shortages? Where do you draw the line? What is the exact amount of food you are allowed to "store up"? Is it biblical to buy food for next week, but not next year? Think about it.

By some people's logic, those who want to be legalistic about these verses, it would mean that it is unbiblical to buy food for tomorrow's dinner because you're not supposed to worry about tomorrow. We all know that is silly and, in my opinion, taking the scriptures out of context. In the same way, I think that if you use these verses against planning for the future, you need to re-evaluate whether or not you should own any kind of insurance. Why would you buy fire insurance for your house? It is extremely unlikely that your particular house will ever catch fire. What are you worrying about? If it does catch on fire and burn down, are you saying that you don't trust God enough to miraculously rebuild it or give you another house? The same principle applies to health insurance or any other type of insurance that could bail you out of a hard time or potential accidents that are highly unlikely to occur. Why are you "worried" about them? Aren't you just worrying about tomorrow then? Why do you spend thousands of dollars a year on insurance policies, "worrying about the future"?

I realize that to some this may seem to be combative. I assure you I am not trying to be. The premise is all the same. If you are a Christian and you have multiple insurance policies protecting you and your family from terrible things that MAY happen in the future, then how could you be against putting some extra food and water in your basement to protect against a likely SHTF scenario and feed your family? The answer is most likely because by today's social norms it is acceptable (actually considered wise) to have those insurance policies, but prepping is not deemed normal or acceptable behavior and therefor it is looked down upon. So why do you buy insurance? Because at the end of the day, you recognize that there is a risk (even if it is extremely slight) that your home could catch fire in your lifetime and you don't want to suffer the consequences of being on the financial hook for that house and all your beloved "stuff" you have in it. I would guess that 99.9% of people don't have the cash in the bank to build a new house and refurnish their house out of pocket. I also believe that, if given enough time, I could easily make the case that there is a much higher likelihood of seeing a financial collapse or grid-down scenario in the near future than the likelihood that your particular house will catch on fire.

However, I do feel that the verses above are still applicable to a lot of Christian preppers. If you've done your research and understand what life is going to look like after the SHTF, it is very easy to fall in to the trap of worrying and stressing over it. That is the overwhelming point of those verses: Do not worry. I am speaking from experience here and something that I struggled with in my early years of prepping. Preparing for hard times should be a peaceful proposition, knowing that you are going to be better prepared to take care of and feed your family when hard times hit. If your preparations revolve around fear, then you are doing it wrong! "But I'm not ready yet!" you say... and I understand. That is where faith steps in. Trust me; I'm not completely ready myself.

In fact, I don't believe you CAN fully prepare for the horrible times that await us after the SHTF. You need to do what you can while still being responsible with the finances God has given you and set things aside as you can. Beyond that, you have to trust in God when the time comes. This is why I specifically tell people not to cash in their kid's college fund or buy survival gear in place of paying your bills. You are still a steward of the money God has bestowed upon your family and required to spend God's money (not yours) responsibly. I believe that you MUST find a balance between preparing and your family's current financial obligations and needs…and every family is different. If you are a rich business man, then maybe that means instead of buying an expensive beach house, you rent a beach house each summer and buy a small secluded cabin in the woods instead. If you are barely getting by, you need to establish a monthly budget and fit in your survival supplies where you can, a little bit each month. Again, everyone is different. Just do what you can in the natural and let God handle the supernatural.

So I have covered the scriptures that I hear most regularly against preparing for hard times, but what does the bible say in support? The first scripture I would point out is in 1 Timothy:

"Anyone who does not provide for their relatives, and especially for their own household, has denied the faith and is worse than an unbeliever." 1Timothy 5:8

Now in context, the surrounding verses are discussing taking care of and providing for widows and your parents in their old age. We are called as Christians to take care of and feed those who can't take care of themselves. How are you supposed to do that after the SHTF if you can't even feed yourself?

However, I also want you to pay special attention to the middle part of the verse. Special emphasis is placed on: "especially for [your] own household." As men, single mothers, or heads of our household, we are specifically called to provide for our immediate families first. Even in its context, I don't know how you can interpret this any different than exactly what it states. I believe there is a hierarchy built into it. I believe that the addition of the word "especially" puts your first priority for your immediate family (your wife and kids, or if single, your parents and siblings). After your immediate family, you have a responsibility to your parents and siblings next. After that are distant relatives, widows, and others who can't take care of themselves.

What do I mean by this and why am I even bringing it up? Without question, at some point in you preparedness planning, unless you are a billionaire, you are going to have to make tough choices on who you are going to help and who you cannot feasibly help. I believe that if you are living paycheck to paycheck, than you must focus on purchasing provisions for your immediate family first while trying to convince your other relatives of the threats so they can prepare on their own. If you are well to do, than I believe that you also have a responsibility to provide supplies for your extended family as well (to the point it is financially responsible to). Even if your parents or siblings aren't on board, or they think you're a little nuts for discussing it at family get-togethers, you still have a responsibility to provide for them if you have the financial means to do so.

On the more controversial side of things, I also believe that if you have family members who refuse to see the light or refuse to leave their city home after the SHTF, you have a responsibility to get your wife and kids out of danger and into a safe environment first. I got hammered by a few critics for the fact that in my first book the main character, Sean, took his pregnant wife and left the family farm (which was very close to a city), escaping to a close friend's fully stocked retreat for her safety and the safety of their unborn child. Some people were very angry about that and said things like, "I was a horrible person, and they would never leave their kin behind." That's perfectly fine with me and I'm not bashing anyone who makes that decision. But again, I believe your first responsibility is to your immediate family.

If your parents stay in their big suburban house outside Washington, D.C., because they don't want to leave, does it make you morally superior to stay behind and watch your wife and kids starve to death or get killed by looters right alongside your parents? I personally don't think so. In fact, this is a very tough and emotional subject for all involved. Do you take your parents, grandparents, cousins....second cousins? Where do you draw the line? In my opinion, you help as many as you can without sacrificing the safety and provisions of your immediate family. There is no easy answer here and you are going to have to make tough decisions. You can't feed or save everyone! Do the best you can.

The next verse I would bring up can be found in Proverbs: "The prudent see danger and take refuge, but the simple keep going and pay the penalty" (22:3). This would fly in the face of the "head in the sand" types that I discussed earlier. If you have done your research and know that hard times are coming, you have a responsibility to provide for your family's needs. If a tornado was coming, you would go into a storm cellar. If you knew a hurricane was coming, you would pack up your family and leave the coastal town you live in. To do otherwise would be crazy and you'd likely pay the penalty of the choice. If you've done your research and know deep down inside that a financial collapse or another SHTF scenario is highly likely, then I think it is crazy not to prepare for it and the penalty paid by you and your loved ones could be severe. It could mean watching your wife and kids die a slow and painful death from starvation and sickness. That last statement is not fear-mongering, it is the truth.

That leads me into the next biblical example, Noah. God told Noah that a cataclysmic event (flood) was coming and to prepare for it by building an enormous boat and putting food in it. God could have easily made the boat miraculously appear with food in it already. Why didn't he? He obviously made the animals miraculously march on board two-by-two. But no, God instructed Noah to prepare for the flood. In fact God specifically told Noah, "You are to take every kind of food that is to be eaten and store it away as food for you and for them (the animals)." Genesis 6:21, NIV

It took Noah over 100 years (by most accounts) to build the enormous structure and provision it, all the while he was being ridiculed by everyone else around him for being the first "prepper" in history. Up to that point it had not yet rained on earth and I could just imagine Noah trying to explain the concept of rain and flooding, all while his neighbors rolled their eyes and talked about him behind his back. God expected Noah to do the natural (building the boat and provisioning it) and He did the supernatural (getting all the animals on board without eating each other on the way). What a sight to have seen! Anyway, I believe that God expects us to build our own life boat, store away food and protect our families to the best of our ability and He will do the rest.

What about Joseph? Egypt was facing seven years of famine in the future, and what did God instruct Joseph to tell Pharaoh? To build enormous grain silos and store up food in the times of plenty. Pharaoh followed Joseph's guidance and it helped the entire country (as well as those countries around it) survive the seven years of famine. If you live in America, you can't argue that this time period is definitely a time of plenty with every possible type of food available 24 hours a day at your local Walmart. If you know hard times are ahead for this country, why are you not building grain silos (putting away food) to provide for your family and to assist the people close to you?

Let's also look at a lesser known famine during the founding of the early church in Acts:

27 "And during these days prophets came down from Jerusalem to Antioch.

28 "And one of them named Agabus stood up and prophesied through the Holy Spirit that a great and severe famine would come upon the whole world. And this did occur during the reign of Claudius.

29 "So the disciples resolved to send relief, each according to his individual ability [in proportion as he had prospered], to the brethren who lived in Judea.

30 "And so they did, sending [their contributions] to the elders by the hand of Barnabas and Saul." Acts 11: 27-30 (Amp)

So a prophet by the name of Agbus prophesized that a great famine would strike the entire world. What was their response? They took head of the warning, took up a collection, and sent relief to their brethren in Judea. Did they send everything they owned? No, they sent relief, "each according to his individual ability [in proportion as he had prospered]." This is another area I want to pay special attention to where prepping is concerned. This is also a very debatable issue with plenty of scripture to back up both sides of the argument. Again, who do you help? How many can you realistically feed? Within a month of a grid-down scenario, with the supermarkets cleaned out after 3-4 days, there will literally be 300+ million starving Americans wandering around looking for any scrap of food they can find. In the early stages, many will be beggars and pleading for food. During the later stages of starvation (weeks in), it is human nature for self-preservation and MOST people will do practically ANYTHING to get food.

This is the biggest area where most survival "experts" are dead wrong because they have never worked with or been around starving, desperate people. They grossly underestimate the threat of the average Joe whose kid is almost dead from starvation. They always discuss building neighborhood coalitions, disregarding the fact that a month into that situation, everyone on their block will literally be starving to death and willing to kill a neighbor at the off-chance that they might have an extra can of soup (let alone if you are the only person on the block with long-term food in your basement). If you think that your entire neighborhood is going to let you lead them through the crisis while you are the only family on the block that is not dying of starvation, you are a fool. Severe starvation causes delusional behavior in most people. The whole "pool our practically non-existent resources together and work together" will NEVER work if there is not enough food to go around. I have seen highly trained soldiers get a little wacky in a training environment when they've gone three days without food (knowing full well that a buffet awaits them back on base after a couple more days in the field). Imagine the average starving family that sees no help or no end in sight.

So in this dangerous time of famine, who do you help? Is it "Christian" to turn people away? What about if the woman is a widow (there will be many of them around after their men are killed while going out to look for food)? Aren't we are specifically called to help widows? These are incredibly tough questions and again, I think you could make a valid argument on either side. Here is my opinion on the matter. As Christians we are called to help feed the poor and take care of the widows. But I also believe that you are called to do this to the best of your ability, like the verse from I Timothy states. If you disagree with me, then I will ask if there is anyone in your neighborhood who is a widow in need or poor. Why? If you have a big screen TV, food on your table, and a roof over your head, why is there anyone in need within a ten mile radius of your home?

What about the starving children in Africa? Are you feeding them as well? You see, you have probably drawn a subconscious, hypothetical line in the sand at some point knowing that YOU CAN'T help everyone and you can't feed EVERY widow in the world, let alone just the ones in your own town. It's impossible. Jesus clearly stated in John 12:8 that "You will always have the poor among you." Especially after a SHTF scenario, there are going to be hundreds of millions of starving people in need. Does the Bible require you to feed them all? Are you supposed to give your wife and child's winter provisions to a wandering widow in need? Is it morally superior to help the widow survive the winter and let your immediate family starve to death?

I would again quote 1 Timothy 5:8, which is discussing widows and the poor yet still clarifies, "Anyone who does not provide for their relatives, and ESPECIALLY for their own household, has denied the faith and is worse than an unbeliever." I think this clearly puts emphasis on your responsibility to take care of your immediate family's needs first. Just like in the story of the early church, it doesn't say that they sold their houses and gave away their own family's food. It says, they sent relief, "each according to his individual ability [in proportion as he had prospered]."

So in my earlier writings, I have laid out what I believe is the best plan to survive the coming collapse, yet at the same time balance that with helping those in need. You are required to do what you can to help others. The first year after the SHTF you do not really know (unless you currently homestead) how much food and supplies it will take to make it through till the next spring and the next growing season (hint, it will be a WHOLE lot more than you think). You must be responsible and cautious and make sure that you don't grow too fast as a group (while at the same time helping the needy) if it means that your immediate family will starve to death before your spring crops come in. In other words, you probably won't be able to help many "outsiders" the first year. But if you are proficient in your preps, a hard worker, and diligent the following year, it is your responsibility to take in or help as many people as your food stores will allow. I actually believe this is the main purpose in having a retreat or advanced plans to survive…to ultimately help others do the same. You may be turning away people at first, but in the long run you are helping the future survivors as you are able and building a larger and larger community as your food stores allow. This is your best chance of helping people long-term without sacrificing your family's safety.

Another way I would explain my theory is like this. Some people will look at giving away their food to the needy immediately after a SHTF as helping those individuals. I know this may sound crass, but you are not really helping them. Without actually taking the individual into your group and by just sharing some of your daily rations with them and sending them on their way, it truly only delays the inevitable. They will still likely starve to death anyway and all you've done is delay that by a couple days while jeopardizing your own family's food stores. I know that is a terrible thing to think about, when as Christians, our heart's desire is to help those in need.

Also don't be naive to think they aren't going to come back every day thereafter. They are going to be just as hungry in two days as they were when they showed up the first time, but this time they will have likely brought other family members with them looking for a handout. Are you going to turn them away on the second, third, or tenth time they come begging? What about the ever growing group of desperate, hungry people that they tell...and that start showing up? Are you only going to feed the first person and turn away the second, the third, or the twenty-third? What happens when the line of beggars grows REALLY long (and it definitely will if word gets out that you have food)? How many people can your family's food stores feed, and for how long? What happens when you start getting low on food and you start turning them away? If you don't think those people will grow angry and resent you for having food while they slowly die from starvation, you are a fool! Word WILL spread that your family has food and eventually a large enough group will come and take it by force, I don't care how many guns your family owns or how John Rambo you think you are.

After all that I've just said, PLEASE don't miss the next paragraph! I am NOT saying to never help anyone, I am just saying that there are very serious risks involved every time you do. You are better to grow your group/retreat slowly and actually take the needy in as you can and help them become self-sufficient on their own for the long-term. Last, I will point out that this is NOT a black and white discussion. These are (in my opinion) wise guidelines to follow and do NOT trump what God is leading you to do individually. I would treat each individual situation you face during these hard times independently and trust the Holy Spirit to help you make the right decision in the moment. Maybe God will instill upon you to give away all your food to your church the day after the SHTF...I don't know. Stay in the Word and pray that God helps guide you through these tough decisions.

In all three stories above (Noah, Joseph, and the early church), at no point did anyone sit around and expect God to miraculously provide manna from above. When God told them of a cataclysmic event in the future, He also gave them specific instructions to make plans and provide for their own future needs. They didn't just sit idly by; they were all proactive, productive, and provided for their families and those in need to the best of their abilities while at the same time growing their faith and trusting in God to see them through it.

Preparing is not just a man's job either. Wives, you are not off the hook. You are called to provide for your household as well. Proverbs 31 discusses the traits for a "Virtuous Wife":

10 A wife of noble character who can find? She is worth far more than rubies. 11 Her husband has full confidence in her and lacks nothing of value. 12 She brings him good, not harm, all the days of her life. 13 She selects wool and flax and works with eager hands. 14 She is like the merchant ships, bringing her food from afar.

15 She gets up while it is still night; she provides food for her family. 16 She considers a field and buys it; out of her earnings she plants a vineyard. 17 She sets about her work vigorously; her arms are strong for her tasks. 18 She sees that her trading is profitable, and her lamp does not go out at night. 19 In her hand she holds the distaff and grasps the spindle with her fingers. 20 She opens her arms to the poor and extends her hands to the needy. 21 When it snows, she has no fear for her household; for all of them are clothed in scarlet. 22 She makes coverings for her bed; she is clothed in fine linen and purple. 24 She makes linen garments and sells them, and supplies the merchants with sashes.

25 She is clothed with strength and dignity; she can laugh at the days to come. 26 She speaks with wisdom, and faithful instruction is on her tongue. 27 She watches over the affairs of her household and does not eat the bread of idleness. 28 Her children arise and call her blessed; her husband also, and he praises her: 29 "Many women do noble things, but you surpass them all." 30 Charm is deceptive, and beauty is fleeting; but a woman who fears the Lord is to be praised. 31 Honor her for all that her hands have done, and let her works bring her praise at the city gate. (Proverbs 31:10-31)

Now as wives, are you supposed to take all that literally? Does this mean that you are supposed to making sashes for the merchants down at the docks? No, of course not. What this means is that God expects you to take an active role in the running of your household. I realize that every household and marriage dynamic is different and I'm not trying to jump into the middle of your relationship with your spouse. But I do believe that God wants you to take an active role in the future of your family and making sure they are properly fed and clothed. On the flipside, men, it is important not to sidestep your wives when preparing for hard times. I realize that prepping is typically a male-dominated segment of society, but it is important to try and get on the same page and include your wives in the decision-making process. Be respectful of each other in the process.

Here are a few more verses I feel are also relevant to the discussion of preparing for hard times:

"Those who work their land will have abundant food but those who chase fantasies will have their fill of poverty." Proverbs 28:19

"The wise store up choice food and olive oil, but fools gulp theirs down." Proverbs 21:20

"Go to the ant, thou sluggard; consider her ways, and be wise: Which having no guide, overseer, or ruler, provideth her meat in the summer, and gathereth her food in the harvest." Proverbs 6:6-9

"A wise man thinks ahead; a fool doesn't, and even brags about it!" Proverbs 13:16

"The prudent sees the evil and hides himself, but the naive go on, and are punished for it." Proverbs 22:3

The last thing that I will mention is that regardless of whether or not you agree with me, a grid-down scenario is going to be awful to live through on all accounts. I don't care how prepared you are or how ready that you think you are. You may eventually find yourself in a place where you have done all you can and you will need God to come through supernaturally to help you get through it. Pray constantly, have faith, and never give up on God. Remember, your wives and children will be watching you and looking for you to remain strong and lead them. Never give in to worry and despair! I find Psalm 91 (TLB) is fitting for this type of scenario.

1 We live within the shadow of the Almighty, sheltered by the God who is above all gods.

2 This I declare, that he alone is my refuge, my place of safety; he is my God, and I am trusting him. 3 For he rescues you from every trap and protects you from the fatal plague. 4 He will shield you with his wings! They will shelter you. His faithful promises are your armor. 5 Now you don't need to be afraid of the dark anymore, nor fear the dangers of the day; 6 nor dread the plagues of darkness, nor disasters in the morning.

7 Though a thousand fall at my side, though ten thousand are dying around me, the evil will not touch me. 8 I will see how the wicked are punished, but I will not share it. 9 For Jehovah is my refuge! I choose the God above all gods to shelter me. 10 How then can evil overtake me or any plague come near? 11 For he orders his angels to protect you wherever you go. 12 They will steady you with their hands to keep you from stumbling against the rocks on the trail. 13 You can safely meet a lion or step on poisonous snakes, yes, even trample them beneath your feet!

14 For the Lord says, "Because he loves me, I will rescue him; I will make him great because he trusts in my name. 15 When he calls on me, I will answer; I will be with him in trouble and rescue him and honor him. 16 I will satisfy him with a full life and give him my salvation."

Good luck in your preps and God Bless.

About the Author

Jonathan Hollerman is a former military S.E.R.E.(Survival, Evasion, Resistance, and Escape) Instructor and expert on survival and prepping. Jonathan currently offers his services as an Emergency Preparedness Consultant specializing in Survival Retreat design and has clients all over the world. He performs on-site survival retreat analysis and designs off-grid infrastructure for families working on a budget up to multi-million dollar compounds. Jonathan also provides his expertise through phone consultation and can be contacted via his company, Grid Down Consulting.

To contact the author or for personalized consulting please visit:
www.GridDownConsulting.com

You can follow *Jonathan Hollerman* on Facebook,
and on Instagram and Twitter **@GridDownPrepper**

Appendix

3-day Bug Out Bag Checklist

- [ ] 1 - Eberlestock Little Brother w/ Belt and Frame
- [ ] 1 - Leatherman Sidekick Multi Tool
- [ ] 1 - EDC Pocket Knife - Kershaw Camber
- [ ] 1 - Full Tang Bolt Knife - Cold Steel SRK
- [ ] 1 - Folding Saw - Silky Ultra Accel
- [ ] 1 - 300 Lumen AA LED Flashlight - Nightcore MT2A
- [ ] 1 - 100' Parachute Cord
- [ ] 2 - Military Surplus Ponchos - Digital Woodland
- [ ] 12 - High Calorie Power Bars - Clif Bars
- [ ] 3 - Mountain House Breakfast Meals
- [ ] 1 - Mountain House Dinner Meal
- [ ] 3 - Military surplus MRE's
- [ ] 1 - Extra Pair of Socks
- [ ] 1 - Extra Moisture Wicking T-shirt
- [ ] 1 - Mosquito Net – Coleman, 3'X3' section
- [ ] 1 - 3-piece ECWS Military Sleeping Bag System

Large Accessory Pouch
- [ ] 1 - Military Cammenga Compass – Tritium
- [ ] 1 - TP Wipes - 40 Wipes
- [ ] 1 - Spork - Toaks Titanium, Long Handle
- [ ] 1 - Set of Extra Batteries for Flashlight
- [ ] 1 - LED Headlamp - Mastervision 5 LED Hat Bill
- [ ] 1 - Emergency Blanket - NDuR Combat Casualty OD
- [ ] 1 - Bump keys and/or Picklock Kit
- [ ] 1 - Travel Roll of Duct Tape
- [ ] 1 - P38 Can Opener
- [ ] 1 - Travel Size Deodorant
- [ ] 1 - Purell Hand Sanitizer
- [ ] 20 - Ibuprofen or other Pain Pill

Fire Kit Pouch
- [ ] 2 - Disposable Lighters – Bic Brand
- [ ] 1 - Metal Match - Bayite 6" Ferro Rod
- [ ] 1 - Tinder - Fire Paste or Vaseline & Cotton Balls
- [ ] 12 - Tinder – Wetfire Cubes

Water Kit
- [ ] 1 - Camelback Water Bladder - 100 oz
- [ ] 30 - Katadyn Micropur MP1 Purification Tablets
- [ ] 1 - Water Filter - Sawer Mini
- [ ] 6 - Instant Coffee Packets
- [ ] 1 - Stainless Canteen - 32oz Nalgene Uninsulated Steel
- [ ] 1 - Esbit CS585HA 3-Piece Lightweight Cook Set
- [ ] 12 - Trioxane Fuel Bars or Esbit Fuel Tablets

First Aid Kit (Mounted on BOB)
- 1 - Condor MOLLE IFAK FRP Rip-Away Pouch
- 1 - Thin H Pressure Bandage 8"
- 1 - Israeli 4" Pressure Bandage
- 1 - Assorted Mix of Band-Aids and Butterfly Closures
- 3 - Iodine Wipes
- 2 – Rolls of Sterilized Gauze
- 1 – Small Tube of Neosporin Antibiotic Cream
- 1 - Small Roll of Medical Tape
- 1 - Celox Rapid Ribbon Z Folded Gauze Package
- 2 - Pair of Latex or Nitrile Gloves
- 1 - Nasopharyngeal Airway (28 Fr., 9.3mm) w/Surgilube
- 1 - Package of Moleskin
- 1 - Tweezers
- 1 - Assorted Medications, Anti-Diarrheal, Pain, etc…

Trauma Kit (Mounted on Battle Belt)
- 1 - HSGI Bleeder Medical Pouch
- 1 - EMT Shears
- 1 - Celox V12090 Granule Plunger Set
- 1 - Celox Rapid Ribbon Z Folded Gauze Package
- 1 - Israeli 4" Pressure Bandage
- 1 – Pair of Latex or Nitrile Gloves
- 1 - NAR Hyfin Vent Chest Seals
- 1 - Combat Application Tourniquet

Optional Items – Lone Wolf Pack
- 1 - 50, 000 Non-Hybrid Organic Seeds
- 1 - Space Pen
- 1 - Write in the Rain tablet
- 1 - Face Camo
- 1 - Signal Mirror - Cohglans 9902
- 1 - Snaring Wire - Military Surplus
- 1 - Fishing Kit – Compact
- 3 - Mechanical Fishing Yo-Yo's
- 1 - Sewing Kit – Compact Size
- 2 - Large HD Black Contractor Trash Bags
- 1 - Bible - Small
- 1 - Survival Manual - USAF 64-4 or Other
- 1 - Edible Plants Book for your Geographical Area
- 1 - Hair and Body Wash Soap
- 1 - Toothpaste/Toothbrush - Travel Size
- 1 - Chaptstick – Healing
- 1 – Tube of Quality Hand Cream
- 1 - Small Hand crank radio - Eton FRX5
- 1 - Goal Zero 41022 Guide 10 Plus Solar Recharging Kit
- 1 - Knife Sharpener - Medium and Fine
- 1 - Extra Clothes - underwear, socks, and undershirts

JONATHAN HOLLERMAN

Made in the USA
Coppell, TX
22 September 2024

37562088R00156